Table of Contents

M000315469

Introduction

Basic Math Skills is based on current NCTM standards and is designed to support any math curriculum that you may be using in your classroom. The standard strands (Number and Operations, Algebra, Geometry, Measurement, and Data Analysis and Probability) and skills within the strand are listed on the overview page for each section of the book. The skill is also shown at the bottom of each reproducible page.

Opportunities to practice the process standards (Problem Solving, Reasoning and Proof, Communication, Connections, and Representations) are also provided as students complete the various types of activities in this resource book.

Basic Math Skills is to be used as a resource providing practice of skills already introduced to students. Any page may be used with an individual child, as homework, with a small group, or by the whole class.

Skill Practice

Each skill is covered in a set of six reproducible pages that include the following:

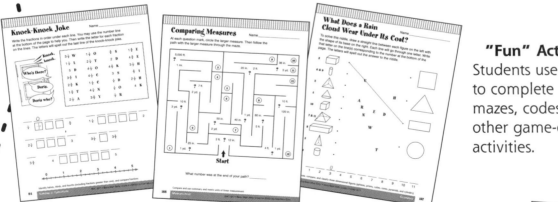

"Fun" Activities
Students use the skill to complete riddles, mazes, codes, and other game-oriented activities.

Drill and Practice
These pages contain straightforward practice of the skill.

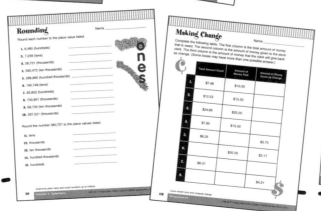

Application/Word Problem Activities

Students use the skill to problem solve and explore real-life situations.

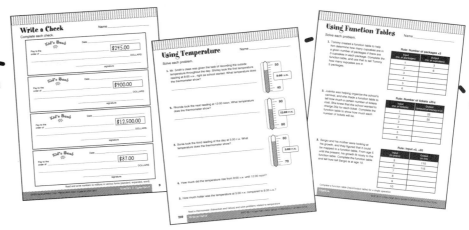

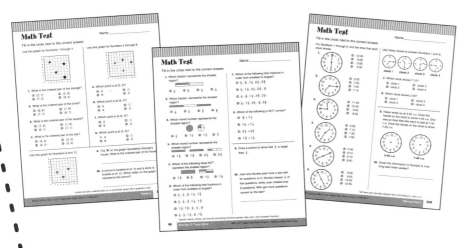

Math Tests

A test in standardized format is provided for each skill.

Additional Resources

The following additional resources are also provided:

- Timed math tests
- Class record sheet
- Test answer form
- Awards
- Reproducible practice cards for multiplication and division facts

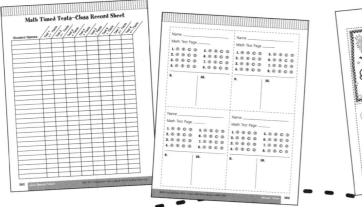

Number and Operations

Read, write, compare, use place value and round numbers

Add, subtract, multiply, and divide whole numbers

Identify odds, evens, primes, composites, factors, and multiples

Identify, compare, add and subtract fractions

Determine common equivalent fractions and decimals

Add and subtract decimals

Compare sets and values using <, >, and =

Where Do Fish Sleep?

Name _____

Match the word form to the standard form for each number. Then write the corresponding letter in the blank. Read the answer to the riddle from top to bottom.

___I___ ten thousand twenty-five

_____ thirty-five thousand three hundred fifty

_____ eight thousand forty-seven

_____ seventy-two thousand three hundred

_____ three hundred seventy-six

_____ five hundred thousand eight

_____ eight hundred forty-seven

_____ three thousand five hundred thirty-five

_____ four thousand six

_____ seven thousand two hundred thirty

_____ thirteen thousand twenty-five

376	T
8,047	W
4,006	E
72,300	A
7,230	D
10,025	I
500,008	E
13,025	S
35,350	N
3,535	B
847	R

YAWN!

Read and write numbers to millions in various forms (standard, expanded, word)

What Kind of Room Has No Windows?

Name _____

Match the expanded form to the standard form. Then write the corresponding letter in the blank. Read the answer to the riddle from top to bottom.

__A__	300 + 40
_____	200 + 70
_____	2,000 + 700
_____	20,000 + 7,000
_____	3,000 + 40
_____	2,000 + 70
_____	30,000 + 4,000
_____	200 + 7
_____	3,000 + 400

270	**M**
34,000	**O**
2,070	**R**
3,040	**H**
2,700	**U**
340	**A**
3,400	**M**
27,000	**S**
207	**O**

Read and write numbers to millions in various forms (standard, expanded, word)

Number & Operations   EMC 3017 • Basic Math Skills, Grade 4 • ©2003 by Evan-Moor Corp.

The Name Is the Same

Name _____

Write each number in word form.

1. 5,000 _____

2. 45,000 _____

3. 3,700 _____

4. 5,835 _____

5. 13,900 _____

6. 497 _____

7. 152,100 _____

_____

8. 4,008 _____

Write each number in standard form.

9. four hundred sixty-eight _____

10. eight thousand three _____

11. six thousand twenty-five _____

12. nine hundred two _____

13. four hundred sixty-one _____

14. five hundred twenty-six thousand _____

15. forty thousand six _____

16. eighty-three thousand two hundred sixty-seven _____

Read and write numbers to millions in various forms (standard, expanded, word)

Number & Operations

Different Forms

Name _____

Write each number in standard form.

1. 5,000 + 60 + 3 = _____

2. 7,000 + 700 = _____

3. 7,000 + 80 + 9 = _____

4. 10,000 + 900 + 6 = _____

5. 300,000 + 80,000 + 4,000 + 300 + 20 + 8 = _____

6. 800 + 90 = _____

7. 40,000 + 600 = _____

8. 80,000 + 7,000 + 500 + 40 + 9 = _____

9. 800 + 3 = _____

10. 90,000 + 90 + 9 = _____

Write each number in expanded form.

11. 4,500 _____

12. 35,000 _____

13. 692 _____

14. 1,090 _____

15. 5,038 _____

16. 6,030 _____

17. 14,972 _____

18. 280,000 _____

Read and write numbers to millions in various forms (standard, expanded, word)

Write a Check

Complete each check.

Kid's Bank

Date _____

Pay to the order of _____ $245.00

_____ DOLLARS

_____
signature

Kid's Bank

Date _____

Pay to the order of _____ $900.00

_____ DOLLARS

_____
signature

Kid's Bank

Date _____

Pay to the order of _____ $12,500.00

_____ DOLLARS

_____
signature

Kid's Bank

Date _____

Pay to the order of _____ $87.00

_____ DOLLARS

_____
signature

Read and write numbers to millions in various forms (standard, expanded, word)

Number & Operations

Math Test

Name _____

Fill in the circle next to the correct answer.

For Numbers 1 through 4, find the standard form.

1. two thousand nine hundred

Ⓐ   29   Ⓒ 2,900
Ⓑ 2,009   Ⓓ   290

2. seventy-two

Ⓐ 702   Ⓒ   720
Ⓑ 72   Ⓓ 72,000

3. five hundred

Ⓐ 500   Ⓒ 5,100
Ⓑ   5   Ⓓ   100

4. six thousand four hundred ninety

Ⓐ 6,090   Ⓒ 6,400
Ⓑ   490   Ⓓ 6,490

For Numbers 5 through 8, find the word form.

5. 40,600

Ⓐ four thousand six hundred
Ⓑ forty thousand six hundred
Ⓒ forty-six hundred
Ⓓ forty thousand six

6. 7,200

Ⓐ seven thousand
Ⓑ seventy-two thousand
Ⓒ seven thousand two hundred
Ⓓ seven thousand two

7. 649

Ⓐ six hundred forty-nine
Ⓑ six thousand forty-nine
Ⓒ six four nine
Ⓓ nine hundred forty-six

8. 820

Ⓐ eighty-two
Ⓑ eight thousand twenty
Ⓒ eight thousand two hundred
Ⓓ eight hundred twenty

9. Write this number in standard form.

twenty-three thousand ninety-seven

_____

10. Write this number in word form.

5,973

_____

_____

_____

Read and write numbers to millions in various forms (standard, expanded, word)

Riddle Time

List the numbers in the box in order from smallest to largest. If you need help, use the number line at the bottom of the page. Then write the corresponding letters in the blanks. Read the answer from top to bottom.

What do you get if you put a dog in the oven?

smallest $1\frac{1}{4}$ A

_____   _____

_____   _____

_____   _____

_____   _____

_____   _____

largest

_____   _____

1.5	H
3.75	O
2	O
$1\frac{1}{4}$	A
$2\frac{1}{2}$	T
$4\frac{1}{2}$	G
2.75	D

0   1   2   3   4   5

Compare and order numbers (including decimals to hundredths and mixed numbers)

Number & Operations

A-Maze-ing!

At each question mark, circle the larger number. Then follow the path
with the larger number through the maze.

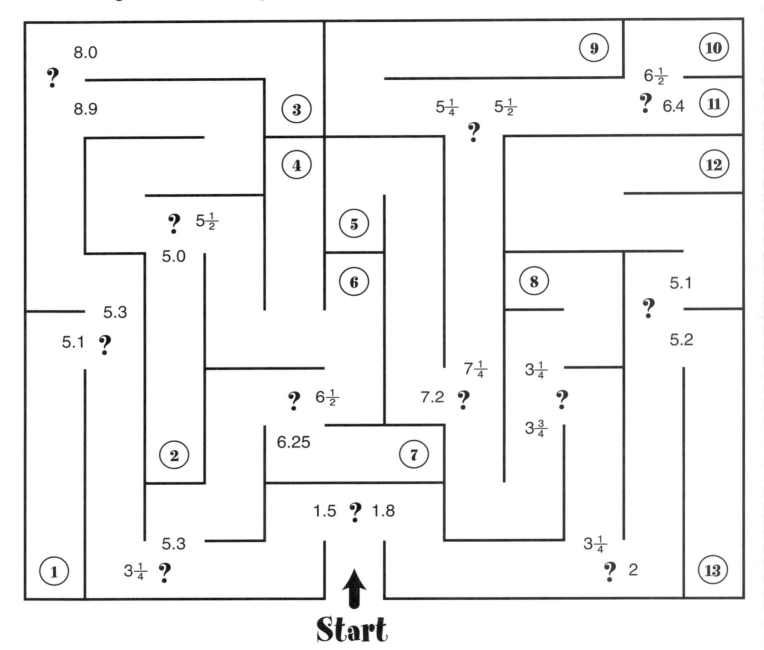

What number was at the end of your path? _____

Compare and order numbers (including decimals to hundredths and mixed numbers)

Largest and Smallest

Name_____

List these numbers in order from least to greatest.

1. 256   842   309   764   310   299

_____   _____   _____   _____   _____   _____

2. 673   674   575   769   599   672

_____   _____   _____   _____   _____   _____

3. 77.5   7.85   80.3   80.29   74.5   79.4

_____   _____   _____   _____   _____   _____

List these numbers in order from largest to smallest.

4. 490   443   485   479   497   482

_____   _____   _____   _____   _____   _____

5. 1,008   1,990   1,010   998   2,000   2,001

_____   _____   _____   _____   _____   _____

6. 10.8   1.9   9.9   8.9   9.2   10.6

_____   _____   _____   _____   _____   _____

7. 4.53   4.51   4.44   4.32   4.61   4.62

_____   _____   _____   _____   _____   _____

8.   42   48.5   48.49   47.0   46.99   43.5   48.43

_____   _____   _____   _____   _____   _____   _____

Compare and order numbers (including decimals to hundredths and mixed numbers)

What's the Order?

Name _____

List these numbers in order from least to greatest.

1. 489   526   500   509   490   492

    _____   _____   _____   _____   _____   _____

2. 602   596   597   524   623   635

    _____   _____   _____   _____   _____   _____

3. 10 $9\frac{5}{8}$ $8\frac{2}{3}$ 9 $8\frac{1}{2}$ $10\frac{1}{2}$

    _____   _____   _____   _____   _____   _____

List these numbers in order from largest to smallest.

4. 800   804   790   791   802   809

    _____   _____   _____   _____   _____   _____

5. 2,006   1,098   1,990   1,987   2,900   2,009

    _____   _____   _____   _____   _____   _____

6. $10\frac{1}{2}$ $9\frac{1}{2}$ 10 $8\frac{1}{2}$ $8\frac{3}{4}$ $10\frac{1}{4}$

    _____   _____   _____   _____   _____   _____

7. $4\frac{3}{4}$ $5\frac{1}{2}$ $3\frac{3}{4}$ $3\frac{1}{4}$ $5\frac{1}{4}$ $4\frac{1}{2}$

    _____   _____   _____   _____   _____   _____

8. $7\frac{3}{4}$ $5\frac{1}{2}$ $6\frac{3}{4}$ $5\frac{1}{4}$ $5\frac{3}{4}$ $6\frac{1}{2}$ $7\frac{1}{2}$

    _____   _____   _____   _____   _____   _____   _____

Compare and order numbers (including decimals to hundredths and mixed numbers)

Number & Operations

EMC 3017 • Basic Math Skills, Grade 4 • ©2003 by Evan-Moor Corp.

Around Town

Name _____

Solve each of the problems.

1. A carpenter has 5 boards that she needs to put in order by length. The boards are the following lengths: 5 feet 6 inches, 5 feet 2 inches, 4 feet 8 inches, 5 feet 9 inches, and 6 feet 1 inch. List the boards in order from the longest to the shortest.

_____

2. A city planning board is concerned about the panoramic view of 5 buildings being built. They would like the tallest building in the middle and the shortest buildings on either end of the row. What is a possible arrangement of the buildings if they have the given number of floors?

      8 floors, 14 floors, 9 floors, 7 floors, and 5 floors

_____

3. A baker is stacking round cakes to make a tiered cake. He wants the cakes to be in order from the largest cake on the bottom to the smallest cake on the top. The diameters of the cakes are 11 inches, 18 inches, 15 inches, 8 inches, and 21 inches. He needs your help to order the cakes. List the cakes in order from the largest to the smallest.

_____

4. When East Elementary School set up a new Computer Lab, they had six extra cables. The extra cables are 3 yards, 4 feet, 10 feet, 5 yards, 6 feet, and 12 feet long. They want to make a list of the cables in order from longest to shortest. List the cables in order from the longest to shortest.

_____

5. A tile store is having a clearance sale. The manager would like to put the boxes of tiles in a row with the first stack having the greatest number of boxes and the last stack having the fewest number of boxes. Help the manager by listing the stacks in order from greatest to fewest.

      27, 89, 105, 62, 96, 108, 32, 29

_____

Compare and order numbers (including decimals to hundredths and mixed numbers)

Math Test

Name_____

Fill in the circle next to the correct answer.

1. Find the numbers listed in order from smallest to largest.

   Ⓐ 400, 460, 490, 501, 478, 499
   Ⓑ 400, 501, 460, 478, 490, 499
   Ⓒ 400, 460, 478, 490, 499, 501
   Ⓓ 501, 499, 490, 478, 460, 400

2. Find the numbers listed in order from smallest to largest.

   Ⓐ 10.8, 9.9, 9.1, 10.2, 11.2
   Ⓑ 9.1, 9.9, 10.2, 10.8, 11.2
   Ⓒ 9.1, 9.9, 11.2, 10.2, 10.8
   Ⓓ 9.9, 9.1, 10.2, 10.8, 11.2

3. Find the numbers listed in order from smallest to largest.

   Ⓐ $\frac{1}{4}, \frac{1}{8}, \frac{1}{2}, \frac{3}{4}, \frac{7}{8}$

   Ⓑ $\frac{1}{4}, \frac{1}{8}, \frac{1}{2}, \frac{7}{8}, \frac{3}{4}$

   Ⓒ $\frac{1}{8}, \frac{1}{4}, \frac{1}{2}, \frac{3}{4}, \frac{7}{8}$

   Ⓓ $\frac{1}{8}, \frac{7}{8}, \frac{1}{4}, \frac{1}{2}, \frac{3}{4}$

4. Which number is largest?

   Ⓐ 985   Ⓑ 975   Ⓒ 974   Ⓓ 903

5. Which number is less than $\frac{1}{4}$?

   Ⓐ $\frac{1}{2}$ Ⓑ $\frac{1}{8}$ Ⓒ $\frac{1}{3}$ Ⓓ $\frac{3}{4}$

6. Find the numbers listed in order from greatest to least.

   Ⓐ 1,999, 1,900, 1,899, 1,880, 1,200
   Ⓑ 1,900, 1,880, 1,899, 1,200, 1,999
   Ⓒ 1,900, 1,899, 1,880, 1,200, 1,999
   Ⓓ 1,999, 1,899, 1,880, 1,900, 1,200

7. Find the numbers listed in order from greatest to least.

   Ⓐ 12.9, 11.8, 11.2, 11.4, 10.9
   Ⓑ 10.9, 11.8, 11.4, 11.2, 12.9
   Ⓒ 10.9, 11.2, 11.4, 11.8, 12.9
   Ⓓ 12.9, 11.8, 11.4, 11.2, 10.9

8. Find the numbers that are NOT in order from smallest to largest.

   Ⓐ 89, 91, 92, 95, 99
   Ⓑ 31, 32, 35, 36, 37
   Ⓒ 78, 79, 80, 82, 81
   Ⓓ 56, 58, 59, 60, 61

9. This table shows the amount sold for 5 different people. List the names in order of their sales, from the greatest to the least amount.

Salesperson	Amount of Sales
Fred	$2,900
Brandon	$2,200
Raul	$2,990
Sharon	$2,889
Maria	$1,500

10. Timothy listed 7 numbers in the following order:

    100, 102, 123, 135, 147, 138, 159

    Has Timothy correctly listed the numbers in order from smallest to largest? Explain your answer.

_____

Compare and order numbers (including decimals to hundredths and mixed numbers)

Number & Operations   EMC 3017 • Basic Math Skills, Grade 4 • ©2003 by Evan-Moor Corp.

Why Is Bowling the Quietest Sport?

Name _____

Round each number to the place value in parentheses. At the bottom of the page, write the corresponding letter on the line above each rounded number to spell out the answer to the riddle.

508,902 (hundred thousands) _____ **A**   108,498 (thousands) _____ **N**

685,602 (thousands) _686,000_ **B**   685,602 (tens) _____ **O**

1,800,990 (thousands) _____ **C**   890 (hundreds) _____ **P**

3,805 (thousands) _____ **D**   674,824 (ten thousands) _____ **R**

2,490,137 (hundred thousands) _____ **E**   5,935 (tens) _____ **S**

1,978 (thousands) _____ **H**   108,905 (tens) _____ **U**

508,902 (tens) _____ **I**   2,905 (tens) _____ **Y**

  B
 ___   ___   ___   ___   ___   ___   ___
686,000 2,500,000 1,801,000 500,000 108,910 5,940 2,500,000

 ___   ___   ___   ___   ___   ___
2,910   685,600 108,910   1,801,000 500,000 108,000

 ___   ___   ___   ___   ___
2,000   2,500,000 500,000 670,000   500,000

 ___   ___   ___   ___   ___   ___   ___
900   508,900 108,000   4,000   670,000 685,600 900

Determine place value and round numbers up to millions

Tongue Twister

Name _____

Find the digit that is in the place value listed. Then write the letter of the corresponding digit in the blank. Read the tongue twister from top to bottom. Try to say it quickly three times.

5,612,973 (ones)   _3_   _G_

679,824 (hundreds) _____ _____

4,870,652 (millions) _____ _____

2,094,137 (thousands) _____ _____

148,965 (tens) _____ _____

7,391 (hundreds) _____ _____

5,812 (hundreds) _____ _____

685,702 (thousands) _____ _____

128,709 (hundreds) _____ _____

1,864,753 (thousands) _____ _____

208,915 (hundred thousands) _____ _____

5	**A**
4	**E**
3	**G**
6	**K**
7	**P**
8	**R**
2	**S**

Determine place value and round numbers up to millions

EMC 3017 • Basic Math Skills, Grade 4 • ©2003 by Evan-Moor Corp.

Digit Search

Name _____

Look for the digit 7 in each number. Then write the place value on the line.

1. 572,163 _____

2. 726,468 _____

3. 268,317 _____

4. 649,752 _____

5. 7,168,259 _____

6. 708,469 _____

7. 46,971 _____

8. 97,802 _____

9. 7,805,821 _____

10. 6,479,520 _____

Write the digit that is in the place value listed.

11. tens digit in 805,317 _____

12. thousands digit in 916,348 _____

13. hundred thousands digit in 915,647 _____

14. hundreds digit in 1,346,592 _____

15. ones digit in 946,310 _____

Determine place value and round numbers up to millions

Number & Operations

Rounding

Round each number to the place value listed.

1. 6,480 (hundreds) _____

2. 7,239 (tens) _____

3. 28,731 (thousands) _____

4. 590,472 (ten thousands) _____

5. 289,962 (hundred thousands) _____

6. 190,749 (tens) _____

7. 83,802 (hundreds) _____

8. 730,801 (thousands) _____

9. 69,730 (ten thousands) _____

10. 287,521 (thousands) _____

Round the number 380,721 to the place values listed.

11. tens _____

12. thousands _____

13. ten thousands _____

14. hundred thousands _____

15. hundreds _____

Determine place value and round numbers up to millions

Number & Operations

EMC 3017 • Basic Math Skills, Grade 4 • ©2003 by Evan-Moor Corp.

Solve It!

Name _____

Solve each problem.

1. Helena was shopping with her mom and saw five things that she wanted to buy. The prices were $24, $19.98, $17.50, $9.45, and $29.90. Helena rounded each price to the nearest ten dollars and added them up to estimate the total cost. What is the estimate for the cost of the 5 items?

   _____

2. Drew was asked to round the number 25,803 to the nearest ten. He said it was 25,810, but Jane said that it is 25,800. Write a note to Drew explaining who was correct, and tell why.

   _____

   _____

3. Roberto was asked to round these numbers to the nearest hundred. Here is his work:

   297,059 became 297,000
   280,460 became 280,400
   109,973 became 109,900

   Do you see a pattern of errors in Roberto's work? What should Roberto do differently next time?

   _____

   _____

4. Angela was asked to identify what digit is in the tens place in the number 12,843. She said it was the 4. Was she correct? If she was, write "correct" on your paper. If not, identify what digit it should have been.

   _____

Determine place value and round numbers up to millions

Math Test

Name _____

Fill in the circle next to the correct answer.

For Numbers 1 through 4, find the place value for the digit 5.

1. 580,392

  Ⓐ hundred thousands
  Ⓑ hundreds
  Ⓒ ones
  Ⓓ ten thousands

2. 490,651

  Ⓐ ten thousands
  Ⓑ hundreds
  Ⓒ tens
  Ⓓ hundred thousands

3. 835,791

  Ⓐ ten thousands
  Ⓑ hundreds
  Ⓒ thousands
  Ⓓ ones

4. 28,735

  Ⓐ thousands
  Ⓑ hundreds
  Ⓒ tens
  Ⓓ ones

5. Round 380,824 to the nearest ten.

  Ⓐ 380,000
  Ⓑ 380,820
  Ⓒ 381,000
  Ⓓ 380,800

6. Round 287,427 to the nearest ten thousand.

  Ⓐ 300,000
  Ⓑ 288,000
  Ⓒ 297,000
  Ⓓ 290,000

7. Round 1,804,579 to the nearest hundred.

  Ⓐ 1,800,000
  Ⓑ 1,804,500
  Ⓒ 1,805,000
  Ⓓ 1,804,600

8. Round 49,246 to the nearest hundred.

  Ⓐ 49,200
  Ⓑ 49,240
  Ⓒ 49,300
  Ⓓ 49,250

9. Juan was asked to round a number to the nearest hundreds place value. Juan rounded the number 359,073 to 359,100. Was Juan correct? If he was, write "correct." If Juan made a mistake, write a note to him explaining his mistake.

_____

_____

_____

10. Shirley was asked to round a number to the nearest ten thousands place value. Shirley rounded the number 1,874,026 to 1,880,000. Was Shirley correct? If she was, write "correct." If Shirley made a mistake, write a note to her explaining the mistake.

_____

_____

_____

Determine place value and round numbers up to millions

EMC 3017 • Basic Math Skills, Grade 4 • ©2003 by Evan-Moor Corp.

Why Can't Bicycles Stand by Themselves?

Name_____

To solve the riddle, find the sum for each addition problem. Then write the corresponding letter on the line above each sum.

T 407 + 209 = _____616_____   **T** 503 + 303 = _____

E 519 + 45 = _____   **T** 802 + 407 + 842 = _____

E 913 + 289 = _____   **E** 735 + 285 + 482 = _____

R 45 + 132 + 84 = _____   **A** 375 + 493 + 263 = _____

I 256 + 250 + 831 = _____   **R** 907 + 32 + 284 = _____

O 290 + 491 + 502 = _____   **W** 280 + 481 + 427 = _____

Y 805 + 204 + 74 = _____   **H** 285 + 429 + 492 = _____

D 89 + 307 + 804 = _____

BECAUSE...

___ ___ ___ ___   ___ ___ ___   T ___ ___
806 1,206 1,202 1,083   1,131 261 1,502   616 1,188 1,283

___ ___ ___ ___ ___
2,051 1,337 1,223 564 1,200

Demonstrate addition with up to 5 three-digit numbers, utilizing regrouping

Tongue Twister

Solve each addition problem. Then write the letter on each line above the sum. Read the tongue twister and try to say it quickly three times.

A 379 + 295 + 49 = _____

E 297 + 45 + 320 = _____

I 234 + 492 + 472 = _____

L 742 + 284 + 423 = _____

M 454 + 485 + 62 = _____

N 402 + 52 + 831 = _____

O 10 + 20 + 420 = ____450____

U 38 + 47 + 620 = _____

____ ____ ____ ____ ____ ____ ____ ____
723 1,449 705 1,001 1,198 1,285 705 1,001

____ ____ ____ _O_ ____ ____ ____ ____
1,449 1,198 1,285 450 1,449 662 705 1,001

Demonstrate addition with up to 5 three-digit numbers, utilizing regrouping

Sum Fun

Name_____

Find the sum for each of the following.

1. 398 + 590 + 490 = _____

2. 290 + 852 + 29 = _____

3. 180 + 9 + 297 = _____

4. 73 + 821 + 820 = _____

5.
```
   173
   925
+  946
```

6.
```
   107
   804
   703
+  983
```

7.
```
   762
   496
   506
+  492
```

8.
```
   602
   721
   613
+   95
```

9.
```
   106
   832
   826
+  381
```

10.
```
   208
   462
   766
   392
+  793
```

Demonstrate addition with up to 5 three-digit numbers, utilizing regrouping

Add Them Up

Name _____

Find the sum for each of the following.

1. 208 + 520 + 286 + 826 = _____	**2.** 601 + 843 + 826 + 825 = _____
3. 926 + 482 + 82 = _____	**4.** 865 + 22 + 862 + 93 = _____

5.
```
   826
   835
   731
 + 651
```

6.
```
   561
   526
   349
 + 496
```

7.
```
   592
   103
   501
 + 600
```

8.
```
   506
    59
   496
 +  34
```

9.
```
   496
   182
   496
 + 768
```

10.
```
   792
   852
   816
   195
 + 463
```

Demonstrate addition with up to 5 three-digit numbers, utilizing regrouping

Number & Operations

EMC 3017 • Basic Math Skills, Grade 4 • ©2003 by Evan-Moor Corp.

Let's Go Shopping

Name_____

Solve each problem.

1. Sally would like to buy 2 cases of candy bars, and each one costs $24. She would also like to buy one twelve-pack of soda for $3. What will be the total of the purchases?

_____

2. Jorge wants to buy a new bike for himself and his sister. His bike costs $216, and his sister's bike costs $190. What will be the total for the two bikes?

_____

3. Helena wants to buy three CD sets for the following prices: $59, $129, and $64. What will be the total of the three CD sets?

_____

4. Brandon and Ian both want to buy new stereos. Each stereo costs $229. In addition, each boy wants to buy a set of speakers for $119. The tax for the 2 stereos and the 2 sets of speakers is $56. What will be the total for these items including tax?

_____

5. Amy and April were shopping and wanted to buy new coats for the winter. Amy found one that cost $56 and April found one that cost $98. What was the total for both coats?

_____

Demonstrate addition with up to 5 three-digit numbers, utilizing regrouping

Math Test

Name _____

Fill in the circle next to the correct answer.

1. 450 + 320 = _____

    Ⓐ 700   Ⓒ 670

    Ⓑ 950   Ⓓ 770

2. 83 + 291 + 582 = _____

    Ⓐ 956   Ⓒ 756

    Ⓑ 856   Ⓓ 7,255

3.
```
    908
    625
    349
  + 584
```
    Ⓐ 2,475   Ⓒ 2,376

    Ⓑ 2,466   Ⓓ 2,476

4.
```
    231
    612
    303
  + 261
```
    Ⓐ 1,400   Ⓒ 2,376

    Ⓑ 1,407   Ⓓ 211,107

5. 465 + 549 + 152 + 101 = _____

    Ⓐ 1,267   Ⓒ 1,257

    Ⓑ 1,260   Ⓓ 1,167

6. 462 + 591 + 201 + 207 = _____

    Ⓐ 1,451   Ⓒ 1,361

    Ⓑ 1,351   Ⓓ 1,461

7.
```
    564
    862
    269
  + 142
```
    Ⓐ 1,847   Ⓒ 1,837

    Ⓑ 1,835   Ⓓ none of the above

8.
```
    264
    492
    297
    464
  + 348
```
    Ⓐ 1,860   Ⓒ 1,864

    Ⓑ 1,866   Ⓓ none of the above

9. Write a story problem that would utilize the following number expression in its solution:

$$528 + 419 + 290 + 410$$

_____

_____

_____

_____

10. Aja's parents are buying 4 new bicycles priced at $259, $199, $159, and $129. What is the total of the 4 bikes?

_____

Demonstrate addition with up to 5 three-digit numbers, utilizing regrouping

Number Games

Name _____

Sally and Juan are playing a game. They have drawn these six number cards:

5   7   2   1   4   8

1. What is the smallest difference they can make if they make two
   3-digit numbers and subtract the smaller one from the larger one?

   _____

2. What is the largest difference they can make if they make two
   3-digit numbers and subtract the smaller one from the larger one?

   _____

3. Why do you think that this is the largest difference?

   _____

Angel and Jeremiah are playing the same game and have drawn the
following six cards:

9   3   6   2   7   5

4. What is the smallest difference they can make if they make two
   3-digit numbers and subtract the smaller one from the larger one?

   _____

5. Why do you think that this is the smallest difference you can make?

   _____

6. What is the largest difference they can make if they make two
   3-digit numbers and subtract the smaller one from the larger one?

   _____

Demonstrate subtraction with three-digit numbers, utilizing regrouping

Football

Name _____

To solve the riddle, solve each subtraction problem. Then write the corresponding letter on the line above the difference. The letters will spell out the answer for you.

T 747 − 235 = ____512____   A 510 − 265 = _____

M 529 − 417 = _____   O 490 − 489 = _____

I 413 − 250 = _____   E 378 − 236 = _____

H 841 − 690 = _____   T 263 − 170 = _____

E 379 − 163 = _____   U 492 − 396 = _____

T 290 − 199 = _____   E 734 − 718 = _____

P 804 − 321 = _____   G 205 − 163 = _____

Why did the football coach send in his second string?

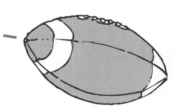

__ __ __   T̲ __ __   __ __
91 1   512 163 216   96 483

__ __ __   __ __ __ __
93 151 142   42 245 112 16

Demonstrate subtraction with three-digit numbers, utilizing regrouping

EMC 3017 • Basic Math Skills, Grade 4 • ©2003 by Evan-Moor Corp.

What's the Difference?

Find the following differences.

1. 109 − 80 = _____

2. 694 − 452 = _____

3. 359 − 126 = _____

4. 298 − 176 = _____

5. 590 − 107 = _____

6. 640 − 150 = _____

7. 480 − 290 = _____

8. 737 − 269 = _____

9. 531 − 284 = _____

10. 630 − 531 = _____

11. 805
    − 102

12. 750
    − 230

13. 620
    − 420

14. 279
    − 180

15. 530
    − 267

16. 497
    − 359

17. 549
    − 524

18. 725
    − 225

19. 737
    − 638

20. 462
    − 421

Demonstrate subtraction with three-digit numbers, utilizing regrouping

Number & Operations

Subtraction Practice

Name _____

Find the following differences.

1. $\begin{array}{r} 562 \\ -\ 162 \\ \hline \end{array}$
2. $\begin{array}{r} 795 \\ -\ 705 \\ \hline \end{array}$
3. $\begin{array}{r} 402 \\ -\ 120 \\ \hline \end{array}$
4. $\begin{array}{r} 603 \\ -\ 546 \\ \hline \end{array}$
5. $\begin{array}{r} 413 \\ -\ 267 \\ \hline \end{array}$

6. $\begin{array}{r} 465 \\ -\ 361 \\ \hline \end{array}$
7. $\begin{array}{r} 156 \\ -\ 149 \\ \hline \end{array}$
8. $\begin{array}{r} 343 \\ -\ 342 \\ \hline \end{array}$
9. $\begin{array}{r} 496 \\ -\ 396 \\ \hline \end{array}$
10. $\begin{array}{r} 726 \\ -\ 627 \\ \hline \end{array}$

11. 456 − 261 = _____

12. 894 − 621 = _____

13. 496 − 261 = _____

14. 895 − 725 = _____

15. 627 − 130 = _____

16. 820 − 419 = _____

17. 597 − 496 = _____

18. 900 − 199 = _____

19. 560 − 250 = _____

20. 764 − 179 = _____

Demonstrate subtraction with three-digit numbers, utilizing regrouping

EMC 3017 • Basic Math Skills, Grade 4 • ©2003 by Evan-Moor Corp.

Solve It!

Name _____

Solve each problem.

1. Sarah had $679 in her savings account. She took $235 out of the account to buy a new stereo. What was the balance after her withdrawal of $235?

   _____

2. The Wildcat Elementary School is going on a field trip to the zoo. They have reserved 8 buses that have a total of 528 seats. There are 470 students in the school and 35 teachers that will be going to the zoo. Are there enough seats for all the students and teachers to ride on the buses?

   _____

3. The fourth-graders at Shawsheen Elementary School were doing their annual fundraiser. They sold $998 worth of candy. The bill they have to pay is $425. How much profit will the fourth-grade class make?

   _____

4. Jeremy has $275 saved up. He wants to buy a CD player for $119 and a TV for $179. Does he have enough for both? Why or why not?

   _____

5. Peter's family was driving to visit his grandparents' house. The entire trip was 642 miles. By lunchtime, they had driven 375 miles. Were they at least halfway there? How many miles were left to go?

   _____

Demonstrate subtraction with three-digit numbers, utilizing regrouping

Math Test

Name_____

Fill in the circle next to the correct answer.

1.
$$305$$
$$- 206$$
   - Ⓐ 100
   - Ⓑ 99
   - Ⓒ 301
   - Ⓓ 101

2.
$$472$$
$$- 190$$
   - Ⓐ 282
   - Ⓑ 322
   - Ⓒ 662
   - Ⓓ 382

3.
$$649$$
$$- 351$$
   - Ⓐ 398
   - Ⓑ 298
   - Ⓒ 351
   - Ⓓ 318

4.
$$842$$
$$- 359$$
   - Ⓐ 517
   - Ⓑ 513
   - Ⓒ 483
   - Ⓓ none of the above

5. 349 − 162 = _____
   - Ⓐ 207
   - Ⓑ 180
   - Ⓒ 227
   - Ⓓ 187

6. 912 − 613 = _____
   - Ⓐ 301
   - Ⓑ 201
   - Ⓒ 299
   - Ⓓ 399

7. Sharon had $815 and spent $621. How much does she have left?
   - Ⓐ $194
   - Ⓑ $214
   - Ⓒ $294
   - Ⓓ $134

8. Brendan picked 254 flowers. He gave away 107 flowers. How many does he have left?
   - Ⓐ 153
   - Ⓑ 147
   - Ⓒ 143
   - Ⓓ 361

9. Roberto started with 295 tickets and gave away 146 of them. Does he have enough left over to give all the 98 fourth-graders tickets? Why or why not?

_____

_____

_____

_____

10. Julia was planning a trip with her Mom. She wants to save $145 to pay her entrance fees for the amusement parks. She has $98 saved. How much more does she need to save? Show how you found your answer.

_____

Demonstrate subtraction with three-digit numbers, utilizing regrouping

Why Aren't Dragons Hungry on Weekends?

Name_____

To solve the riddle, solve each multiplication problem. Then write the letter on the line above each product. The letters will spell out the answer for you.

E $7 \times 8 =$ ___56___   H $6 \times 3 =$ _____

T $3 \times 2 =$ _____   N $7 \times 10 =$ _____

E $9 \times 6 =$ _____   K $8 \times 9 =$ _____

T $1 \times 8 =$ _____   O $7 \times 9 =$ _____

E $2 \times 6 =$ _____   H $8 \times 4 =$ _____

G $9 \times 3 =$ _____   S $6 \times 6 =$ _____

Y $8 \times 8 =$ _____   A $7 \times 6 =$ _____

K $5 \times 9 =$ _____   I $8 \times 6 =$ _____

N $8 \times 3 =$ _____   T $10 \times 5 =$ _____

Y $2 \times 10 =$ _____   L $9 \times 9 =$ _____

W $7 \times 7 =$ _____   A $2 \times 1 =$ _____

___ ___ _E_ ___   ___ ___ ___ ___
 8   32   56   20   63   24   81   64

___ ___ ___   ___ ___ ___ ___
12   42   6   49   54   2   45

___ ___ ___ ___   ___ ___ ___
72   70   48   27   18   50   36

Demonstrate multiplication facts through 10 x 10

Tongue Twister

Solve each multiplication problem. Then write the letter on each line above the product. Read the tongue twister and try to say it quickly three times.

A 8 × 7 = _____56_____		**R** 3 × 6 = _____	
E 6 × 7 = _____		**S** 9 × 6 = _____	
G 7 × 7 = _____		**T** 7 × 9 = _____	
I 5 × 6 = _____		**U** 2 × 5 = _____	
N 9 × 4 = _____		**Y** 9 × 9 = _____	
O 8 × 3 = _____			

___ ___ ___ ___
63   30   36   81

___ ___ A̅ ___   ___ ___ ___ A̅ ___
24   18   56   36   49   10   63   56   36

___ ___ ___ ___ ___ ___ ___
63   24   36   49   10   42   54

Demonstrate multiplication facts through 10 x 10

Multiplication Table

Complete the following multiplication table, but be aware that the numbers are **not** in the usual order. (The first box, 6 x 7, has been done for you.)

✖	6	1	4	9	2	7	3	10	5	8
7	42									
2										
9										
4										
5										
1										
3										
8										
10										
6										

Demonstrate multiplication facts through 10 x 10

Fast Facts

Name _____

Complete the following multiplication problems as quickly as you can.

1. 5 × 6 = _____   2 × 8 = _____   1 × 7 = _____

2. 2 × 7 = _____   8 × 9 = _____   8 × 7 = _____

3. 4 × 8 = _____   7 × 6 = _____   9 × 2 = _____

4. 9 × 6 = _____   3 × 3 = _____   7 × 4 = _____

5. 1 × 6 = _____   10 × 7 = _____   9 × 5 = _____

6. 10 × 5 = _____   8 × 8 = _____   5 × 1 = _____

7. 2 × 9 = _____   9 × 4 = _____   5 × 8 = _____

8. 9 × 9 = _____   4 × 4 = _____   10 × 9 = _____

9. 4 × 1 = _____   8 × 3 = _____   3 × 7 = _____

10. 7 × 7 = _____   2 × 2 = _____   6 × 8 = _____

11. 4 × 10 = _____   6 × 10 = _____   10 × 10 = _____

12. 2 × 1 = _____   5 × 7 = _____   9 × 3 = _____

13. 1 × 8 = _____   7 × 9 = _____

14. 6 × 6 = _____   8 × 2 = _____

How long did it take you to complete all the problems? _____

How many did you get correct? _____

Demonstrate multiplication facts through 10 x 10

 EMC 3017 • Basic Math Skills, Grade 4 • ©2003 by Evan-Moor Corp.

Around the Classroom

Name_____

Solve each problem.

1. There are three boys in Mrs. Johnson's fourth-grade classroom. Each boy brought 9 baseball cards to school with him. How many baseball cards were there in all?

   _____

2. Shirley brought 8 jars, each filled with 5 stuffed frogs. How many frogs did she have in all?

   _____

3. Jason wanted to bring cupcakes for his entire class. He brought 6 packages with 3 cupcakes in each package. If there are 21 students in his class, did he have enough cupcakes? Tell why or why not.

   _____

4. Brett was collecting quarters. He wanted to exchange a five-dollar bill for quarters. How many quarters will he get?

   _____

5. Regina bought packages of markers to share with her after-school club. She bought 7 boxes of the 8 packs of markers. There are 25 girls in her club. Did she have enough markers for each girl to have one?

   _____

6. Maria was climbing up a large flight of stairs, taking 3 steps at a time. If she made 7 strides with her feet, how many steps were there in the flight of stairs?

   _____

Demonstrate multiplication facts through 10 x 10

Math Test

Name _____

Fill in the circle next to the correct answer.

1. 7 × 8 = _____
   - Ⓐ 42
   - Ⓑ 56
   - Ⓒ 48
   - Ⓓ none of the above

2. 9 × 6 = _____
   - Ⓐ 54
   - Ⓑ 56
   - Ⓒ 48
   - Ⓓ none of the above

3. 3 × 8 = _____
   - Ⓐ 12
   - Ⓑ 18
   - Ⓒ 24
   - Ⓓ none of the above

4. 4 × 7 = _____
   - Ⓐ 21
   - Ⓑ 24
   - Ⓒ 27
   - Ⓓ none of the above

5. Which of the following does NOT have a product of 24?
   - Ⓐ 8 × 3
   - Ⓑ 6 × 4
   - Ⓒ 9 × 3
   - Ⓓ 3 × 8

6. Which of the following does NOT have a product of 12?
   - Ⓐ 4 × 3
   - Ⓑ 5 × 2
   - Ⓒ 6 × 2
   - Ⓓ 3 × 4

7. Chad was buying 4 six-packs of soda. How many sodas did he buy in all?
   - Ⓐ 4
   - Ⓑ 6
   - Ⓒ 12
   - Ⓓ 24

8. Suzy has 9 bags of erasers. Each bag has 6 erasers. Does she have enough to give one eraser to each student in her class if there are 27 students in her class?
   - Ⓐ Yes, because she has 30 erasers.
   - Ⓑ No, because she only has 6 erasers.
   - Ⓒ Yes, because she has 54 erasers.
   - Ⓓ No, because she only has 18 erasers.

9. Jake was buying muffins for his birthday treats for his class. There are 32 students in his class. If he buys 9 six-packs of muffins, will he have enough? Tell why or why not.

   _____

   _____

   _____

   _____

10. Michelle has 6 packs of gum. If each pack has 5 pieces, how many pieces does she have?

   _____

Why Did the Spider Get a New Computer?

Name _____

Solve each multiplication problem. Then write each letter on the line above the product. The letters will spell out the answer for you.

T   8 × 7 = ___56___

D   11 × 4 = _____

D   9 × 7 = _____

I   5 × 2 = _____

E   8 × 8 = _____

E   11 × 9 = _____

A   12 × 3 = _____

E   4 × 10 = _____

S   3 × 4 = _____

E   10 × 11 = _____

B   9 × 3 = _____

W   12 × 6 = _____

E   7 × 12 = _____

H   3 × 6 = _____

N   9 × 6 = _____

E   11 × 11 = _____

___ ___
18   84

___ ___ ___ ___ ___ ___
54 110 99   44 121 63

___ ___ ___ ___
36   72   64   27

___ ___ ___ ___
12   10   56   40
            T

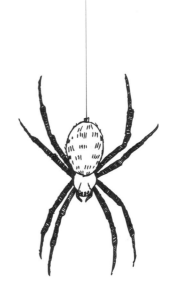

Demonstrate multiplication facts through 12 x 12

Number & Operations

Tongue Twister

Name _____

Solve each multiplication problem. Then write the letter on each line above the product. Read the tongue twister and try to say it quickly three times.

C 12 × 4 = _____48_____

E 9 × 7 = _____

H 11 × 11 = _____

I 5 × 11 = _____

K 8 × 7 = _____

L 11 × 12 = _____

S 9 × 11 = _____

T 12 × 12 = _____

X 10 × 11 = _____

Frank fries freshhhh f-i-s-h f-i-l-l-e-t-s

| ___ | ___ | ___ | | ___ | ___ | ___ | C | ___ |
| 99 | 55 | 110 | | 144 | 121 | 55 | 48 | 56 |

| ___ | ___ | ___ | ___ | ___ | ___ | ___ |
| 144 | 121 | 55 | 99 | 144 | 132 | 63 |

say it quick!

| ___ | ___ | ___ | C | ___ | ___ |
| 99 | 144 | 55 | 48 | 56 | 99 |

Demonstrate multiplication facts through 12 × 12

EMC 3017 • Basic Math Skills, Grade 4 • ©2003 by Evan-Moor Corp.

A Different Multiplication Table

Name_____

Complete the multiplication table, but be aware that the numbers are **not** in the usual order. (The first box, 1 x 2, has been done for you.)

✕	2	12	10	6	8	5	7	1	11	4	9	3
1	2											
6												
12												
4												
7												
10												
3												
8												
11												
9												
5												
2												

Demonstrate multiplication facts through 12 x 12

Number & Operations

Quick as a Wink

Name _____

Complete the multiplication problems as quickly as you can.

1. 5 × 12 = _____   2 × 8 = _____   11 × 7 = _____

2. 2 × 7 = _____   8 × 9 = _____   8 × 7 = _____

3. 4 × 8 = _____   7 × 6 = _____   11 × 2 = _____

4. 9 × 6 = _____   3 × 3 = _____   7 × 4 = _____

5. 1 × 11 = _____   10 × 7 = _____   9 × 5 = _____

6. 10 × 5 = _____   8 × 8 = _____   5 × 1 = _____

7. 12 × 9 = _____   9 × 12 = _____   5 × 8 = _____

8. 9 × 9 = _____   4 × 4 = _____   10 × 9 = _____

9. 4 × 11 = _____   8 × 3 = _____   3 × 7 = _____

10. 7 × 7 = _____   2 × 12 = _____   6 × 8 = _____

11. 4 × 0 = _____   6 × 10 = _____   10 × 10 = _____

12. 12 × 1 = _____   5 × 7 = _____   12 × 12 = _____

13. 11 × 8 = _____   7 × 9 = _____

14. 6 × 6 = _____   8 × 2 = _____

How long did it take you to complete all the problems? _____

How many did you get correct? _____

Demonstrate multiplication facts through 12 x 12

Using Multiplication

Name _____

Solve each problem.

1. George was collecting eggs. He filled 6 cartons that each held one dozen. How many eggs did George collect?

   _____

2. Shawna collected stamps. She found that she could put 10 35-cent stamps on each page. If she had 6 full pages, how many stamps did she have?

   _____

3. Sharise is packing 6 lunches for her family to go on a picnic. She knows that each person wants 2 sandwiches with 2 slices of bread for each sandwich. How many slices of bread does she need?

   _____

4. Leanne was buying six-packs of flowers to plant with her mother. She bought 11 six-packs. Does she have enough flowers if she wants to plant a row with 70 plants in it?

   _____

5. Josh is riding his bike when he notices that there are 12 spokes that attach to the right side of his tire and 12 spokes that attach to the left side of the tire. If the front and back tires are the same, how many spokes are on his two tires? Can you solve the problem two different ways?

   _____

   _____

Demonstrate multiplication facts through 12 x 12

Number & Operations

Math Test

Name _____

Fill in the circle next to the correct answer.

1. 11 × 12 = _____
   - Ⓐ 144
   - Ⓑ 132
   - Ⓒ 121
   - Ⓓ none of the above

2. 9 × 8 = _____
   - Ⓐ 72
   - Ⓑ 84
   - Ⓒ 81
   - Ⓓ none of the above

3. 10 × 12 = _____
   - Ⓐ 121
   - Ⓑ 144
   - Ⓒ 100
   - Ⓓ none of the above

4. 7 × 5 = _____
   - Ⓐ 42
   - Ⓑ 35
   - Ⓒ 56
   - Ⓓ none of the above

5. Which of the following does NOT have a product of 24?
   - Ⓐ 6 × 4
   - Ⓑ 2 × 12
   - Ⓒ 10 × 2
   - Ⓓ 3 × 8

6. Which of the following does NOT have a product of 36?
   - Ⓐ 12 × 3
   - Ⓑ 9 × 4
   - Ⓒ 6 × 6
   - Ⓓ 5 × 7

7. Annie bought 7 six-packs of soda to share with her class of 22 students. Are there enough sodas for each student to receive two?
   - Ⓐ Yes, there are 42 sodas and she needs 22.
   - Ⓑ Yes, there are 48 sodas and she needs 44.
   - Ⓒ Yes, there are 48 sodas and she needs 22.
   - Ⓓ No, there are 42 sodas and she needs 44.

8. Colton is collecting empty milk cartons to make a castle. He needs 12 cartons for each wall and wants to build a castle with 8 walls. How many cartons does he need?
   - Ⓐ 20
   - Ⓑ 96
   - Ⓒ 12
   - Ⓓ 84

9. Alec is sharing gum with his class of 25 students. He has 6 packs with 5 pieces in each pack. Does he have enough gum? Why or why not?

   _____

   _____

   _____

   _____

10. Amanda is bringing bags of cookies to her Girl Scout meeting. She is bringing 4 bags with a dozen cookies in each bag. How many cookies is she bringing?

    _____

Demonstrate multiplication facts through 12 x 12

EMC 3017 • Basic Math Skills, Grade 4 • ©2003 by Evan-Moor Corp.

When Is a Door Not a Door?

Name_____

Solve each multiplication problem. Then write the letter on the line for each product. The letters will spell out the answer for you.

A 12 × 27 = _____324_____   J 49 × 89 = _____

A 63 × 54 = _____   N 615 × 42 = _____

E 120 × 56 = _____   R 713 × 39 = _____

H 430 × 12 = _____   S 46 × 297 = _____

I 951 × 13 = _____   T 55 × 714 = _____

I 342 × 25 = _____   W 342 × 22 = _____

____ ____ ____ ____
7,524 5,160 6,720 25,830

____ ____   ____ ____
8,550 39,270   12,363 13,662

____ ____ _A_ ____
3,402 4,361 324 27,807

Demonstrate multiplication with various numbers up to a three-digit number multiplied by a two-digit number

Maze

Name _____

Solve each problem in order as you find the way through the maze.
Color the path through the maze.

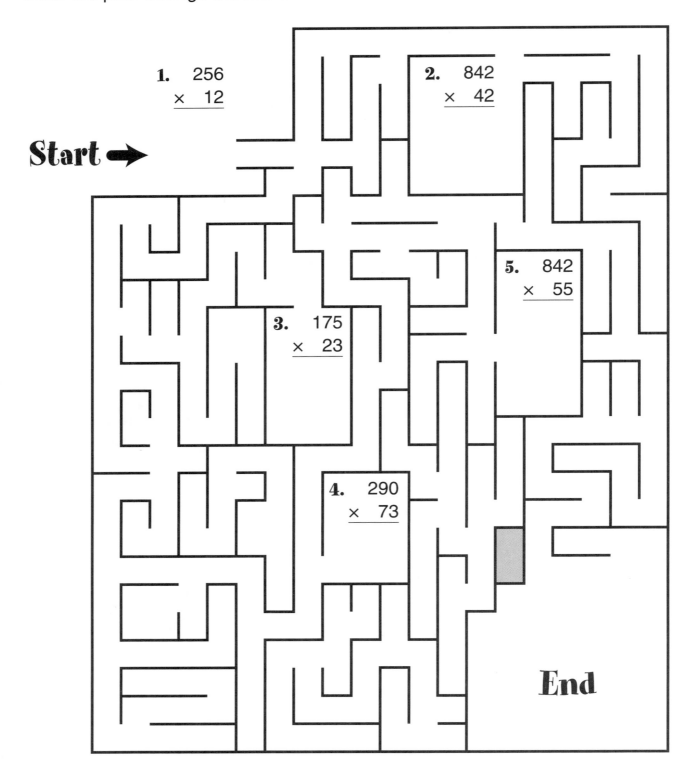

Start ➡

1. 256
    × 12

2. 842
    × 42

3. 175
    × 23

4. 290
    × 73

5. 842
    × 55

End

Demonstrate multiplication with various numbers up to a three-digit number multiplied by a two-digit number

EMC 3017 • Basic Math Skills, Grade 4 • ©2003 by Evan-Moor Corp.

Write the Product

Name _____

Solve the following problems.

1. 25 × 75 = _____

2. 84 × 52 = _____

3. 62 × 38 = _____

4. 128 × 73 = _____

5. 593 × 26 = _____

6. 372 × 73 = _____

7. 274 × 84 = _____

8. 751 × 80 = _____

9. 59 × 991 = _____

10. 734 × 14 = _____

11. 84
    × 90

12. 25
    × 11

13. 64
    × 21

14. 134
    × 16

15. 295
    × 40

16. 249
    × 34

17. 167
    × 59

18. 82
    × 136

19. 148
    × 27

20. 63
    × 120

Demonstrate multiplication with various numbers up to a three-digit number multiplied by a two-digit number

Number & Operations

Multiplication Challenge

Name _____

Solve the following problems.

1. 63 × 51 = _____

2. 43 × 82 = _____

3. 12 × 43 = _____

4. 240 × 67 = _____

5. 382 × 18 = _____

6. 726 × 45 = _____

7. 453 × 34 = _____

8. 123 × 44 = _____

9. 22 × 715 = _____

10. 423 × 50 = _____

11. 47
   × 28

12. 67
   × 66

13. 56
   × 53

14. 285
   × 64

15. 549
   × 52

16. 632
   × 84

17. 194
   × 42

18. 84
   × 267

19. 492
   × 46

20. 18
   × 105

Demonstrate multiplication with various numbers up to a three-digit number multiplied by a two-digit number

EMC 3017 • Basic Math Skills, Grade 4 • ©2003 by Evan-Moor Corp.

At School

Name _____

Solve each problem.

1. Hudson Elementary School is planning their fundraiser. To meet their goal, they have asked every student to raise $25. If there are 492 students in the school, how much money do they want to earn to make their goal?

   _____

2. Shirley has 26 students in her class at school. Each one is bringing in 250 sheets of paper. How many sheets of paper in all will there be in her class? Can you solve the problem in at least two different ways?

   _____

   _____

3. Kevin has 49 books on his shelf. There are an average of 129 pages in each book. About how many pages are on the bookshelf?

   _____

4. In the problem above, if a worm starts at one end of the bookshelf and eats through all the pages to the other end, how many pages will the worm eat through, including the front and back covers of each book?

   _____

5. Ian and Rebecca are stacking newspapers in the corner of their classroom. They need 145 newspapers to reach the height of their window. There are 42 pages in each newspaper, and when stacked, they fold them in half. How many sheets of paper does it take to reach the window's height?

   _____

Demonstrate multiplication with various numbers up to a three-digit number multiplied by a two-digit number

Number & Operations

Math Test

Name _____

Fill in the circle next to the correct answer.

1. 11 × 29 is about _____
   - Ⓐ 200
   - Ⓒ 150
   - Ⓑ 300
   - Ⓓ 400

2. 49 × 26 = _____
   - Ⓐ 294
   - Ⓒ 1,274
   - Ⓑ 392
   - Ⓓ 338

3. 164 × 29 = _____
   - Ⓐ 4,756
   - Ⓒ 328
   - Ⓑ 1,476
   - Ⓓ 1,804

4. 198 × 11 = _____
   - Ⓐ 198
   - Ⓒ 2,078
   - Ⓑ 396
   - Ⓓ 2,178

5. Which problem does NOT have a product of 1,680?
   - Ⓐ 42 × 40
   - Ⓑ 24 × 70
   - Ⓒ 42 × 48
   - Ⓓ 48 × 35

6. Which problem does NOT have a product of 2,450?
   - Ⓐ 24 × 50
   - Ⓑ 245 × 10
   - Ⓒ 49 × 50
   - Ⓓ 70 × 35

7. Charles is buying 14 boxes of sports cards. If each box contains 125 cards, how many cards is he purchasing?
   - Ⓐ 1,750
   - Ⓒ 625
   - Ⓑ 500
   - Ⓓ none of the above

8. Samantha has 84 CDs on her shelf. The average length of her CDs is 72 minutes. If she listened to all the CDs nonstop, how many minutes would it take her?
   - Ⓐ 7,258
   - Ⓒ 756
   - Ⓑ 864
   - Ⓓ 6,048

9. There are 25 classrooms in Heath Elementary School. Each classroom has one phone and the office has 5 phones. There are 12 buttons on each phone. How many buttons are there in all?

   _____

10. Centennial Elementary School wants to raise $19,000 for some new playground equipment. There are 579 students in the school. If each student raises $30, will they have enough money? Justify your answer.

   _____

   _____

   _____

   _____

Demonstrate multiplication with various numbers up to a three-digit number multiplied by a two-digit number

What Kind of Key Won't Work in a Lock?

Name _____

Write the letter for each division problem on the line above the model.
The letters will spell out the answer for you.

A $16 \div 2 = \underline{8}$ **N** $18 \div 3 = \underline{}$

E $24 \div 4 = \underline{}$ **O** $24 \div 3 = \underline{}$

K $12 \div 2 = \underline{}$ **Y** $16 \div 4 = \underline{}$

M $18 \div 2 = \underline{}$

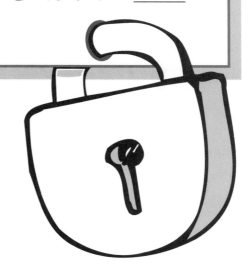

A

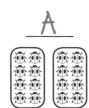

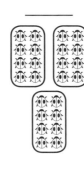

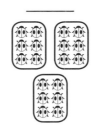

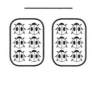

Demonstrate division in conceptual form (single-digit divisors)

Number & Operations

What Is It?

Write two division facts for each model. Then color the spaces in the picture.

✶✶✶✶✶✶✶✶✶✶✶✶
✶✶✶✶✶✶✶✶✶✶✶✶
Yellow

$24 \div 2 = 6$

$24 \div 12 = 2$

✶✶✶✶✶✶
✶✶✶✶✶✶ _____
Blue _____

✶✶✶✶
✶✶✶✶ _____
✶✶✶✶ _____
✶✶✶✶
✶✶✶✶
✶✶✶✶
Blue

✶✶✶✶
✶✶✶✶ _____
✶✶✶✶ _____
Yellow

✶✶✶✶✶✶
✶✶✶✶✶✶ _____
✶✶✶✶✶✶ _____
Blue

$18 \div 6 =$

$12 \div 2 =$

$12 \div 6 =$

$24 \div 6 =$

$24 \div 4 =$

$18 \div 6 =$

$18 \div 3 =$

$18 \div 6 =$

$24 \div 2 =$

$18 \div 3 =$

$24 \div 6 =$

$12 \div 2 =$

$18 \div 3 =$

$24 \div 4 =$

$24 \div 4 =$

$24 \div 6 =$

$24 \div 2 =$

$12 \div 3 =$

$18 \div 6 =$

$12 \div 6 =$

$24 \div 12 =$

$24 \div 4 =$

$12 \div 4 =$

$12 \div 3 =$

$12 \div 4 =$

$18 \div 6 =$

$12 \div 3 =$

$24 \div 2 =$

$12 \div 2 =$

$12 \div 6 =$

$18 \div 3 =$

$24 \div 4 =$

$24 \div 4 =$

$18 \div 6 =$

$18 \div 6 =$

$24 \div 4 =$

$18 \div 3 =$

$24 \div 6 =$

$24 \div 6 =$

$24 \div 6 =$

Demonstrate division in a conceptual form (single-digit divisors)

Division Facts

Name _____

Each model represents two different division facts.

This model could represent
12 ÷ 6 or **12 ÷ 2**.

✿✿✿✿✿✿
✿✿✿✿✿✿

Write two division facts for each model.

1. ✿✿✿✿✿✿ _____
   ✿✿✿✿✿✿ _____
   ✿✿✿✿✿✿

3. ✿✿✿ _____
   ✿✿✿ _____
   ✿✿✿
   ✿✿✿
   ✿✿✿

2. ✿✿✿✿✿✿ _____
   ✿✿✿✿✿✿ _____
   ✿✿✿✿✿✿
   ✿✿✿✿✿✿

Draw a model to represent each division fact.

4. 8 ÷ 4 = 2	**5.** 12 ÷ 3 = 4

Demonstrate division in a conceptual form (single-digit divisors)

Division Models

Name _____

Each model represents two different division facts.

```
This model could represent
    18 ÷ 6 or 18 ÷ 3.
```

Write two division facts for each model.

1. ✐ ✐ ✐ ✐   _____
    ✐ ✐ ✐ ✐
    ✐ ✐ ✐ ✐   _____
    ✐ ✐ ✐ ✐

3. ☎ ☎ ☎   _____

    ☎ ☎ ☎   _____

    ☎ ☎ ☎

2. ☆☆☆☆☆☆☆☆   _____
    ☆☆☆☆☆☆☆☆
    ☆☆☆☆☆☆☆☆   _____

Draw a model to represent each division fact.

4. $18 ÷ 6 = 3$	5. $9 ÷ 3 = 3$

Demonstrate division in a conceptual form (single-digit divisors)

Draw a Picture

Name _____

Draw a picture to illustrate each problem. Then solve each problem.

1. Jerry has 18 candy bars that he would like to divide evenly between himself and 5 other friends. How many candy bars will each person receive?

   _____

2. Carol and her 4 sisters earned $25 for baby-sitting. How much should each one receive if they divide the money evenly?

   _____

3. Beverly has a bag of candy and wants to share it with the 6 students in her reading group (the 6 includes Beverly). If there are 30 pieces of candy in the bag, how many pieces of candy does each person get?

   _____

4. John has 28 stickers. He wants to put one sticker on each of the 4 corners of each page in his notebook. How many pages will have stickers?

   _____

   If there are 10 pages in the book, how many more stickers does he need to put stickers on every page?

   _____

Demonstrate division in a conceptual form (single-digit divisors)

Number & Operations

Math Test

Name _____

Fill in the circle next to the correct answer.

1. Which of these represents 6 ÷ 2 = 3?

Ⓐ

Ⓑ

Ⓒ

Ⓓ

2. Which of these does NOT represent 12 ÷ 3 = 4 ?

Ⓐ

Ⓑ

Ⓒ

Ⓓ

3. Which of these represents 5 ÷ 1 = 5 ?

Ⓐ

Ⓑ

Ⓒ

Ⓓ

4. Which of these is illustrated by this model?

Ⓐ 9 ÷ 3 = 3   Ⓒ 18 ÷ 3 = 6
Ⓑ 18 ÷ 9 = 2   Ⓓ 15 ÷ 3 = 5

5. Which of the following is illustrated by this model?

Ⓐ 24 ÷ 8 = 3   Ⓒ 16 ÷ 8 = 2
Ⓑ 18 ÷ 3 = 6   Ⓓ 12 ÷ 3 = 4

6. 24 ÷ 3 = _____
Ⓐ 6   Ⓒ 12
Ⓑ 4   Ⓓ none of the above

7. 12 ÷ 4 = _____
Ⓐ 3   Ⓒ 6
Ⓑ 4   Ⓓ none of the above

8. 15 ÷ 5 = _____
Ⓐ 10   Ⓒ 3
Ⓑ 5   Ⓓ none of the above

9. Draw a picture of what 21 divided by 7 means.

10. Juanita has 27 pieces of gum to divide evenly among 9 people. Draw a picture to show how many pieces of gum each person will get.

Demonstrate division in a conceptual form (single-digit divisors)

EMC 3017 • Basic Math Skills, Grade 4 • ©2003 by Evan-Moor Corp.

What Did the Car Have on Its Toast This Morning?

Solve each division problem. Then write the letter on the line for each answer. The letters will spell out the answer to the riddle.

A	12 ÷ 6 = __2__	**J**	28 ÷ 7 = _____
C	54 ÷ 9 = _____	**M**	64 ÷ 8 = _____
F	20 ÷ 4 = _____	**R**	49 ÷ 7 = _____
I	36 ÷ 4 = _____	**T**	27 ÷ 9 = _____

___ ___ A ___ ___ ___ ___
 3   7   2   5   5   9   6

___ A ___
 4   2   8

Demonstrate division facts (through divisors of nine)

Number & Operations

What Kind of House Weighs the Least?

Name _____

Solve each division problem. Then write the letter on the line for each answer. The letters will spell out the answer to the riddle.

$8 \div 8 =$ __1__   __A__

$48 \div 8 =$ ____   ____

$25 \div 5 =$ ____   ____

$9 \div 3 =$ ____   ____

$12 \div 3 =$ ____   ____

$27 \div 3 =$ ____   ____

$24 \div 6 =$ ____   ____

$49 \div 7 =$ ____   ____

$0 \div 5 =$ ____   ____

$56 \div 7 =$ ____   ____

$16 \div 8 =$ ____   ____

1	A
2	E
3	G
4	H
5	I
6	L
7	O
8	S
9	T
0	U

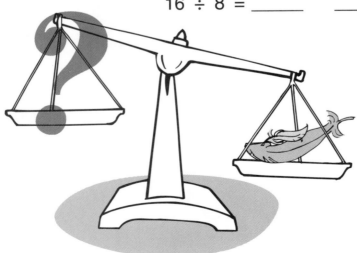

Demonstrate division facts (through divisors of nine)

Quick Answers

Name _____

Complete the following division problems as quickly as you can.

1. $24 \div 8 =$ _____ $12 \div 6 =$ _____ $8 \div 8 =$ _____

2. $42 \div 7 =$ _____ $63 \div 7 =$ _____ $21 \div 7 =$ _____

3. $27 \div 9 =$ _____ $72 \div 8 =$ _____ $3 \div 1 =$ _____

4. $35 \div 5 =$ _____ $7 \div 7 =$ _____ $45 \div 9 =$ _____

5. $63 \div 9 =$ _____ $0 \div 7 =$ _____ $7 \div 1 =$ _____

6. $49 \div 7 =$ _____ $64 \div 8 =$ _____ $15 \div 5 =$ _____

7. $18 \div 6 =$ _____ $25 \div 5 =$ _____ $30 \div 5 =$ _____

8. $9 \div 3 =$ _____ $36 \div 6 =$ _____ $10 \div 5 =$ _____

9. $14 \div 7 =$ _____ $12 \div 2 =$ _____ $10 \div 2 =$ _____

10. $45 \div 5 =$ _____ $18 \div 9 =$ _____ $54 \div 6 =$ _____

11. $24 \div 6 =$ _____ $12 \div 4 =$ _____ $8 \div 2 =$ _____

12. $40 \div 5 =$ _____ $20 \div 5 =$ _____ $9 \div 1 =$ _____

13. $48 \div 8 =$ _____ $16 \div 8 =$ _____

14. $42 \div 6 =$ _____ $0 \div 5 =$ _____

How long did it take you to complete all the problems? _____

How many did you get correct? _____

Demonstrate division facts (through divisors of nine)

Number & Operations

Division Facts

Name _____

Complete the following division problems as quickly as you can.

1. $28 \div 4 =$ _____ $6 \div 2 =$ _____ $21 \div 7 =$ _____

2. $15 \div 5 =$ _____ $72 \div 8 =$ _____ $9 \div 3 =$ _____

3. $30 \div 5 =$ _____ $24 \div 6 =$ _____ $24 \div 4 =$ _____

4. $3 \div 1 =$ _____ $0 \div 7 =$ _____ $28 \div 7 =$ _____

5. $49 \div 7 =$ _____ $72 \div 9 =$ _____ $36 \div 9 =$ _____

6. $27 \div 3 =$ _____ $8 \div 8 =$ _____ $32 \div 8 =$ _____

7. $40 \div 8 =$ _____ $12 \div 4 =$ _____ $35 \div 5 =$ _____

8. $20 \div 5 =$ _____ $18 \div 6 =$ _____ $6 \div 6 =$ _____

9. $4 \div 4 =$ _____ $48 \div 6 =$ _____ $0 \div 9 =$ _____

10. $16 \div 8 =$ _____ $25 \div 5 =$ _____ $24 \div 8 =$ _____

11. $18 \div 2 =$ _____ $6 \div 3 =$ _____ $40 \div 5 =$ _____

12. $5 \div 5 =$ _____ $10 \div 5 =$ _____ $64 \div 8 =$ _____

13. $54 \div 9 =$ _____ $14 \div 7 =$ _____

14. $0 \div 2 =$ _____ $18 \div 3 =$ _____

How long did it take you to complete all the problems? _____

How many did you get correct? _____

Demonstrate division facts (through divisors of nine)

NUMBER & Operations   EMC 3017 • Basic Math Skills, Grade 4 • ©2003 by Evan-Moor Corp.

Using Division

Solve each problem.

1. Jennifer was dividing 64 cookies between herself and her 7 cousins. How many cookies does each get if she divides them evenly?

   _____

2. John has 24 brownies. He would like to divide them evenly into groups. What are some possible groups that he could divide them into evenly?

   _____

3. Virginia has 48 balloons. In her class are 8 tables. She wants to put the same number of balloons on each table for a class party at 3:00. How many balloons should she put on each table?

   _____

4. Paul is writing a book to give to a guest teacher. He has 8 pages in the book and wants all 72 students to sign the book. How many signatures should he get on each page so that all pages have the same number of signatures?

   _____

5. Bill has 2 dozen cupcakes that he wants to divide equally between himself, his 5 brothers, 3 sisters, and 3 friends. How many cupcakes should each person get? Show how you found your answer.

   _____

Demonstrate division facts (through divisors of nine)

Math Test

Fill in the circle next to the correct answer.

1. $42 \div 7 =$ _____

  Ⓐ 8   Ⓒ 6

  Ⓑ 7   Ⓓ none of the above

2. $72 \div 9 =$ _____

  Ⓐ 8   Ⓒ 9

  Ⓑ 7   Ⓓ none of the above

3. $35 \div 5 =$ _____

  Ⓐ 8   Ⓒ 6

  Ⓑ 7   Ⓓ none of the above

4. $24 \div 4 =$ _____

  Ⓐ 5   Ⓒ 8

  Ⓑ 3   Ⓓ none of the above

5. Which of the following does NOT equal 6?

  Ⓐ $24 \div 4$

  Ⓑ $18 \div 3$

  Ⓒ $30 \div 5$

  Ⓓ none of the above

6. Which of the following does NOT equal 3?

  Ⓐ $18 \div 6$

  Ⓑ $12 \div 4$

  Ⓒ $16 \div 4$

  Ⓓ none of the above

7. Which of the following equals 8?

  Ⓐ $72 \div 8$

  Ⓑ $56 \div 7$

  Ⓒ $49 \div 7$

  Ⓓ none of the above

8. Which of the following equals 5?

  Ⓐ $30 \div 5$

  Ⓑ $42 \div 7$

  Ⓒ $24 \div 6$

  Ⓓ none of the above

9. Write three division problems that all have the answer of 4.

_____

_____

_____

10. Jeremy has 75 tickets. He wants to give 3 to his little sister and divide the remaining tickets between himself and his 7 friends. How many tickets will each of his friends get?

_____

Demonstrate division facts (through divisors of nine)

Tongue Twister

Name _____

Solve each division problem. Then write the letter for each remainder on the line. Read the tongue twister and try to say it quickly three times.

Frank fries freshhhh f-i-s-h f-i-l-l-e-t-s

A = remainder of 1   N = remainder of 4

B = remainder of 2   O = remainder of 5

M = remainder of 3

17 ÷ 5 = __3__ remainder of __2__   __B__

15 ÷ 7 = _____ remainder of _____   _____

26 ÷ 4 = _____ remainder of _____   _____

54 ÷ 7 = _____ remainder of _____   _____

61 ÷ 8 = _____ remainder of _____   _____

44 ÷ 5 = _____ remainder of _____   _____

20 ÷ 9 = _____ remainder of _____   _____

6 ÷ 5 = _____ remainder of _____   _____

18 ÷ 5 = _____ remainder of _____   _____

10 ÷ 4 = _____ remainder of _____   _____

69 ÷ 8 = _____ remainder of _____   _____

37 ÷ 8 = _____ remainder of _____   _____

Demonstrate division with remainders (single-digit divisors)

What's Hiding?

Name _____

Complete each division problem in the picture below. Then look at each remainder and color each space, using this key.

Red = remainder of 1   **Red** = remainder of 3

Blue = remainder of 2   **Blue** = remainder of 4

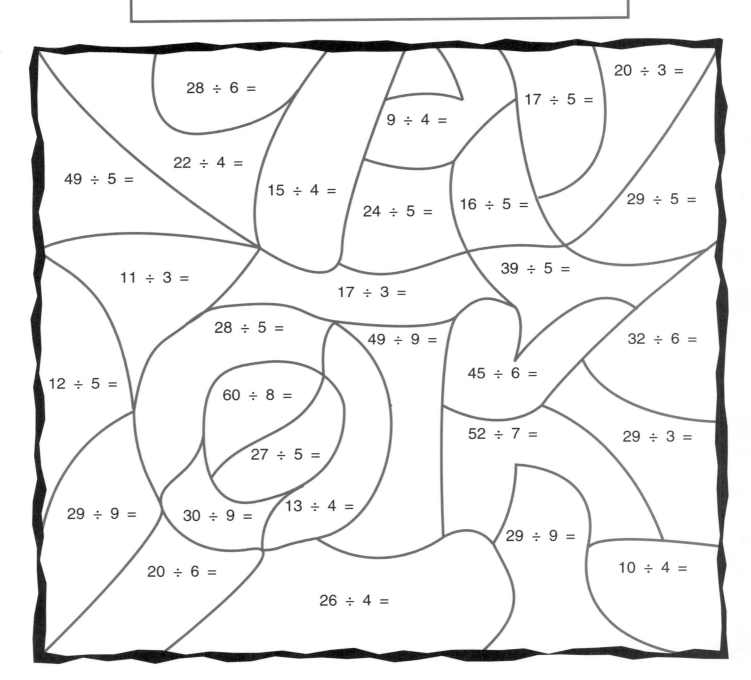

Demonstrate division with remainders (single-digit divisors)

Is There a Remainder?

Name _____

Solve each division problem. If there is a remainder, be sure to include that in your answer.

1. $84 \div 9 =$ _____

2. $49 \div 5 =$ _____

3. $37 \div 5 =$ _____

4. $29 \div 7 =$ _____

5. $84 \div 7 =$ _____

6. $62 \div 8 =$ _____

7. $28 \div 4 =$ _____

8. $73 \div 9 =$ _____

9. $68 \div 8 =$ _____

10. $15 \div 7 =$ _____

$$20 \div 6$$

$$35 \div 7$$

11. Write a sentence answering this question: What is a remainder?

_____

_____

_____

12. Write a sentence explaining what is meant if there is no remainder.

_____

_____

_____

Demonstrate division with remainders (single-digit divisors)

Remainders

Name _____

Solve each division problem. If there is a remainder, be sure to include that in your answer.

1. $9\overline{)62}$ 2. $8\overline{)42}$ 3. $9\overline{)46}$ 4. $6\overline{)27}$ 5. $4\overline{)84}$

6. $9\overline{)55}$ 7. $8\overline{)28}$ 8. $6\overline{)59}$ 9. $7\overline{)52}$ 10. $8\overline{)15}$

11. Write a sentence explaining what division is.

_____

_____

_____

12. Write a sentence explaining what is meant if there is a remainder.

_____

_____

_____

Demonstrate division with remainders (single-digit divisors)

EMC 3017 • Basic Math Skills, Grade 4 • ©2003 by Evan-Moor Corp.

Interpreting Remainders

Name_____

What is the most appropriate thing to do with any remainders in each of these situations?

1. Susy and her friends are sharing cookies among the four of them, and there are two left over.

_____

2. Mark and his friend are sharing dimes that they found, and there is one left over.

_____

3. Juan and Julia are sharing balloons from a package the teacher gave them, and there is one left over.

_____

4. Shane and Sarah are sharing time playing video games, and there are 8 minutes left over.

_____

Solve each of these problems.

5. Sherry's mom is making banners for the students in Sherry's class. She needs 9 inches of fabric for each one and has 8 feet of fabric. How many banners can she make from the 8 feet of fabric? How much fabric will be left over?

_____

6. Tristan is packaging cupcakes for the school bake sale. Julie brought in 16 cupcakes, Mary brought in 20 cupcakes, and Mark brought in 28 cupcakes. If Tristan is packaging them with 9 on a plate, how many cupcakes will be left over for the kids to snack on?

_____

7. Amber is passing out markers to the students in her reading group. There are 7 students in her group. If she starts with a canister of 55 markers, how many will each student get? Will there be any extras? If so, how many are left over?

_____

Demonstrate division with remainders (single-digit divisors)

Number & Operations

Math Test

Name _____

Fill in the circle next to the correct answer.

1. 84 ÷ 9 = _____

Ⓐ 9 remainder 3
Ⓑ 8 remainder 4
Ⓒ 9 remainder 4
Ⓓ 8 remainder 3

2. 56 ÷ 9 = _____

Ⓐ 5 remainder 6
Ⓑ 6 remainder 2
Ⓒ 6 remainder 4
Ⓓ none of the above

3. 73 ÷ 9 = _____

Ⓐ 8 remainder 2
Ⓑ 7 remainder 1
Ⓒ 8 remainder 3
Ⓓ none of the above

4. 35 ÷ 8 = _____

Ⓐ 3 remainder 3
Ⓑ 4 remainder 3
Ⓒ 4 remainder 4
Ⓓ none of the above

5. Which of the following has a remainder of 2?

Ⓐ 83 ÷ 9
Ⓑ 42 ÷ 6
Ⓒ 35 ÷ 8
Ⓓ 24 ÷ 9

6. Which of the following has a remainder of 3?

Ⓐ 25 ÷ 5
Ⓑ 32 ÷ 9
Ⓒ 28 ÷ 9
Ⓓ none of the above

7. Which of the following does NOT have a remainder of 2?

Ⓐ 9 ÷ 4
Ⓑ 12 ÷ 5
Ⓒ 18 ÷ 4
Ⓓ none of the above

8. Which of the following does NOT have a remainder of 4?

Ⓐ 24 ÷ 5
Ⓑ 40 ÷ 6
Ⓒ 30 ÷ 8
Ⓓ none of the above

---

9. What is a remainder?

_____

_____

_____

10. Henry and Louise are gathering shells to share with their family. There are a total of 5 people in their family. If they collect 97 shells, how many should they give to each family member? Will there be any extras? If so, what could they do with the extras?

_____

_____

_____

Demonstrate division with remainders (single-digit divisors)

EMC 3017 • Basic Math Skills, Grade 4 • ©2003 by Evan-Moor Corp.

Amusement Park

Name _____

Using a crayon, draw a path through the maze. At each circled number, decide if the number is odd or even and continue through the maze to the Amusement Park.

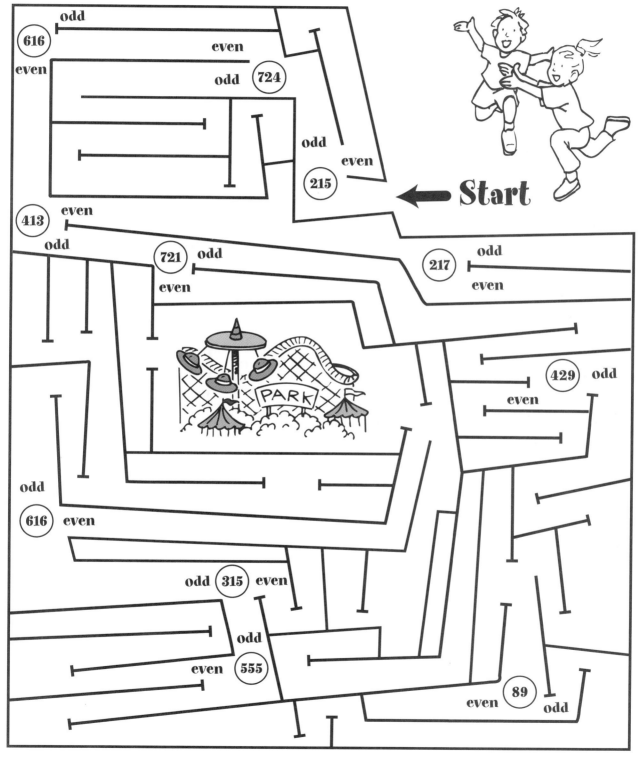

Identify any number as odd or even, and numbers under 100 as prime or composite

Candy Store

Name _____

Using a crayon, draw a path through the maze. At each circled number, decide if the number is prime (P) or composite (C) and continue your path until you get to the Candy Store.

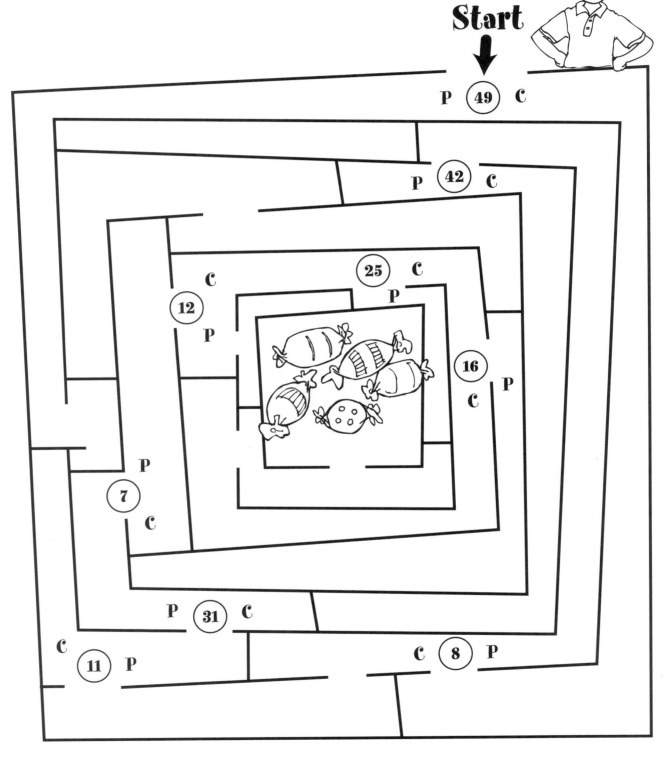

Start

P (49) C

P (42) C

(25) C

C

(12)

P

P

(16)

C

P

P

7

C

P (31) C

C

(11) P

C (8) P

Identify any number as odd or even, and numbers under 100 as prime or composite

Number & Operations

EMC 3017 • Basic Math Skills, Grade 4 • ©2003 by Evan-Moor Corp.

Odd or Even?

Name _____

Look at each of the following numbers. Circle **odd** or **even** for each number.

1. 285	**odd**	**even**	
2. 482	**odd**	**even**	
3. 97	**odd**	**even**	
4. 31	**odd**	**even**	
5. 53	**odd**	**even**	
6. 523	**odd**	**even**	
7. 624	**odd**	**even**	
8. 56	**odd**	**even**	
9. 63	**odd**	**even**	
10. 3	**odd**	**even**	
11. 32	**odd**	**even**	
12. 25	**odd**	**even**	

13. 216	**odd**	**even**	
14. 624	**odd**	**even**	
15. 134	**odd**	**even**	
16. 827	**odd**	**even**	
17. 501	**odd**	**even**	
18. 419	**odd**	**even**	
19. 481	**odd**	**even**	
20. 820	**odd**	**even**	
21. 480	**odd**	**even**	
22. 28	**odd**	**even**	
23. 7	**odd**	**even**	
24. 6	**odd**	**even**	

Identify any number as odd or even, and numbers under 100 as prime or composite

Number & Operations

Finding Prime Numbers

Name_____

Follow the directions to find prime numbers.

1. Use a black crayon to cross out the number 1 since it is neither prime nor composite.

2. Use a red crayon to circle the number 2. This number is the first prime number.

3. Use a blue crayon to cross out all even numbers since 2 goes into all even numbers.

4. Use a red crayon to circle the 3. This is the next-smallest prime number.

5. Use the blue crayon to cross out all multiples of 3 that have not already been marked out.

6. Continue alternating between the red and blue crayon following steps 4 and 5 until all the numbers on the chart have either been crossed out or circled.

1	2	3	4	5	6	7	8	9	10
11	12	13	14	15	16	17	18	19	20
21	22	23	24	25	26	27	28	29	30
31	32	33	34	35	36	37	38	39	40
41	42	43	44	45	46	47	48	49	50
51	52	53	54	55	56	57	58	59	60
61	62	63	64	65	66	67	68	69	70
71	72	73	74	75	76	77	78	79	80
81	82	83	84	85	86	87	88	89	90
91	92	93	94	95	96	97	98	99	100

List all the prime numbers (circled in red) between 1 and 100._____

_____

Identify any number as odd or even, and numbers under 100 as prime or composite

EMC 3017 • Basic Math Skills, Grade 4 • ©2003 by Evan-Moor Corp.

Problem Solving

Name _____

Solve each problem.

1. Julie, a carpenter, has two measuring sticks. The lengths of the two measuring sticks are the two prime numbers between 4 and 10. What are the lengths of the measuring sticks? If Julie wants to cut a length of 1 unit, how can this be done with the fewest number of cuts?

   _____

2. Kyle is another carpenter. He has three measuring sticks. The lengths of his sticks are the prime numbers between 6 and 15. He needs to create a length of 8. How might Kyle do this with his three measuring sticks?

   _____

3. Shirley claims that any time you add two odd numbers together that the answer is always even. Do you think that she is correct? Write a few examples and see what the answers are.

   _____

4. Similarly, Jonathan notices that if you add two even numbers together that the sum is always even. Do you think that is always true? Write a few examples and see what the answers are.

   _____

5. Juan says that if you add an even number and an odd number together, that the answer will always be odd. Do you agree with this claim? If so, why do you think that is true? If not, give an example of an even number and an odd number that when added together, give you an even sum instead of an odd sum.

   _____

Identify any number as odd or even, and numbers under 100 as prime or composite

Math Test

Fill in the circle next to the correct answer.

1. Which of the following is an odd number?

Ⓐ 26   Ⓒ 29
Ⓑ 44   Ⓓ 36

2. Which of the following is an even number?

Ⓐ 51   Ⓒ 72
Ⓑ 83   Ⓓ 77

3. Which of the following is NOT an odd number?

Ⓐ 45   Ⓒ 95
Ⓑ 31   Ⓓ 98

4. Which of the following is NOT an even number?

Ⓐ 31   Ⓒ 42
Ⓑ 62   Ⓓ 96

5. Which of the following is a prime number?

Ⓐ 9   Ⓒ 18
Ⓑ 16   Ⓓ 11

6. Which of the following is a composite number?

Ⓐ 13   Ⓒ 19
Ⓑ 17   Ⓓ 15

7. Which of the following is NOT a prime number?

Ⓐ 6   Ⓒ 7
Ⓑ 3   Ⓓ 5

8. Which of the following is NOT a composite number?

Ⓐ 14   Ⓒ 19
Ⓑ 16   Ⓓ 18

9. List five even numbers greater than 45.

_____

10. List all the prime numbers between 10 and 30.

_____

_____

_____

Identify any number as odd or even, and numbers under 100 as prime or composite

Baseball Riddle

Name _____

Each set of numbers is a list of factors. Find the smallest number (larger than all the given factors) that has all of these numbers as factors. Then write the letter on the line above that number. The letters will spell out the answer.

A 1, 3, 4 __12__   **N** 1, 3, 5 ____

C 1, 5, 7 ____   **P** 1, 2, 3, 6, 9 ____

E 1, 2, 4 ____   **R** 1, 2, 4, 7, 14 ____

G 1, 2, 4, 8 ____   **S** 1, 3 ____

H 1, 2, 3 ____   **T** 1, 2, 4, 8, 16 ____

I 1, 2, 3, 5, 6 ____   **W** 1, 3, 11 ____

L 1, 2, 3, 4, 6, 8, 12 ____   **Y** 1, 2, 3, 6, 7, 14, 21 ____

Why did the young baseball player chase his sister around the field?

____ ____   ____ _A_ ____
 6   8   33   12   9

____ ____ _A_ ____ ____ ____ ____
18   24   12   42   30   15   16

____ _A_ ____ ____ ____   ____ ____ ____
35   12   32   35   6   6   8   28

Identify factors of numbers less than 100 and multiples of single-digit numbers

Riddle

Each set of numbers is a list of multiples of a certain number. Find the largest number (smaller than all the given multiples) that has all of these numbers as multiples. Write that number next to the multiples. Then write the letter on the line above the number. The letters will spell out the answer for you.

A   10, 20, 35, 40 _____

B   28, 14, 35, 49 _____

D   12, 24, 36, 30 _____

E   12, 16, 28, 32 _____

I   12, 9, 15, 21 _____

P   24, 16, 40, 56 _____

R   36, 54, 27, 18 _____

What did the Boy Scout say after fixing his neighbor's bicycle horn?

____ ____ ____ ____
 7   4   4   8

____ ____ ____ ____ ____ ____ ____ ____
 9   4   8   5   3   9   4   6

Identify factors of numbers less than 100 and multiples of single-digit numbers

Find the Multiples

Name _____

Use the hundreds table as you follow the directions.

1. Use a red crayon and circle all the multiples of 5. Look for a pattern.

2. Use a blue crayon and cross out all the multiples of 3. Look for a pattern.

3. Use a green crayon and draw a triangle on all the multiples of 2. Look for a pattern.

1	2	3	4	5	6	7	8	9	10
11	12	13	14	15	16	17	18	19	20
21	22	23	24	25	26	27	28	29	30
31	32	33	34	35	36	37	38	39	40
41	42	43	44	45	46	47	48	49	50
51	52	53	54	55	56	57	58	59	60
61	62	63	64	65	66	67	68	69	70
71	72	73	74	75	76	77	78	79	80
81	82	83	84	85	86	87	88	89	90
91	92	93	94	95	96	97	98	99	100

Identify factors of numbers less than 100 and multiples of single-digit numbers

Finding Factors

Name _____

List all the factors for each number.

1. 8 _____

2. 12 _____

3. 15 _____

4. 21 _____

5. 24 _____

6. 9 _____

7. 32 _____

8. 7 _____

9. 6 _____

10. 16 _____

11. 35 _____

12. 40 _____

13. 25 _____

14. 45 _____

15. 42 _____

16. 31 _____

17. 22 _____

18. 18 _____

19. 5 _____

20. 10 _____

Skill practice copy here Identify factors of numbers less than 100 and multiples of single-digit numbers

Using Factors and Multiples

Name _____

Solve each problem.

1. Gerald has 24 baseball cards and wants to know all the different ways that he can divide them evenly. What are all the ways that he can stack his baseball cards with each stack having the same number of cards?

_____

2. Cupcakes from the Hilltop Bakery are wrapped in packages of 3. The bakers want to put several packages into a larger box. What are four possible numbers of cupcakes that could appear in this larger box?

_____

3. Julie has a stamp collection and would like to arrange 12 stamps on each page of her new book. What are all the possible arrangements of stamps that she could use if she wants to have the same number of stamps in every row? Which arrangement do you think would be the best and why?

_____

_____

4. Christy saw some packages of erasers at the grocery store. Each package had 9 erasers in it. Christy grabbed a handful of packages, less than 8 but more than 3. List all the possible numbers of erasers she could be holding in her hand.

_____

5. In the library are some magazine holders. There are 6 magazine holders and each one holds the same number of magazines, at least 8. What are the four smallest possible numbers of magazines that are held in all 6 holders?

_____

Identify factors of numbers less than 100 and multiples of single-digit numbers

Math Test

Name _____

Fill in the circle next to the correct answer.

1. Which of the following is a multiple of 5?

Ⓐ 27 　　　Ⓒ 85
Ⓑ 93 　　　Ⓓ 16

2. Which of the following is a factor of 8?

Ⓐ 4 　　　Ⓒ 5
Ⓑ 3 　　　Ⓓ 6

3. Which of the following is NOT a multiple of 3?

Ⓐ 15 　　　Ⓒ 31
Ⓑ 27 　　　Ⓓ 60

4. Which of the following is NOT a factor of 40?

Ⓐ 3 　　　Ⓒ 20
Ⓑ 8 　　　Ⓓ 10

5. Which of the following lists the first five multiples of 2?

Ⓐ 4, 8, 12, 16, 20
Ⓑ 2, 4, 6, 8, 10
Ⓒ 1, 2, 4, 6, 8
Ⓓ 1, 3, 5, 7, 9

6. Which of the following lists the first five multiples of 6?

Ⓐ 12, 24, 30, 48, 60
Ⓑ 1, 2, 3, 4, 6
Ⓒ 12, 18, 24, 30, 36
Ⓓ 6, 12, 18, 24, 30

7. Which of the following lists all the factors of 12?

Ⓐ 1, 2, 3, 4, 6, 12
Ⓑ 2, 3, 4, 6, 12
Ⓒ 2, 3, 4, 6
Ⓓ 1, 2, 3, 4, 6, 8, 12

8. Which of the following lists all the factors of 17?

Ⓐ 1, 2, 8, 17
Ⓑ 1, 3, 17
Ⓒ 1, 17
Ⓓ 1, 5, 17

9. List the smallest eight prime numbers.

_____

_____

10. List the first five multiples of 8.

_____

Identify factors of numbers less than 100 and multiples of single-digit numbers

Tongue Twister

Name _____

Write the letter for each fraction model on the lines above each fraction. This will spell out a tongue twister. Try to say it quickly three times in a row.

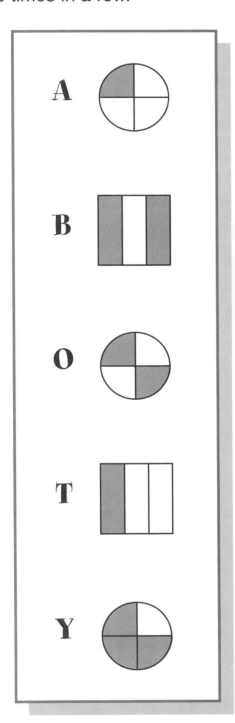

A

B

O

T

Y

_____ _____ _____
$\frac{1}{3}$ $\frac{2}{4}$ $\frac{3}{4}$

_____ _____ _____ _____
$\frac{2}{3}$ $\frac{1}{2}$ $\frac{1}{4}$ $\frac{1}{3}$

Identify halves, thirds, and fourths (including fractions greater than one), and compare fractions

Number & Operations

Knock-Knock Joke

Write the fractions in order under each line. You may use the number line at the bottom of the page to help you. Then write the letter for each fraction on the lines. The letters will spell out the last line of the knock-knock joke.

Knock, knock.

Who's there?

Doris.

Doris who?

$3\frac{1}{3}$ **W**	$1\frac{1}{3}$ **O**	$\frac{3}{4}$ **S**	$1\frac{3}{4}$ **E**
$1\frac{1}{4}$ **L**	$2\frac{1}{4}$ **T**	2 **D**	$4\frac{3}{4}$ **E**
5 **D**	$4\frac{1}{3}$ **O**	$4\frac{2}{3}$ **K**	$3\frac{1}{2}$ **H**
$3\frac{3}{4}$ **I**	$4\frac{1}{2}$ **C**	3 **S**	$\frac{2}{3}$ **I**
$2\frac{3}{4}$ **K**	$1\frac{1}{2}$ **C**	$\frac{1}{4}$ **D**	$2\frac{1}{3}$ **H**
$1\frac{2}{3}$ **K**	$4\frac{1}{4}$ **N**	$\frac{1}{3}$ **O**	4 **K**
$2\frac{1}{2}$ **A**	$3\frac{2}{3}$ **Y**	$\frac{1}{2}$ **R**	

___ _O_ ___ ___ ___   ___ ___ ___ ___ ___
$\frac{1}{4}$ $\boxed{\frac{1}{3}}$ $\boxed{}$ $\boxed{}$ $\frac{3}{4}$ $1\frac{1}{4}$ $\boxed{}$ $\boxed{}$ $\boxed{}$ $\boxed{}$ 2

,

___ ___ ___ ___ ___   ___ ___ ___
$2\frac{1}{4}$ $\boxed{}$ $\boxed{}$ $\boxed{}$ 3 $3\frac{1}{3}$ $\boxed{}$ $3\frac{2}{3}$

___ ___ ___ ___ ___ ___ ___
$3\frac{3}{4}$ 4 $\boxed{}$ $\boxed{}$ $\boxed{}$ $\boxed{}$ $\boxed{}$ 5

Identify halves, thirds, and fourths (including fractions greater than one), and compare fractions

Naming Fractions

Name _____

Write the fraction that is represented by the shaded part(s) in each figure.
Are there any other fraction names that could name the same region?

1. 　　　　　_____

2. 　　　　　_____

3. 　　　　　_____

4. 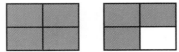　　　　　_____

5. 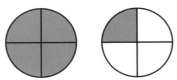　　　　　_____

6. 　_____

7. 　　_____

8. 　　_____

Identify halves, thirds, and fourths (including fractions greater than one), and compare fractions

Number & Operations

Comparing Fractions

Name _____

Write <, >, or = in the blank for each math sentence.

1. $1\frac{2}{3}$ _____ $2\frac{1}{3}$

2. $4\frac{1}{4}$ _____ $4\frac{1}{2}$

3. $6\frac{1}{3}$ _____ $6\frac{1}{2}$

4. $9\frac{1}{4}$ _____ $9\frac{3}{4}$

5. $2\frac{3}{4}$ _____ $3\frac{1}{2}$

6. $\frac{3}{4}$ _____ $1\frac{1}{2}$

7. $2\frac{1}{2}$ _____ $2\frac{2}{4}$

8. $8\frac{1}{3}$ _____ $5\frac{3}{4}$

9. $2\frac{1}{2}$ _____ $2\frac{3}{4}$

10. $5\frac{1}{2}$ _____ $5\frac{3}{4}$

11. $6\frac{1}{2}$ _____ $6\frac{1}{3}$

12. $7\frac{1}{3}$ _____ $6\frac{2}{3}$

13. $8\frac{1}{4}$ _____ $8\frac{2}{4}$

14. $5\frac{2}{4}$ _____ $5\frac{1}{2}$

15. $3\frac{1}{2}$ _____ $4\frac{1}{2}$

Identify halves, thirds, and fourths (including fractions greater than one), and compare fractions

EMC 3017 • Basic Math Skills, Grade 4 • ©2003 by Evan-Moor Corp.

Using Fractions

Name _____

Solve each problem.

1. Shirley is baking bread and wants to make just half of the recipe. The original recipe calls for 4 eggs. How many eggs will she need for half the recipe?

   _____

2. Molly and Jose took a spelling test with 10 questions. If Molly missed half of the words and Jose missed 6 of the words, who missed more?

   _____

3. Jimmy and Marisol took a math test with 100 questions. Jimmy missed $\frac{1}{4}$ of the questions while Marisol got $\frac{3}{4}$ of the questions right. Who had the better score?

   _____

4. Alec brought two quarters to school with him. Sandy brought one half-dollar with her. Alec and Sandy disagreed about who had more money. Write a short note to these two students telling them who has more money.

   _____

   _____

   _____

5. Adam missed half of the questions on his test while Katie missed 7 of the 10 questions on her test. Clare said that Adam missed more questions. Is it possible that Clare could be telling the truth?

   _____

Identify halves, thirds, and fourths (including fractions greater than one), and compare fractions

Math Test

Name _____

Fill in the circle next to the correct answer.

1. Which fraction represents the shaded region?

   Ⓐ $\frac{1}{4}$ Ⓑ $\frac{3}{4}$ Ⓒ $\frac{1}{2}$ Ⓓ $\frac{1}{3}$

2. Which fraction represents the shaded region?

   Ⓐ $\frac{1}{3}$ Ⓑ $\frac{1}{4}$ Ⓒ $\frac{2}{4}$ Ⓓ $\frac{2}{3}$

3. Which mixed number represents the shaded region?

   Ⓐ $\frac{1}{4}$ Ⓑ $1\frac{1}{4}$ Ⓒ $1\frac{1}{2}$ Ⓓ 2

4. Which mixed number represents the shaded region?

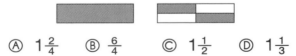

   Ⓐ $1\frac{1}{3}$ Ⓑ $1\frac{2}{3}$ Ⓒ $2\frac{1}{3}$ Ⓓ $2\frac{1}{2}$

5. Which of the following does NOT represent the shaded region?

   Ⓐ $1\frac{2}{4}$ Ⓑ $\frac{6}{4}$ Ⓒ $1\frac{1}{2}$ Ⓓ $1\frac{1}{3}$

6. Which of the following lists fractions in order from smallest to largest?

   Ⓐ $\frac{1}{2}, \frac{1}{4}, \frac{3}{4}, 1\frac{1}{2}, 1\frac{3}{4}$

   Ⓑ $\frac{1}{4}, \frac{1}{2}, \frac{3}{4}, 1\frac{1}{2}, 1\frac{3}{4}$

   Ⓒ $1\frac{1}{2}, 1\frac{3}{4}, \frac{1}{2}, \frac{1}{4}, \frac{3}{4}$

   Ⓓ $\frac{1}{4}, \frac{1}{2}, 1\frac{1}{2}, \frac{3}{4}, 1\frac{3}{4}$

7. Which of the following lists fractions in order from smallest to largest?

   Ⓐ $\frac{1}{3}, \frac{2}{3}, 1\frac{1}{3}, 2\frac{1}{3}, 2\frac{2}{3}$

   Ⓑ $\frac{1}{3}, 1\frac{1}{3}, 2\frac{1}{3}, 2\frac{2}{3}, \frac{2}{3}$

   Ⓒ $\frac{1}{3}, \frac{2}{3}, 1\frac{1}{3}, 2\frac{2}{3}, 2\frac{1}{3}$

   Ⓓ $\frac{1}{3}, 1\frac{1}{3}, 2\frac{1}{3}, \frac{2}{3}, 2\frac{2}{3}$

8. Which of the following is NOT correct?

   Ⓐ $\frac{2}{3} < 1\frac{1}{4}$

   Ⓑ $1\frac{1}{2} > 1\frac{1}{3}$

   Ⓒ $2\frac{1}{2} > 2\frac{2}{3}$

   Ⓓ $1\frac{3}{4} > 1\frac{1}{3}$

9. Draw a picture to show that $\frac{1}{3}$ is larger than $\frac{1}{4}$.

10. Juan and Mureta each took a test with 24 questions on it. Mureta missed $\frac{1}{4}$ of the questions, while Juan missed only 9 questions. Who got more questions correct on the test?

   _____

Identify halves, thirds, and fourths (including fractions greater than one), and compare fractions

EMC 3017 • Basic Math Skills, Grade 4 • ©2003 by Evan-Moor Corp.

Riddle

Name _____

Find the sum for each addition problem. Then write the corresponding letter at the bottom of the page on the line above the sum. The letters will spell out the answer for you.

A $1\frac{1}{4} + \frac{2}{4} =$ _____

E $\frac{1}{4} + \frac{3}{4} =$ _____

G $\frac{1}{8} + \frac{6}{8} =$ _____

H $1\frac{1}{3} + 1\frac{1}{3} =$ _____

I $\frac{2}{5} + \frac{2}{5} =$ _____

L $\frac{1}{7} + \frac{4}{7} =$ _____

M $2\frac{1}{8} + 2\frac{4}{8} =$ _____

N $\frac{2}{7} + 1\frac{2}{7} =$ _____

O $\frac{1}{9} + \frac{4}{9} =$ _____

R $\frac{4}{7} + 1\frac{1}{7} =$ _____

T $2\frac{1}{5} + 1\frac{2}{5} =$ _____

W $1\frac{2}{4} + 1\frac{1}{4} =$ _____

Go?

Stop?

When should you go at red and stop at green?

_____ _____ _____ _____   _____ _____ _____ _____ _____ _____
$2\frac{3}{4}$ $2\frac{2}{3}$ $\frac{4}{4}$ $1\frac{4}{7}$ 1 $1\frac{3}{4}$ $3\frac{3}{5}$ $\frac{4}{5}$ $1\frac{4}{7}$ $\frac{7}{8}$

_____ _____ _____ _____ _____ _____ _____ _____ _____ _____
$2\frac{3}{4}$ $1\frac{3}{4}$ $3\frac{3}{5}$ $\frac{4}{4}$ $1\frac{5}{7}$ $4\frac{5}{8}$ 1 $\frac{5}{7}$ $\frac{5}{9}$ $1\frac{4}{7}$

Demonstrate addition and subtraction using fractions with like denominators (including mixed numbers)

Tongue Twister

Name _____

Solve each subtraction problem. Write the letter on each line above the difference. Read the tongue twister and try to say it quickly three times.

A $\frac{5}{7} - \frac{3}{7} =$ _____   L $\frac{4}{7} - \frac{1}{7} =$ _____

C $\frac{5}{6} - \frac{4}{6} =$ _____   P $\frac{4}{9} - \frac{2}{9} =$ _____

D $\frac{7}{8} - \frac{6}{8} =$ _____   R $\frac{6}{7} - \frac{1}{7} =$ _____

E $\frac{3}{4} - \frac{2}{4} =$ _____   S $\frac{4}{5} - \frac{1}{5} =$ _____

F $\frac{8}{9} - \frac{4}{9} =$ _____   V $\frac{7}{8} - \frac{2}{8} =$ _____

H $\frac{2}{3} - \frac{1}{3} =$ _____   Y $\frac{5}{9} - \frac{4}{9} =$ _____

I $\frac{2}{5} - \frac{1}{5} =$ _____

,

___ ___ ___ ___ ___ ___ ___   ___ ___ ___ ___
$\frac{4}{9}$ $\frac{5}{7}$ $\frac{1}{5}$ $\frac{1}{8}$ $\frac{2}{7}$ $\frac{1}{9}$ $\frac{3}{5}$ $\frac{4}{9}$ $\frac{1}{5}$ $\frac{5}{8}$ $\frac{1}{4}$

___ ___ ___ ___ ___   ___ ___ ___ ___
$\frac{4}{9}$ $\frac{5}{7}$ $\frac{1}{4}$ $\frac{3}{5}$ $\frac{1}{3}$ $\frac{4}{9}$ $\frac{1}{5}$ $\frac{3}{5}$ $\frac{1}{3}$

___ ___ ___ ___ ___ ___ ___ ___
$\frac{3}{5}$ $\frac{2}{9}$ $\frac{1}{4}$ $\frac{1}{6}$ $\frac{1}{5}$ $\frac{2}{7}$ $\frac{3}{7}$ $\frac{3}{5}$

Demonstrate addition and subtraction using fractions with like denominators (including mixed numbers)

EMC 3017 • Basic Math Skills, Grade 4 • ©2003 by Evan-Moor Corp.

Adding Fractions and Mixed Numbers

Name _____

Add the following fractions.

1. $\frac{1}{7} + \frac{5}{7}$ = _____

2. $\frac{3}{7} + \frac{3}{7}$ = _____

3. $\frac{1}{6} + \frac{4}{6}$ = _____

4. $\frac{2}{3} + \frac{1}{3}$ = _____

5. $\frac{6}{9} + \frac{1}{9}$ = _____

6. $\frac{7}{12} + \frac{4}{12}$ = _____

7. $\frac{2}{7} + \frac{4}{7}$ = _____

8. $\frac{3}{8} + \frac{4}{8}$ = _____

9. $\frac{1}{5} + \frac{2}{5}$ = _____

10. $\frac{1}{4} + \frac{2}{4}$ = _____

Add the following mixed numbers.

11. $1\frac{1}{5} + 2\frac{2}{5}$ = _____

12. $3\frac{1}{4} + 1\frac{2}{4}$ = _____

13. $1\frac{5}{9} + 2\frac{2}{9}$ = _____

14. $4 + 2\frac{3}{7}$ = _____

15. $8\frac{1}{9} + 4$ = _____

Demonstrate addition and subtraction using fractions with like denominators (including mixed numbers)

Number & Operations

Subtracting Fractions and Mixed Numbers

Name _____

Subtract the following fractions.

1. $\frac{5}{9} - \frac{1}{9} =$ _____

2. $\frac{6}{7} - \frac{1}{7} =$ _____

3. $\frac{3}{4} - \frac{2}{4} =$ _____

4. $\frac{8}{9} - \frac{1}{9} =$ _____

5. $\frac{4}{5} - \frac{2}{5} =$ _____

6. $\frac{6}{7} - \frac{3}{7} =$ _____

7. $\frac{7}{8} - \frac{6}{8} =$ _____

8. $\frac{5}{6} - \frac{4}{6} =$ _____

9. $\frac{9}{10} - \frac{2}{10} =$ _____

10. $\frac{8}{9} - \frac{6}{9} =$ _____

Subtract the following mixed numbers.

11. $6\frac{3}{4} - 1\frac{1}{4} =$ _____

12. $5\frac{4}{9} - 1\frac{2}{9} =$ _____

13. $6\frac{6}{7} - 2\frac{1}{7} =$ _____

14. $5\frac{4}{5} - 2\frac{1}{5} =$ _____

15. $8\frac{7}{8} - 5\frac{6}{8} =$ _____

Demonstrate addition and subtraction using fractions with like denominators (including mixed numbers)

EMC 3017 • Basic Math Skills, Grade 4 • ©2003 by Evan-Moor Corp.

Using Fractions and Mixed Numbers

Name _____

Solve each problem.

1. Mike brought $5\frac{3}{4}$ packages of gum to school for his birthday party. He gave away $2\frac{2}{4}$ packages during the party. How much does he have left?

   _____

2. Brenda and Jodee each had $3\frac{1}{3}$ boxes of candy. How much do they have in all?

   _____

3. Joe has a sister that likes to take his candy. After he got home from the store, he had $5\frac{3}{4}$ bags of candy. When he got home from school the next day, there were only $3\frac{1}{4}$ bags left. How much candy did his sister eat?

   _____

4. Amanda is riding her bike to school and then back home after school. She figures that the one-way trip is $2\frac{1}{5}$ miles. How far is the round trip?

   _____

5. Jason is writing a report for school that must be at least 5 pages long. He wrote $2\frac{3}{4}$ pages on Friday and then another $2\frac{2}{4}$ pages on Saturday. Is his paper long enough yet? Why or why not?

   _____

   _____

Demonstrate addition and subtraction using fractions with like denominators (including mixed numbers)

Math Test

Name_____

Fill in the circle next to the correct answer.

1. $\frac{1}{5} + \frac{2}{5} =$ _____
   - Ⓐ $\frac{2}{5}$
   - Ⓒ $\frac{3}{10}$
   - Ⓑ $\frac{3}{5}$
   - Ⓓ $\frac{1}{5}$

2. $5\frac{1}{7} + 2\frac{4}{7} =$ _____
   - Ⓐ $\frac{5}{7}$
   - Ⓒ $7\frac{5}{14}$
   - Ⓑ 7
   - Ⓓ $7\frac{5}{7}$

3. $\frac{8}{9} - \frac{4}{9} =$ _____
   - Ⓐ $\frac{4}{9}$
   - Ⓒ $\frac{5}{9}$
   - Ⓑ 4
   - Ⓓ $\frac{3}{9}$

4. $5\frac{7}{8} - 2\frac{6}{8} =$ _____
   - Ⓐ 3
   - Ⓒ $3\frac{1}{8}$
   - Ⓑ $5\frac{1}{8}$
   - Ⓓ 4

5. Which number sentence is correct?
   - Ⓐ $5\frac{1}{4} + 4\frac{2}{4} = 9\frac{3}{4}$
   - Ⓑ $3\frac{1}{3} + 3\frac{1}{3} = 6\frac{2}{6}$
   - Ⓒ $4\frac{1}{2} + 2\frac{1}{2} = 6\frac{1}{2}$
   - Ⓓ $8\frac{1}{7} + 1\frac{2}{7} = 8\frac{3}{7}$

6. Which number sentence is correct?
   - Ⓐ $7\frac{5}{9} - 4\frac{4}{9} = 3\frac{2}{9}$
   - Ⓑ $4\frac{3}{4} - 4\frac{2}{4} = 4\frac{1}{4}$
   - Ⓒ $6\frac{2}{8} - 1\frac{1}{8} = 6\frac{1}{8}$
   - Ⓓ $4\frac{5}{7} - 2\frac{3}{7} = 2\frac{2}{7}$

7. Which number sentence is NOT correct?
   - Ⓐ $7\frac{1}{5} + 2\frac{2}{5} = 9\frac{3}{5}$
   - Ⓑ $2\frac{1}{9} + 4\frac{3}{9} = 6\frac{4}{9}$
   - Ⓒ $8\frac{2}{5} + 4\frac{1}{5} = 8\frac{3}{5}$
   - Ⓓ $3 + 4\frac{1}{4} = 7\frac{1}{4}$

8. Which number sentence is NOT correct?
   - Ⓐ $3\frac{7}{9} - 1\frac{6}{9} = 2\frac{1}{9}$
   - Ⓑ $4\frac{5}{8} - 2\frac{4}{8} = 2\frac{1}{8}$
   - Ⓒ $4\frac{4}{5} - 1\frac{2}{5} = 3\frac{2}{5}$
   - Ⓓ $6\frac{5}{7} - 3\frac{2}{7} = 3\frac{2}{7}$

9. Brandon has 5 pages to write for a school report. If he has written $2\frac{1}{4}$ pages, how many more does he have to write?

   _____

10. Aja brought $2\frac{1}{4}$ packages of cards to school. Miranda gave her another $2\frac{3}{4}$ packages. How many packages does she have now?

    _____

Demonstrate addition and subtraction using fractions with like denominators (including mixed numbers)

Number & Operations   EMC 3017 • Basic Math Skills, Grade 4 • ©2003 by Evan-Moor Corp.

Riddle

Name _____

To solve the riddle, draw a straight line between each fraction on the left and an equivalent fraction on the right. Each line will go through one number and one letter. At the bottom of the page, write the letter on each line above the number.

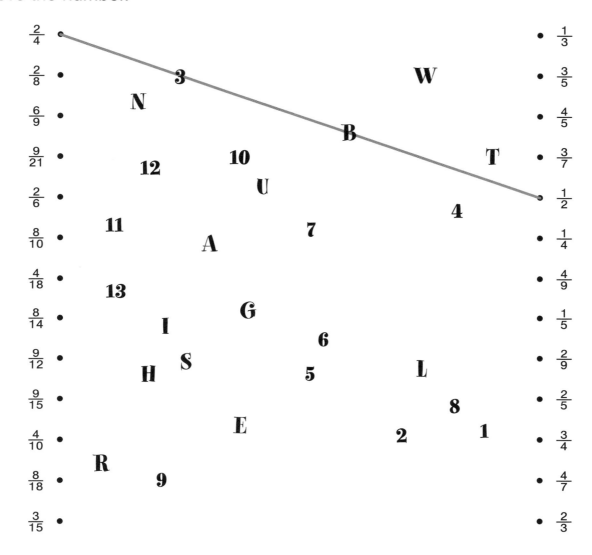

What did Mrs. Margarine think about her sister's husband?

| 1 | 8 | | 7 | 2 | | 6 | | 13 | 5 | 8 | 6 | 10 |

B

| 3 | 11 | 10 | 10 | 8 | 5 | - | 7 | 4 | - | 9 | 6 | 12 |

Determine common equivalent fractions and decimals (fractions equivalent to other fractions and fractions equivalent to decimals)

Where Do Dogs Refuse to Shop?

Name _____

To solve the riddle, draw a straight line between each fraction on the left and an equivalent fraction on the right. Each line will go through one number and one letter. At the bottom of the page, write the letter on each line above the number.

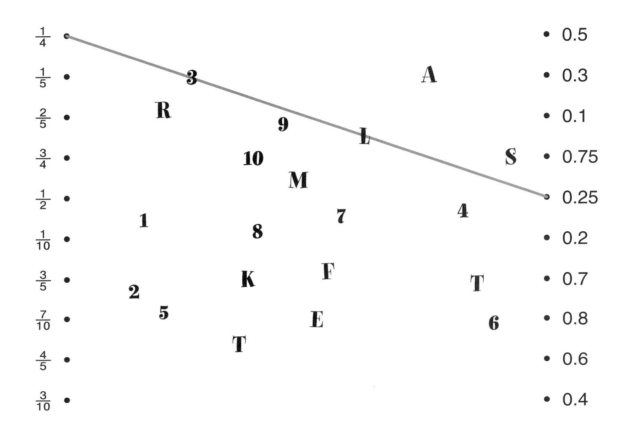

$\frac{1}{4}$ •   • 0.5

$\frac{1}{5}$ •   **3**   **A**   • 0.3

$\frac{2}{5}$ •   **R**   **9**   • 0.1

$\frac{3}{4}$ •   **10**   **L**   **S** • 0.75

$\frac{1}{2}$ •   **M**   • 0.25

    1   **8**   **7**   **4**

$\frac{1}{10}$ •   • 0.2

$\frac{3}{5}$ •   **K**   **F**   **T** • 0.7

   2

$\frac{7}{10}$ •   **5**   **E**   **6** • 0.8

   T

$\frac{4}{5}$ •   • 0.6

$\frac{3}{10}$ •   • 0.4

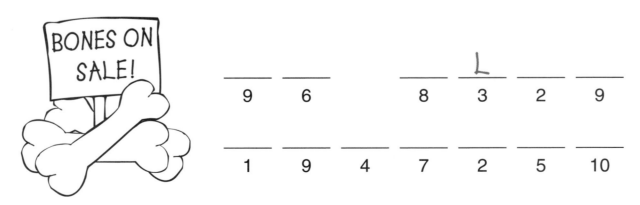

BONES ON SALE!

___ ___   ___ _L_ ___ ___
9   6   8   3   2   9

___ ___ ___ ___ ___ ___ ___
1   9   4   7   2   5   10

Determine common equivalent fractions and decimals (fractions equivalent to other fractions and fractions equivalent to decimals)

Equivalent Fractions

Name _____

Write two fractions that are equivalent to each of the following fractions.

1. $\frac{1}{2}$ _____

2. $\frac{1}{3}$ _____

3. $\frac{1}{5}$ _____

4. $\frac{2}{3}$ _____

5. $\frac{4}{5}$ _____

6. $\frac{3}{7}$ _____

7. $\frac{1}{4}$ _____

8. $\frac{1}{7}$ _____

9. $\frac{3}{4}$ _____

10. $\frac{2}{5}$ _____

Reduce the following fractions to lowest terms.

11. $\frac{2}{4}$ _____

12. $\frac{3}{9}$ _____

13. $\frac{2}{6}$ _____

14. $\frac{4}{12}$ _____

15. $\frac{12}{16}$ _____

16. $\frac{10}{15}$ _____

17. $\frac{8}{12}$ _____

18. $\frac{9}{21}$ _____

19. $\frac{15}{20}$ _____

20. $\frac{5}{15}$ _____

$\frac{1}{4}$ 0.25 $\frac{2}{8}$

Determine common equivalent fractions and decimals (fractions equivalent to other fractions and fractions equivalent to decimals)

Make a Match

Name _____

Match each fraction on the left to the equivalent decimal on the right.

1. $\frac{1}{2}$ **A**   0.4

2. $\frac{1}{4}$ **B**   0.6

3. $\frac{1}{5}$ **C**   0.8

4. $\frac{2}{5}$ **D**   0.5

5. $\frac{3}{10}$ **E**   0.3

6. $\frac{4}{5}$ **F**   0.75

7. $\frac{3}{4}$ **G**   0.25

8. $\frac{3}{5}$ **H**   0.2

Determine common equivalent fractions and decimals (fractions equivalent to other fractions and fractions equivalent to decimals)

Using Fractions and Decimals

Solve each problem.

1. Holly was shopping at Clothing World and found two sales, but she didn't know which was a better buy. The first sale was $\frac{1}{4}$ off the original price and the second sale was 0.3 off the original price. Which was a larger discount?

   _____

2. Lori is making cookies and the recipe calls for 0.25 cups of milk. All she has are measuring cups that are marked in fractions. What amount of milk (in fraction form) does she need to put into the recipe?

   _____

3. What is one way to remember that one-fourth ($\frac{1}{4}$) is the same as 0.25? Next, explain how $\frac{1}{2}$ is the same as 0.5.

   _____

   _____

4. Gen is making a quilt and needs to measure out 0.25 feet. What fraction of a foot is that, and how many inches is that equivalent to?

   _____

Determine common equivalent fractions and decimals (fractions equivalent to other fractions and fractions equivalent to decimals)

Math Test

Name _____

Fill in the circle next to the correct answer.

1. Which fraction is equivalent to $\frac{3}{6}$?

   (A) $\frac{2}{3}$ (C) $\frac{1}{4}$

   (B) $\frac{1}{3}$ (D) $\frac{1}{2}$

2. Which fraction is equivalent to $\frac{4}{12}$?

   (A) $\frac{1}{2}$ (C) $\frac{1}{4}$

   (B) $\frac{1}{3}$ (D) $\frac{1}{12}$

3. Which fraction is NOT equivalent to $\frac{1}{3}$?

   (A) $\frac{2}{6}$ (C) $\frac{5}{15}$

   (B) $\frac{4}{12}$ (D) $\frac{3}{6}$

4. Which fraction is NOT equivalent to $\frac{1}{2}$?

   (A) $\frac{5}{10}$ (C) $\frac{4}{8}$

   (B) $\frac{2}{5}$ (D) $\frac{3}{6}$

5. Which decimal is equivalent to $\frac{1}{4}$?

   (A) 0.2 (C) 0.5

   (B) 0.4 (D) 0.25

6. Which decimal is equivalent to $\frac{2}{5}$?

   (A) 0.25 (C) 0.4

   (B) 0.2 (D) 0.5

7. Which fraction is NOT equivalent to 0.5?

   (A) $\frac{1}{2}$ (C) $\frac{3}{6}$

   (B) $\frac{5}{8}$ (D) $\frac{6}{12}$

8. Which fraction is NOT equivalent to 0.2?

   (A) $\frac{1}{5}$ (C) $\frac{4}{20}$

   (B) $\frac{2}{10}$ (D) $\frac{2}{5}$

9. List four fractions equivalent to 0.5.

   _____

   _____

10. Explain how $\frac{1}{4}$ is the same as 0.25.

   _____

   _____

   _____

Determine common equivalent fractions and decimals (fractions equivalent to other fractions and fractions equivalent to decimals)

EMC 3017 • Basic Math Skills, Grade 4 • ©2003 by Evan-Moor Corp.

What Goes Tick-Tick, Woof-Woof?

Name _____

Solve each addition problem. Then write the letter on each line above the answer. The letters will spell out the answer for you.

A $0.5 + 0.3 =$ _____

A $0.4 + 0.2 =$ _____

C $0.25 + 0.52 =$ _____

D $4.0 + 0.2 =$ _____

G $0.5 + 3.0 =$ _____

H $2.5 + 5.2 =$ _____

O $2.5 + 0.52 =$ _____

T $0.25 + 5.2 =$ _____

W $0.52 + 0.71 =$ _____

tick-tick   woof-woof

‾‾‾‾‾   ‾‾‾‾ ‾‾‾‾ ‾‾‾‾ ‾‾‾‾ ‾‾‾‾   ‾‾‾‾ ‾‾‾‾ ‾‾‾‾
0.6   1.23 0.8 5.45 0.77 7.7   4.2 3.02 3.5

Demonstrate addition and subtraction with decimals to the hundredths

Tongue Twister

Name_____

Solve each subtraction problem below. Then write the letter on each line above the difference. Read the tongue twister and try to say it quickly three times.

A	2.5 – 1.2 = _____	**N**	6.54 – 6.3 = _____
C	5.3 – 2.1 = _____	**O**	6.25 – 4.5 = _____
D	4.6 – 1.3 = _____	**S**	5.2 – 3.14 = _____
E	9.5 – 8.4 = _____	**T**	8.69 – 1.26 = _____
H	5.2 – 4.8 = _____	**V**	6.49 – 5.2 = _____
I	4.12 – 3.09 = _____	**W**	6.2 – 4.16 = _____
K	5.26 – 4.13 = _____	**Y**	5.5 – 1.26 = _____
L	6.24 – 2.59 = _____		

___ ___ ___ ___ ___   ___ ___ ___ ___ ___
2.06 1.1 1.29 1.1 0.24   2.06 1.03 3.65 3.65 4.24

___ ___ ___ ___ ___ ___   ___ ___ ___ ___
2.06 1.3 0.24 7.43 1.3 2.06   2.06 3.65 1.03 3.3

___ ___   ___ ___ ___
1.75 0.24 7.43 0.4 1.1

___ ___ ___ ___ ___   ___ ___ ___ ___
2.06 3.65 1.03 3.2 1.13   2.06 0.24 1.75 2.04

Demonstrate addition and subtraction with decimals to the hundredths

Adding Decimals

Name_____

Find the following sums.

1. $1.2 + 2.6 = $ _____

2. $5.3 + 6.4 = $ _____

3. $2.8 + 6.1 = $ _____

4. $2.5 + 6.4 = $ _____

5. $6.0 + 2.6 = $ _____

6. $4.0 + 8.2 = $ _____

7. $6.1 + 9.0 = $ _____

8. $5.2 + 8.0 = $ _____

9. $2.63 + 1.64 = $ _____

10. $2.94 + 8.16 = $ _____

11. $8.64 + 6.15 = $ _____

12. $6.28 + 8.64 = $ _____

13. $6.5 + 5.29 = $ _____

14. $7.41 + 8.9 = $ _____

15. $8.2 + 8.46 = $ _____

16. $5.29 + 8.1 = $ _____

17. $8.2 + 0.64 = $ _____

18. $4.46 + 8.29 = $ _____

19. $5.5 + 9.47 = $ _____

20. $8.2 + 49.64 = $ _____

Demonstrate addition and subtraction with decimals to the hundredths

Subtracting Decimals

Name _____

Find the following differences.

1. 5.2 – 4.1 = _____

2. 9.4 – 6.2 = _____

3. 8.4 – 5.1 = _____

4. 8.7 – 6.4 = _____

5. 9.46 – 8.41 = _____

6. 7.95 – 4.16 = _____

7. 8.26 – 4.19 = _____

8. 8.94 – 4.0 = _____

9. 9.5 – 7.2 = _____

10. 4.5 – 3.09 = _____

11. 8.5 – 4.62 = _____

12. 4.8 – 1.29 = _____

13. 5.49 – 2.4 = _____

14. 8.49 – 6.82 = _____

15. 8.5 – 6.18 = _____

16. 49.5 – 6.4 = _____

17. 84.42 – 64.15 = _____

18. 94.62 – 49.98 = _____

19. 49.52 – 48.98 = _____

20. 6.19 – 5.2 = _____

Demonstrate addition and subtraction with decimals to the hundredths

EMC 3017 • Basic Math Skills, Grade 4 • ©2003 by Evan-Moor Corp.

Using Decimals

Name _____

Solve each problem.

1. Julie had $6.25 before she went to the candy store. She bought $3.89 worth of candy at the store. How much money does she have left?

   _____

2. Chad was helping his dad build a shed. They measured a board that was 2.6 meters long. They need to cut it to measure 2.35 meters long. How much should they cut off?

   _____

3. Darla baked a three-layer cake with her father. Each of the layers was 5.3 centimeters high. If they put 0.8 centimeters of frosting between each layer and then on the top of the cake, how tall was the entire three-layer cake?

   _____

4. Peggy and Michelle are planting a garden. They figure that each row must be about 0.8 feet across with 0.5 feet space between each row. If they are planting 5 rows in their garden, what is the total width of the garden (distance from the beginning of the first row to the far side of the last row)?

   _____

5. Paula and her brother were making a ramp to ride their bikes on. She put two boards with lengths of 2.6 feet and 1.5 yards together end to end. After putting these boards together, she decided that it was a little too long, so she cut off 1.8 feet. What was the final length of the ramp?

   _____

Demonstrate addition and subtraction with decimals to the hundredths

Math Test

Name _____

Fill in the circle next to the correct answer.

1. 4.3 + 2.7 = _____
   - Ⓐ 7.0
   - Ⓒ 6.11
   - Ⓑ 7.10
   - Ⓓ 6.10

2. 6.2 + 0.92 = _____
   - Ⓐ 15.4
   - Ⓒ 6.12
   - Ⓑ 6.94
   - Ⓓ 7.12

3. 5.9 − 3.6 = _____
   - Ⓐ 1.3
   - Ⓒ 2.4
   - Ⓑ 2.3
   - Ⓓ 3.2

4. 6.3 − 4.8 = _____
   - Ⓐ 1.5
   - Ⓒ 2.8
   - Ⓑ 2.5
   - Ⓓ 2.3

5. Which of the following equals 2.9?
   - Ⓐ 1.3 + 1.5
   - Ⓑ 2.1 + 0.7
   - Ⓒ 7.1 − 4.2
   - Ⓓ 8.4 − 5.6

6. Which of the following does NOT equal 5.2?
   - Ⓐ 3.1 + 2.1
   - Ⓑ 4.8 + 0.4
   - Ⓒ 9.6 − 4.4
   - Ⓓ 8.9 − 3.6

7. Which of the following equals 12.08?
   - Ⓐ 16.8 − 4.72
   - Ⓑ 18.8 − 6.0
   - Ⓒ 15.08 − 4.2
   - Ⓓ 19.26 − 7.16

8. Which of the following does NOT equal 15.84?
   - Ⓐ 6.23 + 9.59
   - Ⓑ 8.19 + 7.65
   - Ⓒ 5.47 + 10.37
   - Ⓓ 9.94 + 5.9

9. Raymond has two boards with lengths of 2.6 feet and 4.8 feet. If he glues them end to end, what will be the total length of the new board?

   _____

10. Angel is cutting some fabric to sew a new skirt. She bought 5.5 yards of the fabric. She needs 2.8 yards for the skirt. What length of fabric will be left over?

   _____

Demonstrate addition and subtraction with decimals to the hundredths

What Do You Call a Burning Jacket?

Name _____

To solve the riddle, draw a straight line between each math sentence on the left and the correct symbol on the right. Each line will go through one number and one letter. Write the letter on the line above the number to spell out the answer to the riddle.

4.3 __<__ 7.0

5.2 _____ 5.1

4.9 _____ 5.1

4.2 _____ 4.20

3.68 _____ 3.71

8.53 _____ 8.49

4.0 _____ 4.0

6

E

A

1

B

5   Z

R

2   • =

L   7

A   4   • >

3

<

___
1

___ ___ ___ ___ E ___
2   3   4   5   6   7

Compare sets and values using <, >, and =

Through the Maze

Name _____

Help the mouse find its way through the maze. Decide if each number sentence is true (T) or false (F). Draw a path through the maze to the cheese.

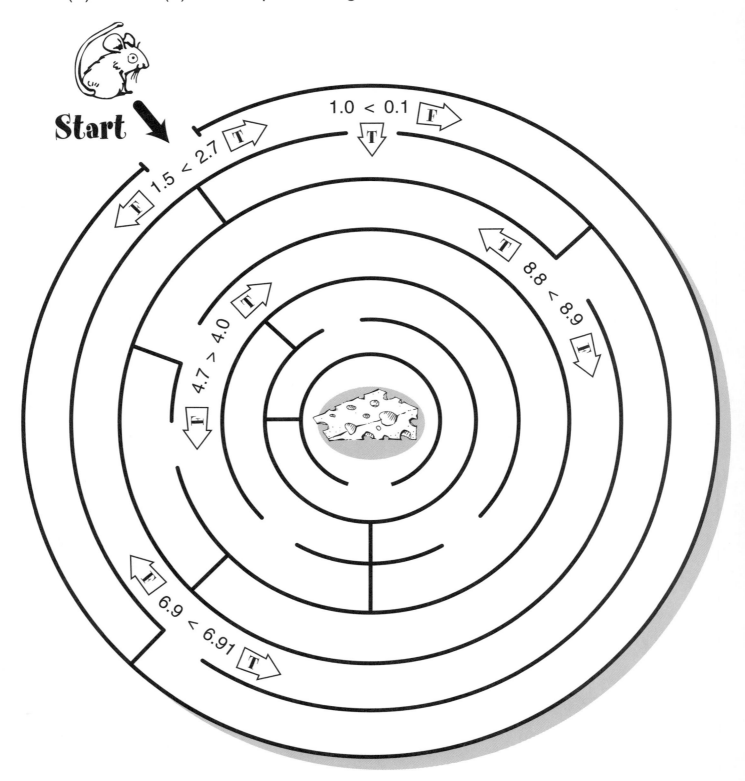

Start

1.0 < 0.1

1.5 < 2.7

8.8 < 8.9

4.7 > 4.0

6.9 < 6.91

Compare sets and values using <, >, and =

EMC 3017 • Basic Math Skills, Grade 4 • ©2003 by Evan-Moor Corp.

Use Symbols

Name _____

Write <, >, or = in each blank to compare the shaded regions.

1. _____

2. _____

3. _____

4. _____

5. _____

6. _____

7. _____

8. _____

9. _____

10. _____

Compare sets and values using <, >, and =

Greater Than, Less Than, or Equal

Name _____

Write <, >, or = in the blank to complete each number sentence.

1. 3.0 _____ 5

2. 8.0 _____ 4

3. 3 _____ 3.0

4. 2.1 _____ 3

5. 4.1 _____ 4.10

6. 5.9 _____ 2.4

7. 49 _____ 4.9

8. 100 _____ 100.3

9. 8.9 _____ 89

10. 35.0 _____ 35

11. 18 _____ 17.1

12. 2.45 _____ 2.61

13. 4.2 _____ 5.08

14. 18.40 _____ 18.4

15. 294 _____ 2.94

16. 3.2 _____ 4.2

17. 8.4 _____ 21.0

18. 94.3 _____ 93.9

19. 16 _____ 15.9

20. 3.69 _____ 3.71

Compare sets and values using <, >, and =

Making Comparisons

Solve each problem.

1. Tim and Julie are arguing about who has the longer piece of string. Tim's string is 3.5 feet long, while Julie's string is 3.4 feet long. Who has the longer piece of string?

   _____

2. Amy has two layers of cake that have diameters of 18.5 centimeters and 24 centimeters. If she wants to put the larger cake on the bottom, which diameter cake should she use?

   _____

3. Students in Mrs. Vierow's class were given the following math sentence and asked to complete it with a <, >, or = symbol: 4.5 _____ 4.50. Gerardo thinks that it should be a < since 45 is less than 450. Do you agree with him? If not, write a note explaining your reasoning.

   _____

   _____

4. Konna and Eva were arguing about the following problem: 3.60 < 3.72. Konna said that it is correct since 6 tenths is smaller than 7 tenths. Eva said that 60 hundredths is smaller than 72 hundredths. Which student has the correct reasoning for the answer?

   _____

5. Brandon says that 5.19 is more than 5.2. He claims that both have 5s for the whole numbers, but 19 is more than 2, so 5.19 is more than 5.2. Do you agree with Brandon? If not, write a note explaining your reasoning.

   _____

   _____

Compare sets and values using <, >, and =

Number & Operations

Math Test

Fill in the circle next to the correct answer.

1. 5.2 _____ 4.9

   (A) <   (C) =
   (B) >   (D) none of the above

2. 3.6 _____ 4.2

   (A) <   (C) =
   (B) >   (D) none of the above

3. 2.61 _____ 3.1

   (A) <   (C) =
   (B) >   (D) none of the above

4. 4.93 _____ 4.96

   (A) <   (C) =
   (B) >   (D) none of the above

5. 8.1 _____ 8.10

   (A) <   (C) =
   (B) >   (D) none of the above

6. 7.84 _____ 7.8

   (A) <   (C) =
   (B) >   (D) none of the above

7. Which of the following is correct?

   (A) 5.9 > 5.91
   (B) 6.9 < 6.89
   (C) 7.30 = 7.03
   (D) 8.2 = 8.20

8. Which of the following is NOT correct?

   (A) 4.5 < 4.51
   (B) 5.03 = 5.30
   (C) 3.5 = 3.50
   (D) 6.38 > 6.35

9. Juan collected two ropes. One rope measured 4.2 feet, while the other measured 5.9 feet. Which rope is the longer rope?

   _____

10. Ivan and Roberto attempted to complete the math sentence 4.5 _____ 4.50 by using a < symbol. Their reasoning was that the 4s are the same for the whole numbers. They thought that since 5 is less than 50, that the 4.5 must be less than the 4.50. Do you agree? If not, write a note explaining your reasoning.

    _____

    _____

    _____

Compare sets and values using <, >, and =

Algebra

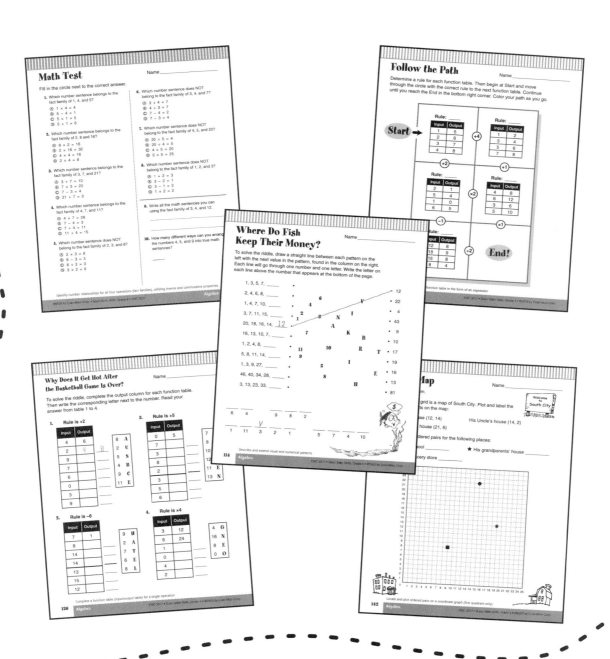

Where Do Fish Keep Their Money?

Name _____

To solve the riddle, draw a straight line between each pattern on the left with the next value in the pattern, found in the column on the right. Each line will go through one number and one letter. Write the letter on each line above the number that appears at the bottom of the page.

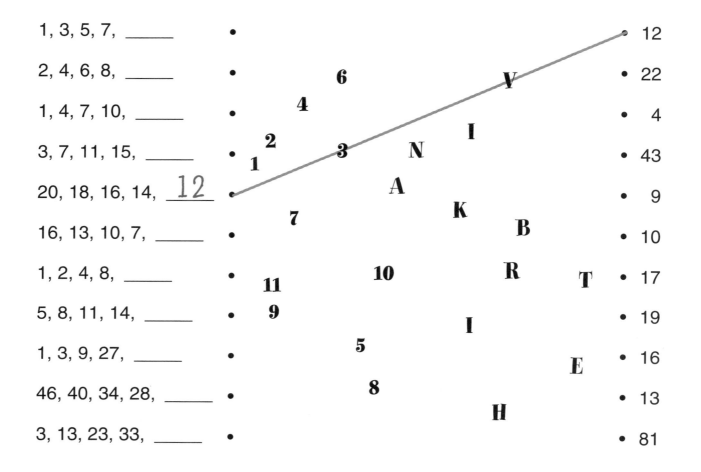

1, 3, 5, 7, _____ •

2, 4, 6, 8, _____ •

1, 4, 7, 10, _____ •

3, 7, 11, 15, _____ •

20, 18, 16, 14, _12_ •

16, 13, 10, 7, _____ •

1, 2, 4, 8, _____ •

5, 8, 11, 14, _____ •

1, 3, 9, 27, _____ •

46, 40, 34, 28, _____ •

3, 13, 23, 33, _____ •

• 12
• 22
• 4
• 43
• 9
• 10
• 17
• 19
• 16
• 13
• 81

2 6 4 3 N I V A K B R T 1 7 11 9 10 I 5 E 8 H

___ ___ ___ ___ ___ ___
 6   4   9   8   2

___ ___ _V_ ___ ___ ___ ___ ___ ___ ___
 1   11   3   2   1   5   7   4   10

Describe and extend visual and numerical patterns

Algebra

EMC 3017 • Basic Math Skills, Grade 4 • ©2003 by Evan-Moor Corp.

Tongue Twister

Name _____

Find the next figure in each pattern below. Then write the corresponding letter on each line above the correct figure. Read the tongue twister and try to say it quickly three times.

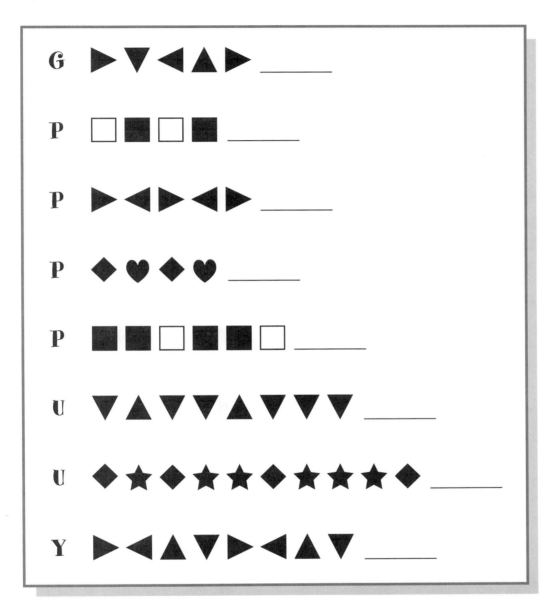

Describe and extend visual and numerical patterns

What's the Rule?

Name _____

List the next three numbers in each pattern. Then write the rule you used to find those numbers.

1. 1, 3, 5, 7, 9, _11_ , _13_ , _15_   **Rule** _+ 2_____

2. 3, 7, 11, 15, ____, ____, ____   **Rule** _____

3. 5, 11, 17, 23, ____, ____, ____   **Rule** _____

4. 1, 2, 4, 8, ____, ____, ____   **Rule** _____

5. 28, 25, 22, 19, ____, ____, ____   **Rule** _____

6. 59, 53, 47, 41, ____, ____, ____   **Rule** _____

7. 1, 2, 4, 7, 11, 16, ____, ____, ____   **Rule** _____

8. 94, 89, 84, 79, ____, ____, ____   **Rule** _____

9. 52, 60, 68, 76, ____, ____, ____   **Rule** _____

10. 2, 4, 7, 9, 12, 14, ____, ____, ____   **Rule** _____

Describe and extend visual and numerical patterns

Algebra   EMC 3017 • Basic Math Skills, Grade 4 • ©2003 by Evan-Moor Corp.

Describe the Patterns

Name _____

Draw the next figure in each pattern. Then write a sentence describing each pattern.

1.  ⇦ ⇧ ⇨ ⇩ _____

   Rule _____

2.  ◤ ◢ ◤ ◢ _____

   Rule _____

3.  ▦ ▦ ▦ ▦ _____

   Rule _____

4.  ⊘ ⊖ ⊘ ⊖ _____

   Rule _____

5.  ◺ ◿ ◺ ◹ _____

   Rule _____

6.  ▲ ▶ ▼ ◀ ▲ ▶ ▼ ◀ _____

   Rule _____

7. ☐ ■ ☐ ■ ■ ☐ ■ ■ ■ _____

   Rule _____

8.  ● ○ ● ● ○ ● ○ _____

   Rule _____

Describe and extend visual and numerical patterns

Using Patterns

Name_____

Solve each problem.

1. Sarah is making a quilt with her mother. She would like to use a pattern of triangles facing different directions around the border of the quilt. Draw a pattern using triangles that could repeat all the way around the quilt.

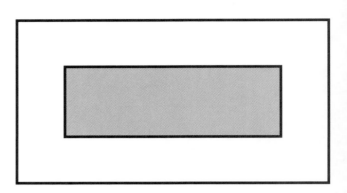

2. Adam is making a brick fence with his dad around their front yard. He has started the top border of the fence with the following pattern of bricks, showing some bricks lengthwise and some showing the end of the brick.

   How should Adam place the next brick on the right side to continue the pattern?

   _____

3. Tim has identified his pattern as having the format A, B, B, A, B, B, and so on. If the first item in his pattern is red followed by blue, what is the color of the next two items in his pattern?

   _____

4. Joan is writing a song that is in a pattern. The first thing she sings is the chorus. The next part is the first verse of her song. This is followed by a repeat of the chorus. Then she sings the second verse. If her pattern continues, what will she sing next?

   _____

5. Using red and blue crayons, as well as squares and circles, create a pattern using both attributes.

Describe and extend visual and numerical patterns

EMC 3017 • Basic Math Skills, Grade 4 • ©2003 by Evan-Moor Corp.

Math Test

Name _____

Fill in the circle next to the correct answer.

1. 2, 4, 6, 8, _____
   - Ⓐ 9
   - Ⓑ 10
   - Ⓒ 11
   - Ⓓ 12

2. 4, 7, 10, 13, _____
   - Ⓐ 13
   - Ⓑ 14
   - Ⓒ 15
   - Ⓓ 16

3. 65, 59, 53, 47, _____
   - Ⓐ 43
   - Ⓑ 41
   - Ⓒ 42
   - Ⓓ 40

4. 1, 2, 4, 8, _____
   - Ⓐ 24
   - Ⓑ 16
   - Ⓒ 10
   - Ⓓ 12

5. 35, 31, 27, 23, _____
   - Ⓐ 21
   - Ⓑ 19
   - Ⓒ 24
   - Ⓓ 20

6. 14, 19, 24, 29, _____
   - Ⓐ 34
   - Ⓑ 39
   - Ⓒ 35
   - Ⓓ 24

7. ▲▶▼◀▲▶ _____
   - Ⓐ ▲
   - Ⓑ ▶
   - Ⓒ ▼
   - Ⓓ ◀

8. □■●○□ _____
   - Ⓐ □
   - Ⓑ ■
   - Ⓒ ●
   - Ⓓ ○

9. Julie is making a brick fence with her dad around their front yard. She started the top border of the fence with the following pattern of bricks:

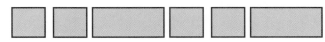

Describe the pattern and explain what should come next.

_____

_____

_____

10. Use red and orange crayons to create a pattern using two attributes (color and shape). Draw the pattern using squares and triangles in the two colors.

Describe and extend visual and numerical patterns

Tongue Twister

Name _____

Using fact families, draw straight lines from the numbers on the left to all the math sentences on the right that belong to that number family. Each line will pass through one number. On that numbered space at the bottom of the page, write the letter. Read the tongue twister and try to say it quickly three times.

A   1, 2, 3

H   1, 2, 2

S   2, 4, 8

R   2, 5, 10

T   2, 7, 14

K   4, 7, 11

M   4, 6, 10

P   6, 7, 13

X   8, 9, 17

I   4, 5, 20

S   3, 3, 9

- $1 \times 2 = 2$
- $2 \times 4 = 8$
- $10 \div 2 = 5$
- $14 \div 7 = 2$
- $1 + 2 = 3$
- $9 \div 3 = 3$
- $8 + 9 = 17$
- $13 - 7 = 6$
- $3 \times 3 = 9$
- $8 \div 4 = 2$
- $2 + 1 = 3$
- $2 \times 5 = 10$
- $2 \div 2 = 1$
- $4 \times 5 = 20$
- $11 - 7 = 4$
- $3 - 1 = 2$
- $10 - 6 = 4$
- $8 \div 2 = 4$
- $5 \times 2 = 10$

5   1   6   7   13   11   19   17   12   4   18   8   14   16   15   3   9   10   2

___ ___ ___   ___ ___ A̸ ___ ___
1   2   3   4   5   6   7   8

___ ___ ___ ___ ___   ___ ___ ___ ___ ___ ___
9   10 11 12 13   14 15 16 17 18 19

Identify number relationships for all four operations (fact families), utilizing inverse and commutative properties

EMC 3017 • Basic Math Skills, Grade 4 • ©2003 by Evan-Moor Corp.

How Do You Stop a Skunk From Smelling?

Name _____

Identify which number family each number sentence belongs to. Write the letter for the number family next to each number sentence. Read the answer to the riddle from top to bottom.

_____ $25 \div 5 = 5$

_____ $6 - 4 = 2$

_____ $2 \times 6 = 12$

_____ $3 + 5 = 8$

_____ $4 + 2 = 6$

_____ $18 \div 3 = 6$

_____ $1 \times 2 = 2$

_____ $8 \div 4 = 2$

_____ $11 - 7 = 4$

_____ $6 + 3 = 9$

_____ $5 \times 2 = 10$

_____ $2 + 4 = 6$

_____ $9 - 3 = 6$

_____ $5 - 3 = 2$

D	1, 2, 2	**N**	2, 5, 10
E	2, 3, 5	**O**	2, 4, 6
H	3, 5, 8	**S**	3, 6, 9
I	2, 4, 8	**T**	4, 7, 11
L	3, 6, 18	**U**	2, 6, 12
M	1, 5, 5	**Y**	5, 5, 25

Go! take a bath!

Identify number relationships for all four operations (fact families), utilizing inverse and commutative properties

Inverse Operations

Name _____

Answer each question.

1. What is the inverse operation for addition?

   _____

2. What is the inverse operation for multiplication?

   _____

3. Using the numbers 3, 6, and 9, write four correct number sentences.

   _____

   _____

4. Using the numbers 1, 3, and 3, write four correct number sentences.

   _____

   _____

5. Using the numbers 5, 5, and 25, write two correct number sentences.

   _____

6. Using the numbers 5, 6, and 11, write four correct number sentences.

   _____

   _____

7. Looking at number 6 above, why can you write only two unique number sentences?

   _____

Identify number relationships for all four operations (fact families), utilizing inverse and commutative properties

Algebra

EMC 3017 • Basic Math Skills, Grade 4 • ©2003 by Evan-Moor Corp.

Families

Answer each question.

1. What is the inverse operation for subtraction?

   _____

2. What is the inverse operation for division?

   _____

Use the fact families and the inverse operations to write at least two other number sentences that are related to each of the following sentences.

3. $3 + 4 = 7$ _____

4. $5 \times 2 = 10$ _____

5. $6 \div 3 = 2$ _____

6. $8 - 2 = 6$ _____

7. $7 + 8 = 15$ _____

8. $12 \div 3 = 4$ _____

9. $3 \times 6 = 18$ _____

10. $17 - 9 = 8$ _____

Identify number relationships for all four operations (fact families), utilizing inverse and commutative properties

Arrange the Numbers

Name _____

1. How many different ways can you arrange the numbers 5, 6, and 30 into true math sentences?

   _____

2. How many different ways can you arrange the numbers 3, 4, and 7 into true math sentences?

   _____

3. How many different ways can you arrange the numbers 4, 4, and 8 into true math sentences?

   _____

4. How many different ways can you arrange the numbers 3, 3, and 9 into true math sentences?

   _____

5. Why can't you arrange any set of numbers into four unique math sentences?

   _____

   _____

Identify number relationships for all four operations (fact families), utilizing inverse and commutative properties

EMC 3017 • Basic Math Skills, Grade 4 • ©2003 by Evan-Moor Corp.

Math Test

Name _____

Fill in the circle next to the correct answer.

1. Which number sentence belongs to the fact family of 1, 4, and 5?

   Ⓐ $1 \times 4 = 4$
   Ⓑ $5 - 4 = 1$
   Ⓒ $5 \times 1 = 5$
   Ⓓ $5 + 1 = 6$

2. Which number sentence belongs to the fact family of 2, 8, and 16?

   Ⓐ $8 \times 2 = 16$
   Ⓑ $2 \times 16 = 32$
   Ⓒ $4 \times 4 = 16$
   Ⓓ $2 \times 4 = 8$

3. Which number sentence belongs to the fact family of 3, 7, and 21?

   Ⓐ $3 + 7 = 10$
   Ⓑ $7 \times 3 = 20$
   Ⓒ $7 - 3 = 4$
   Ⓓ $21 \div 7 = 3$

4. Which number sentence belongs to the fact family of 4, 7, and 11?

   Ⓐ $4 \times 7 = 28$
   Ⓑ $7 - 4 = 3$
   Ⓒ $7 + 4 = 11$
   Ⓓ $11 + 4 = 15$

5. Which number sentence does NOT belong to the fact family of 2, 3, and 6?

   Ⓐ $2 \times 3 = 6$
   Ⓑ $6 - 3 = 3$
   Ⓒ $6 \div 2 = 3$
   Ⓓ $3 \times 2 = 6$

6. Which number sentence does NOT belong to the fact family of 3, 4, and 7?

   Ⓐ $3 + 4 = 7$
   Ⓑ $4 + 3 = 7$
   Ⓒ $7 - 4 = 2$
   Ⓓ $7 - 3 = 4$

7. Which number sentence does NOT belong to the fact family of 4, 5, and 20?

   Ⓐ $20 \div 5 = 4$
   Ⓑ $20 \div 4 = 5$
   Ⓒ $4 \times 5 = 20$
   Ⓓ $5 \times 5 = 25$

8. Which number sentence does NOT belong to the fact family of 1, 2, and 3?

   Ⓐ $1 + 2 = 3$
   Ⓑ $3 - 2 = 1$
   Ⓒ $3 - 1 = 2$
   Ⓓ $1 \times 2 = 2$

9. Write all the math sentences you can using the fact family of 3, 4, and 12.

   _____

   _____

10. How many different ways can you arrange the numbers 4, 5, and 9 into true math sentences?

   _____

Identify number relationships for all four operations (fact families), utilizing inverse and commutative properties

Why Does It Get Hot After the Basketball Game Is Over?

Name _____

To solve the riddle, complete the output column for each function table. Then write the corresponding letter next to the number. Read your answer from table 1 to 4.

1. Rule is +2

Input	Output
4	6
2	4
9	
7	
6	
0	
3	
9	

____ B
____
____
____
____
____
____

8	A
2	U
5	S
4	B
9	C
11	E

3. Rule is +5

Input	Output
0	5
7	
3	
8	
2	
3	
5	
6	

____
____
____
____
____
____
____

7	S
8	A
10	R
12	F
11	E
13	N

2. Rule is −6

Input	Output
7	1
8	
14	
14	
13	
15	
12	

____
____
____
____
____
____

9	H
2	A
7	T
6	E
8	L

4. Rule is ×4

Input	Output
3	12
6	24
1	
0	
4	
2	

____
____
____
____

4	G
16	N
8	E
0	O

Complete a function table (input/output table) for a single operation

Algebra   EMC 3017 • Basic Math Skills, Grade 4 • ©2003 by Evan-Moor Corp.

Tongue Twister

Name _____

Complete the output column for each function table. Then write the corresponding letter next to the number. Read the tongue twister from table 1 to 2 and try to say it quickly three times.

1. Rule is +4

Input	Output
2	6
7	11
5	9
3	
4	
1	
9	
6	

13	**O**
5	**M**
7	**L**
8	**E**
10	**N**

2. Rule is ×2

Input	Output
2	4
7	14
8	
6	
1	
0	
3	
5	
9	
4	

8	**T**
6	**M**
16	**L**
10	**E**
12	**I**
0	**I**
2	**N**
18	**N**

Frank fries Frank freshhhh f-i-s-h f-i-l-l-e-t-s

say it quick!

Complete a function table (input/output table) for a single operation

Algebra

Function Tables

Name _____

Complete each function table.

1. Rule is +4

Input	Output
1	
2	
3	
4	
5	
6	

2. Rule is ×2

Input	Output
1	
2	
3	
4	
5	
6	

3. Rule is –7

Input	Output
8	
10	
12	
15	
16	
19	

4. Rule is –3

Input	Output
9	
8	
7	
6	
5	
4	

5. Rule is +5

Input	Output
2	
4	
5	
7	
9	
10	

6. Rule is +10

Input	Output
7	
15	
6	
0	
9	
10	

Complete a function table (input/output table) for a single operation

Algebra

EMC 3017 • Basic Math Skills, Grade 4 • ©2003 by Evan-Moor Corp.

Input/Output

Name _____

Complete each function table.

1. Rule is +3

Input	Output
1	
2	
4	
6	
8	
10	

2. Rule is ×3

Input	Output
6	
2	
5	
9	
15	
21	

3. Rule is −4

Input	Output
2	
19	
0	
5	
9	
16	

4. Rule is −2

Input	Output
9	
6	
5	
3	
6	
12	

5. Rule is +12

Input	Output
5	
16	
13	
18	
5	
12	

6. Rule is ÷2

Input	Output
10	
2	
8	
12	
20	
14	

Complete a function table (input/output table) for a single operation

Using Function Tables

Name _____

Solve each problem.

1. Tommy created a function table to help him determine how many cupcakes are in a given number of packages if there are 3 cupcakes in each package. Complete the function table, and use that to tell Tommy how many cupcakes are in 5 packages.

Rule: Number of packages ×3

Input (no. of packages)	Output (no. of cupcakes)
1	3
2	6
3	
4	
5	
6	

2. Juanita was helping organize the school's carnival, and she made a function table to tell how much a certain number of tickets cost. She knew that the school wanted to charge 25¢ for each ticket. Complete the function table to show how much each number of tickets will be.

Rule: Number of tickets ×25¢

Input (no. of tickets)	Output (amount of money in ¢)
1	25
2	50
3	
4	
5	
6	

3. Sergio and his mother were looking at his growth, and they figured that it could be mapped to a function table. From age 5 until the present, his growth fit nicely to the function table. Complete the function table and tell how tall Sergio is at age 10.

Rule: Input ×5, +85

Input (in years)	Output (in cm)
5	110
6	115
7	
8	
9	
10	

Complete a function table (input/output table) for a single operation

EMC 3017 • Basic Math Skills, Grade 4 • ©2003 by Evan-Moor Corp.

Math Test

Name _____

Fill in the circle next to the correct answer.

For Numbers 1 through 4, use this function table.

Rule is +3

Input	Output
1	4
5	8
2	
7	
0	
3	

1. What is the output when the input is 2?

- Ⓐ 12
- Ⓑ 6
- Ⓒ 4
- Ⓓ 5

2. What is the output when the input is 7?

- Ⓐ 16
- Ⓑ 10
- Ⓒ 13
- Ⓓ 9

3. What is the output when the input is 0?

- Ⓐ 0
- Ⓑ 3
- Ⓒ 6
- Ⓓ 20

4. What is the output when the input is 3?

- Ⓐ 6
- Ⓑ 3
- Ⓒ 24
- Ⓓ 5

For Numbers 5 through 8, use this function table.

Rule is ÷2

Input	Output
10	5
6	3
2	
8	
0	
4	

5. What is the output when the input is 2?

- Ⓐ 1
- Ⓑ 2
- Ⓒ 4
- Ⓓ none of the above

6. What is the output when the input is 8?

- Ⓐ 16
- Ⓑ 10
- Ⓒ 4
- Ⓓ none of the above

7. What is the output when the input is 0?

- Ⓐ 2
- Ⓑ 0
- Ⓒ 1
- Ⓓ none of the above

8. What is the output when the input is 4?

- Ⓐ 0
- Ⓑ 6
- Ⓒ 4
- Ⓓ none of the above

9. Draw a function table with five inputs and five outputs, utilizing the rule −2.

10. Draw a function table with five inputs and five outputs, utilizing the rule ×5.

Complete a function table (input/output table) for a single operation

©2003 by Evan-Moor Corp. • Basic Math Skills, Grade 4 • EMC 3017

Algebra

Follow the Path

Determine a rule for each function table. Then begin at Start and move through the circle with the correct rule to the next function table. Continue until you reach the End in the bottom right corner. Color your path as you go.

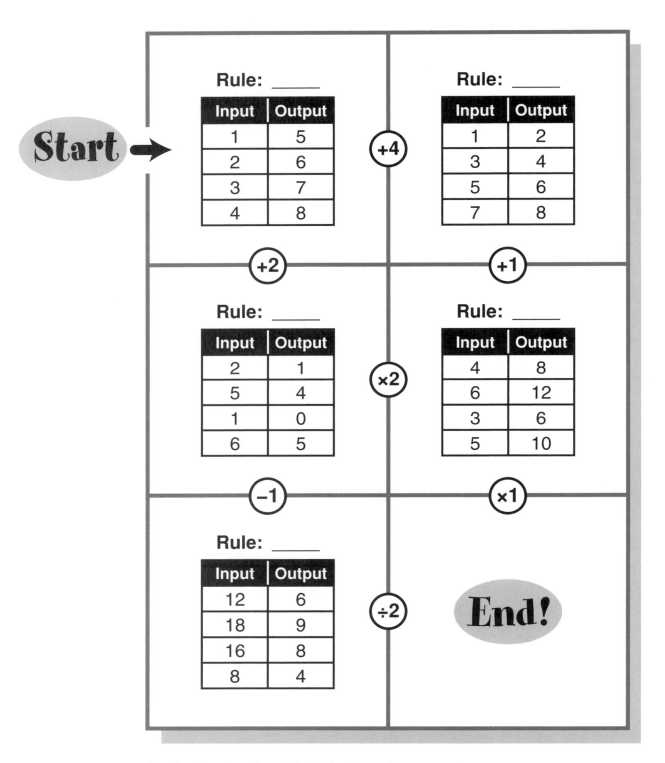

Write simple rules for a function table in the form of an expression

What Is of Most Use When It Is Used Up?

Name_____

Find the rule for each function table below. Then look for the rule at the bottom of the page. Write the letter from the function table on the line above the rule. This will spell out the solution to the riddle.

A Rule: _____

Input	Output
1	3
6	8
3	5
4	6

R Rule: _____

Input	Output
2	8
6	24
4	16
7	28

M Rule: _____

Input	Output
9	4
16	11
14	9
8	3

E Rule: _____

Input	Output
12	6
24	12
18	9
4	2

B Rule: _____

Input	Output
4	2
8	6
5	3
9	7

U Rule: _____

Input	Output
9	3
3	1
24	8
18	6

L Rule: _____

Input	Output
6	10
9	13
1	5
5	9

L Rule: _____

Input	Output
4	12
3	9
9	27
5	15

____ ____ ____ ____ ____ ____ ____ ____
÷3   −5   −2   ×4   ÷2   ×3   +4   +2

Write simple rules for a function table in the form of an expression

Algebra   **133**

What's the Rule?

Name _____

Write the rule for each completed function table.

1. Rule: _____

Input	Output
1	5
2	6
3	7
4	8
5	9
6	10

2. Rule: _____

Input	Output
1	2
2	4
3	6
4	8
5	10
6	12

3. Rule: _____

Input	Output
10	8
9	7
8	6
7	5
6	4
5	3

4. Rule: _____

Input	Output
1	5
3	7
6	10
8	12
10	14
12	16

5. Rule: _____

Input	Output
10	5
22	17
16	11
19	14
8	3
28	23

6. Rule: _____

Input	Output
6	18
3	9
0	0
5	15
2	6
7	21

Write simple rules for a function table in the form of an expression

Algebra   EMC 3017 • Basic Math Skills, Grade 4 • ©2003 by Evan-Moor Corp.

Find the Rule

Name _____

Write the rule for each function table and fill in the missing numbers.

1. Rule: _____

Input	Output
1	5
2	6
3	7
4	8
	9
6	

2. Rule: _____

Input	Output
2	6
3	9
5	15
9	27
	30
15	

3. Rule: _____

Input	Output
18	15
12	9
16	13
6	
	3
3	

4. Rule: _____

Input	Output
2	5
6	9
7	10
12	15
	17
16	19

5. Rule: _____

Input	Output
12	3
20	5
40	10
48	
	13
60	

6. Rule: _____

Input	Output
19	14
8	3
12	7
90	
	61
	49

Write simple rules for a function table in the form of an expression

Algebra

Using Function Tables

Name _____

Solve each problem.

1. Juanita was thinking of a rule for a function table. When she was given the input of 2, she said that the output would be 4. What are two different rules that Juanita could be thinking of for her function table?

   _____

   _____

2. Tim had this function table, and he was asked to determine the rule. Tim thinks that the rule is to add 2 since 1 + 2 equals 3. Write a note to Tim either agreeing with him, or explaining to him the correct rule.

   _____

   _____

   Rule: _____

Input	Output
1	3
0	0
3	9
5	15

3. Anne Marie knows that three bananas cost 93¢. She also knows that 5 bananas cost $1.55. She started to create a function table, but needs your help to determine the rule. Write the rule and then complete the remaining spaces on her function table.

   Rule: _____

Input (# of bananas)	Output (cost)
3	93¢
5	$1.55
8	
10	

4. Herald had this function table and was asked to determine the rule. In addition, the teacher said that one of the outputs was incorrect. Herald thinks that the rule is to divide by 2 since 6 ÷ 2 equals 3. Write a note to Herald either agreeing with him, or explaining to him the correct rule. Include in your note a sentence telling Herald which one of the outputs is incorrect, and what it should be.

   _____

   Rule: _____

Input	Output
6	3
14	11
16	8
4	2

Write simple rules for a function table in the form of an expression

EMC 3017 • Basic Math Skills, Grade 4 • ©2003 by Evan-Moor Corp.

Math Test

Name _____

Fill in the circle next to the correct answer.

For Numbers 1 through 4, use the following function table. The input stays the same, but the output is different for each column.

	#1	#2	#3	#4
Input	**Output**	**Output**	**Output**	**Output**
4	7	2	4	8
5	8	3	5	10
6	9	4	6	12
7	10	5	7	14

1. What is the rule for output column #1?

Ⓐ ×2   Ⓒ +3
Ⓑ +4   Ⓓ none of the above

2. What is the rule for output column #2?

Ⓐ ÷2   Ⓒ −2
Ⓑ ×1   Ⓓ none of the above

3. What is the rule for output column #3?

Ⓐ +1   Ⓒ −1
Ⓑ ×1   Ⓓ none of the above

4. What is the rule for output column #4?

Ⓐ ×2   Ⓒ +5
Ⓑ +4   Ⓓ none of the above

For Numbers 5 through 8, use the following function table. The input stays the same, but the output is different for each column.

	#5	#6	#7	#8
Input	**Output**	**Output**	**Output**	**Output**
12	14	6	48	9
16	18	8	64	13
6	8	3	24	3
10	12	5	40	7

5. What is the rule for output column #5?

Ⓐ +2   Ⓒ +1
Ⓑ +3   Ⓓ none of the above

6. What is the rule for output column #6?

Ⓐ −6   Ⓒ ÷2
Ⓑ −8   Ⓓ none of the above

7. What is the rule for output column #7?

Ⓐ +18   Ⓒ +30
Ⓑ ×3   Ⓓ none of the above

8. What is the rule for output column #8?

Ⓐ −3   Ⓒ ÷2
Ⓑ −4   Ⓓ none of the above

9. Joe is thinking of a function machine. He says that the output is 12 if the input is 4. What are two rules that he could be thinking of for his function machine?

_____

_____

10. Laura is thinking of another function machine. She said that the output is 2 if the input is 6. What are two rules that she could be thinking of for her function machine?

_____

_____

Write simple rules for a function table in the form of an expression

All Smiles

Name _____

Plot the ordered pairs of numbers on the graph in the order in which they are listed, connecting them with straight lines. Start each new set of points with a new line.

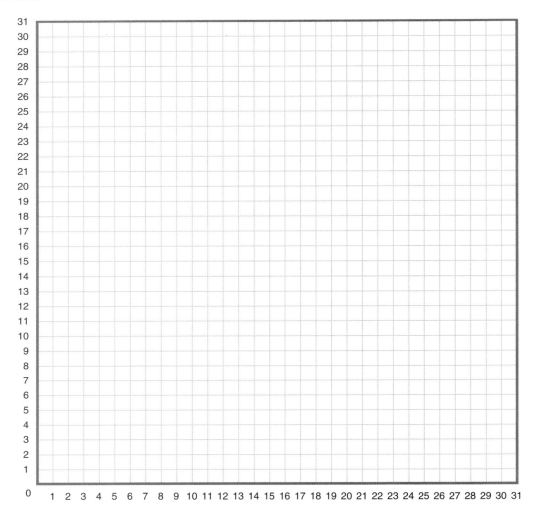

▶ (13, 0) (13, 9) (10, 9) (6, 12) (6, 17) (5, 17) (4, 16) (3, 16) (3, 21) (4, 21) (5, 20) (6, 20) (6, 22) (9, 29) (21, 29) (24, 22) (24, 20) (25, 20) (26, 21) (27, 21) (27, 16) (26, 16) (25, 17) (24, 17) (24, 12) (20, 9) (17, 9) (17, 0)

▶ (9, 16) (11, 11) (19, 11) (21, 16) (19, 16) (17, 14) (13, 14) (11, 16) (9, 16)

▶ (12, 25) (10, 23) (11, 22) (13, 24) (12, 25)

▶ (17, 24) (18, 25) (20, 23) (19, 22) (17, 24)

▶ (14, 22) (14, 17) (16, 17) (17, 18)

Locate and plot ordered pairs on a coordinate graph (first quadrant only)

EMC 3017 • Basic Math Skills, Grade 4 • ©2003 by Evan-Moor Corp.

Mystery Picture

Name_____

Plot the ordered pairs of numbers on the graph in the order in which they are listed, connecting them with straight lines. Start each new set of points with a new line.

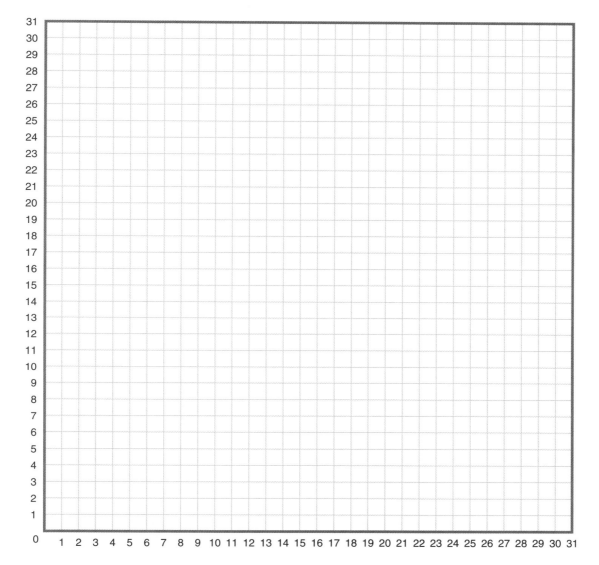

▶ (16, 6) (7, 21) (5, 21) (2, 24) (2, 27) (4, 29) (7, 29) (10, 26) (10, 24) (21, 11) (16, 12) (16, 6)

▶ (22, 17) (22, 22) (18, 23) (22, 24) (22, 28) (24, 25) (28, 26) (26, 23) (28, 19) (25, 21) (22, 17)

▶ (6, 23) (8, 25)

▶ (4, 25) (4, 27) (7, 24)

Locate and plot ordered pairs on a coordinate graph (first quadrant only)

Algebra

Plot the Ordered Pairs

Name _____

Plot each of the following ordered pairs and label them with the corresponding letter.

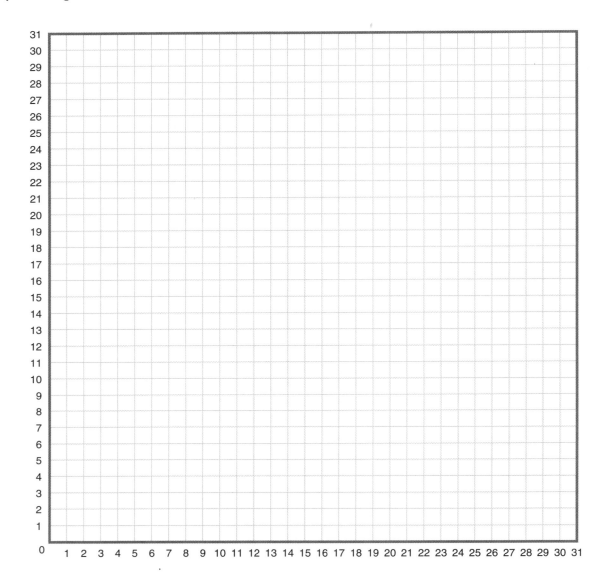

A (2, 6)	**D** (26, 5)	**G** (29, 20)	**J** (10, 29)
B (4, 9)	**E** (15, 30)	**H** (0, 0)	
C (21, 20)	**F** (18, 5)	**I** (17, 15)	

Locate and plot ordered pairs on a coordinate graph (first quadrant only)

Plot the Points

Name _____

Plot each of the following ordered pairs and label them with the corresponding letter.

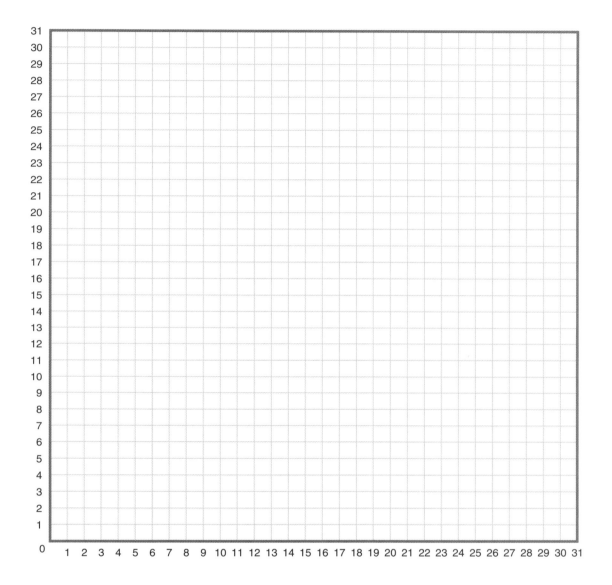

A	(15, 0)	D	(4, 20)	G	(12, 28)	J	(28, 5)
B	(14, 29)	E	(6, 2)	H	(18, 17)		
C	(16, 20)	F	(10, 10)	I	(25, 22)		

Locate and plot ordered pairs on a coordinate graph (first quadrant only)

Algebra

On the Map

Name _____

Solve each problem.

1. The following grid is a map of South City. Plot and label the following points on the map:

   Sam's house (12, 14)   His Uncle's house (14, 2)

   His Aunt's house (21, 6)

2. Identify the ordered pairs for the following places:

   ■ The school _____   ★ His grandparents' house _____

   ● The grocery store _____

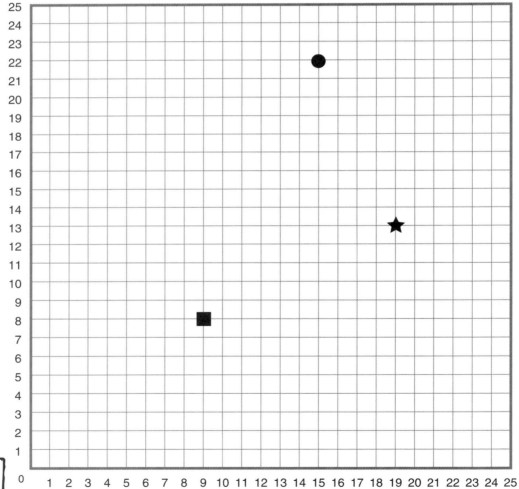

Locate and plot ordered pairs on a coordinate graph (first quadrant only)

Math Test

Name _____

Fill in the circle next to the correct answer.

Use this graph for Numbers 1 through 4.

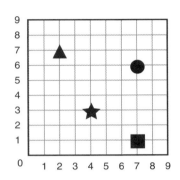

Use this graph for Numbers 5 through 8.

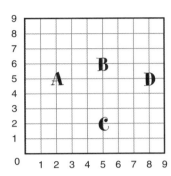

1. What is the ordered pair of the triangle?

Ⓐ (2, 7)   Ⓒ (2, 6)

Ⓑ (7, 2)   Ⓓ (8, 2)

2. What is the ordered pair of the circle?

Ⓐ (6, 6)   Ⓒ (7, 6)

Ⓑ (7, 7)   Ⓓ (6, 7)

3. What is the ordered pair of the square?

Ⓐ (7, 0)   Ⓒ (1, 6)

Ⓑ (6, 1)   Ⓓ (7, 1)

4. What is the ordered pair of the star?

Ⓐ (4, 4)   Ⓒ (3, 3)

Ⓑ (4, 3)   Ⓓ (3, 4)

5. Which point is at (5, 2)?

Ⓐ A   Ⓒ C

Ⓑ B   Ⓓ D

6. Which point is at (8, 5)?

Ⓐ A   Ⓒ C

Ⓑ B   Ⓓ D

7. Which point is at (2, 5)?

Ⓐ A   Ⓒ C

Ⓑ B   Ⓓ D

8. Which point is at (5, 6)?

Ⓐ A   Ⓒ C

Ⓑ B   Ⓓ D

Use this graph for Numbers 9 and 10.

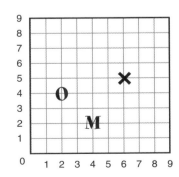

9. The ✖ on the graph represents George's house. What is the ordered pair of his house?

_____

10. A school is located at (2, 4) and a store is located at (4, 2). Which letter on the graph represents the school?

_____

Locate and plot ordered pairs on a coordinate graph (first quadrant only)

Algebra

Geometry

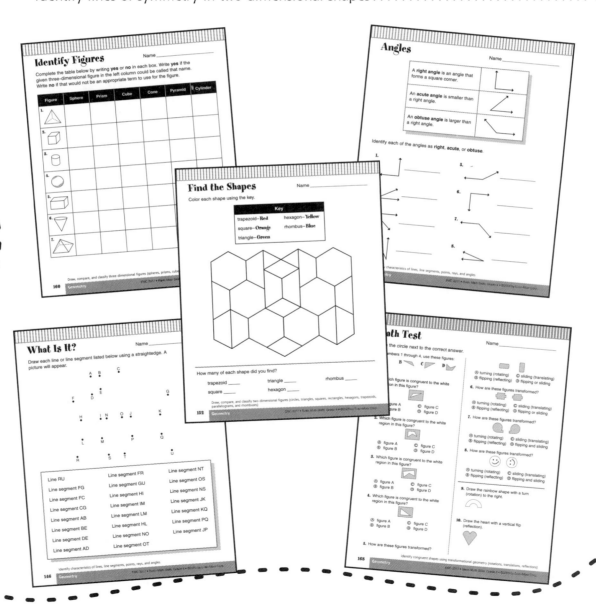

EMC 3017 • Basic Math Skills, Grade 4 • ©2003 by Evan-Moor Corp.

Riddle

Name _____

To answer the riddle, draw a straight line connecting each term on the left with its appropriate example. The line will go through a letter and a number. Write the letter in the numbered space at the bottom to find the solution to the riddle.

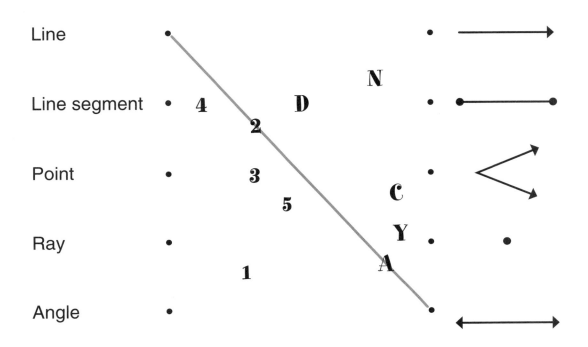

Line

Line segment   4   D

   2

Point   3

   5

Ray

   1

Angle

N   C   Y   A

How can you spell candy using only two letters?

____   A̲   ____ ____   ____
1   2   3   4   5

Identify characteristics of lines, line segments, points, rays, and angles

What Is It?

Draw each line or line segment listed below using a straightedge.
A picture will appear.

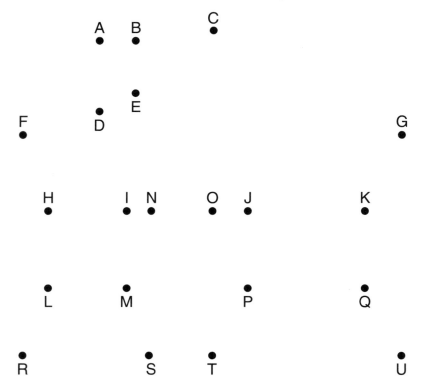

Line RU	Line segment FR	Line segment NT
Line segment FG	Line segment GU	Line segment OS
Line segment FC	Line segment HI	Line segment NS
Line segment CG	Line segment IM	Line segment JK
Line segment AB	Line segment LM	Line segment KQ
Line segment BE	Line segment HL	Line segment PQ
Line segment DE	Line segment NO	Line segment JP
Line segment AD	Line segment OT	

Identify characteristics of lines, line segments, points, rays, and angles

EMC 3017 • Basic Math Skills, Grade 4 • ©2003 by Evan-Moor Corp.

Definitions

Name _____

Find the best definition for each term. Draw a star in the box where the term and the definition intersect.

	Line	Line Segment	Point	Ray	Angle
An exact location in space.					
An infinite set of points forming a straight line that extends in two directions.					
A part of a line that has one endpoint and extends in one direction.					
Two rays that share an endpoint.					
A part of a line defined by two endpoints.					

Identify characteristics of lines, line segments, points, rays, and angles

Angles

A **right angle** is an angle that forms a square corner.	
An **acute angle** is smaller than a right angle.	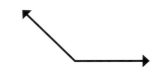
An **obtuse angle** is larger than a right angle.	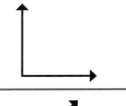

Identify each of the angles as **right**, **acute**, or **obtuse**.

1. _____

5. 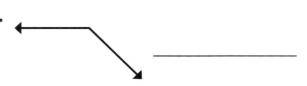 _____

2.  _____

6. 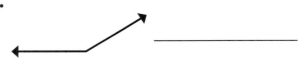 _____

3.  _____

7. 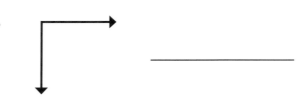 _____

4.  _____

8.  _____

Identify characteristics of lines, line segments, points, rays, and angles

EMC 3017 • Basic Math Skills, Grade 4 • ©2003 by Evan-Moor Corp.

Lines, Rays, Angles

Name _____

Solve each problem.

1. On a football field, we call the end line the goal line. Is it really a line? Justify your answer.

   _____

   _____

2. A baseball diamond is shaped like a square with a base at each corner. Think of each base as a point. How many line segments does a baseball runner follow as he runs around all the bases and back to home plate?

   _____

3. Think about a set of telephone lines that you see suspended by telephone poles. Would you describe them as lines? Why or why not?

   _____

   _____

4. Think of a sun's ray. Would you describe this as a ray? Why or why not?

   _____

   _____

5. On a clockface, there are two hands: a minute hand and an hour hand. How many times between 8:00 in the morning and 2:00 in the afternoon do the two hands form right angles?

   _____

Identify characteristics of lines, line segments, points, rays, and angles

Math Test

Name _____

Fill in the circle next to the correct answer.

1. An infinite set of points forming a straight line that extends in two directions is a(an) _____.
   - Ⓐ line
   - Ⓑ line segment
   - Ⓒ ray
   - Ⓓ angle

2. A part of a line that has one endpoint and extends in one direction is a(an) _____.
   - Ⓐ line
   - Ⓑ line segment
   - Ⓒ ray
   - Ⓓ angle

3. A part of a line that has two endpoints is a(an) _____.
   - Ⓐ line
   - Ⓑ line segment
   - Ⓒ ray
   - Ⓓ angle

4. Two rays that share a common endpoint form a(an) _____.
   - Ⓐ line
   - Ⓑ line segment
   - Ⓒ ray
   - Ⓓ angle

For Numbers 1 through 8, name the figure.

5. ●————●
   - Ⓐ line
   - Ⓑ line segment
   - Ⓒ ray
   - Ⓓ angle

6. ←————→
   - Ⓐ line
   - Ⓑ line segment
   - Ⓒ ray
   - Ⓓ angle

7.
   - Ⓐ line
   - Ⓑ line segment
   - Ⓒ ray
   - Ⓓ angle

8. ————→
   - Ⓐ line
   - Ⓑ line segment
   - Ⓒ ray
   - Ⓓ angle

9. What is one way that a line is the same as a ray?

   _____

   _____

10. What is one difference between a line and a line segment?

    _____

    _____

Identify characteristics of lines, line segments, points, rays, and angles

Geometry

EMC 3017 • Basic Math Skills, Grade 4 • ©2003 by Evan-Moor Corp.

Identify the Shapes

Name _____

Color each shape using the key. Some shapes will need more than one color.

Key	
trapezoid–**Red**	circle–**Pink**
square–**Yellow**	hexagon–**Black**
rectangle–**Blue**	all other boxes–**Leave White**
triangle–**Brown**	

1.	4.	7.	10.
2.	5.	8.	11.
3.	6.	9.	12.

Draw, compare, and classify two-dimensional figures (circles, triangles, squares, rectangles, hexagons, trapezoids, parallelograms, and rhombuses)

Find the Shapes

Name _____

Color each shape using the key.

Key	
trapezoid–**Red**	hexagon–**Yellow**
square–**Orange**	rhombus–**Blue**
triangle–**Green**	

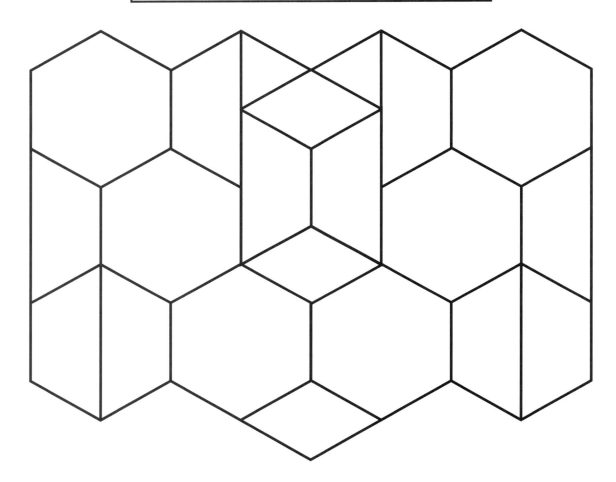

How many of each shape did you find?

trapezoid _____   triangle _____   rhombus _____

square _____   hexagon _____

Draw, compare, and classify two-dimensional figures (circles, triangles, squares, rectangles, hexagons, trapezoids, parallelograms, and rhombuses)

EMC 3017 • Basic Math Skills, Grade 4 • ©2003 by Evan-Moor Corp.

Draw the Shapes

Name _____

Draw each of the following figures.

1. circle	**2.** triangle	**3.** trapezoid
4. square	**5.** hexagon	**6.** parallelogram
7. rectangle	**8.** rhombus	**9.** quadrilateral

10. List four correct mathematical terms _____
that could describe this shape.

_____

_____

_____

_____

Draw, compare, and classify two-dimensional figures (circles, triangles, squares, rectangles, hexagons, trapezoids, parallelograms, and rhombuses)

Name the Shapes

Name _____

Complete the table. Write **yes** in all boxes that name each shape.
Some shapes will have more than one name.

Shape	Circle	Triangle	Square	Rectangle	Hexagon	Trapezoid	Parallel-ogram	Rhombus
1.								
2.								
3.								
4.								
5.								
6.								
7.								
8.								

Draw, compare, and classify two-dimensional figures (circles, triangles, squares, rectangles, hexagons, trapezoids, parallelograms, and rhombuses)

EMC 3017 • Basic Math Skills, Grade 4 • ©2003 by Evan-Moor Corp.

Shapes All Around Us

Name _____

Look around the classroom for objects that have the shapes listed below. Draw a picture of the object and outline the shape.

Square	Rectangle
Triangle	**Circle**
Trapezoid	**Rhombus**

Draw, compare, and classify two-dimensional figures (circles, triangles, squares, rectangles, hexagons, trapezoids, parallelograms, and rhombuses)

Math Test

Name _____

Fill in the circle next to the correct answer.

For Numers 1 and 2, name the figure.

1. ⬜

   Ⓐ square   Ⓒ trapezoid
   Ⓑ rectangle   Ⓓ none of the above

2. ⬜

   Ⓐ square   Ⓒ parallelogram
   Ⓑ rectangle   Ⓓ all of the above

3. If you draw a diagonal across a rectangle, what do you end up with?

   Ⓐ 2 squares   Ⓒ 2 triangles
   Ⓑ 2 rectangles   Ⓓ 2 trapezoids

4. A square is a rectangle.

   Ⓐ This is always true.
   Ⓑ This is true some of the time, but not very often.
   Ⓒ This is true most of the time, but there are exceptions.
   Ⓓ This is never true.

5. A trapezoid has _____.

   Ⓐ four congruent sides
   Ⓑ one pair of parallel sides
   Ⓒ four right angles
   Ⓓ two pairs of parallel sides

6. A circle has _____.

   Ⓐ four sides
   Ⓑ one right angle
   Ⓒ two parallel sides
   Ⓓ none of the above

7. A triangle has _____.

   Ⓐ three sides
   Ⓑ three right angles
   Ⓒ four congruent sides
   Ⓓ all of the above

8. A hexagon has _____.

   Ⓐ four sides
   Ⓑ six angles
   Ⓒ three angles
   Ⓓ none of the above

9. Draw a quadrilateral that has the following characteristics: one pair of parallel sides, two sides that are congruent, and two sides that are not congruent.

10. Draw a figure that has the following characteristics: four congruent sides and no right angles.

Draw, compare, and classify two-dimensional figures (circles, triangles, squares, rectangles, hexagons, trapezoids, parallelograms, and rhombuses)

What Does a Rain Cloud Wear Under Its Coat?

Name _____

To solve this riddle, draw a straight line between each figure on the left with the shape of its base on the right. Each line will go through one letter. Write that letter on the line(s) corresponding to the number at the bottom of the page. The letters will spell out the answer to the riddle.

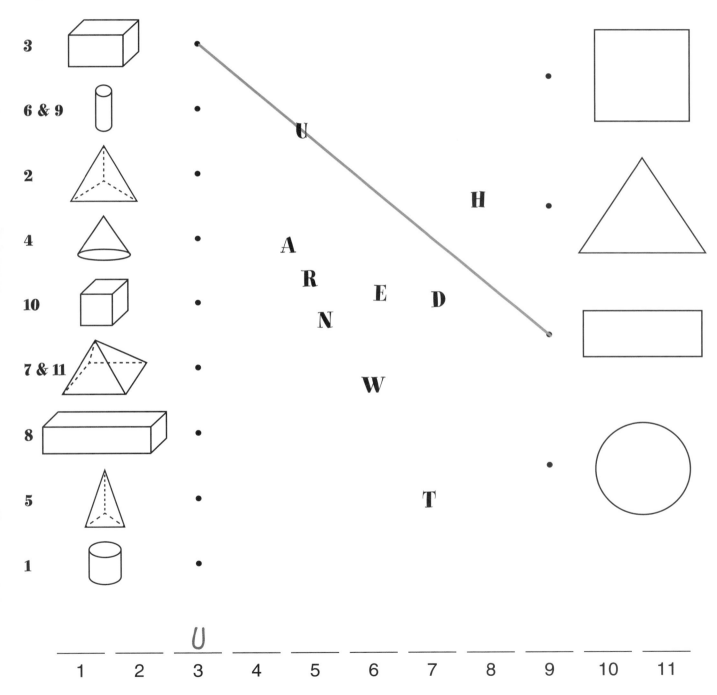

____ ____ $\overset{U}{\_\_\_\_}$ ____ ____ ____ ____ ____ ____ ____ ____
 1   2   3   4   5   6   7   8   9   10   11

Draw, compare, and classify three-dimensional figures (spheres, prisms, cubes, cones, pyramids, and cylinders)

Tongue Twister

Name _____

Draw a straight line connecting each figure on the left with the correct term on the right. Each line will go through one letter. Write that letter on the line(s) corresponding to the number in front of each figure. The letters will spell out a tongue twister. Try to say it fast three times.

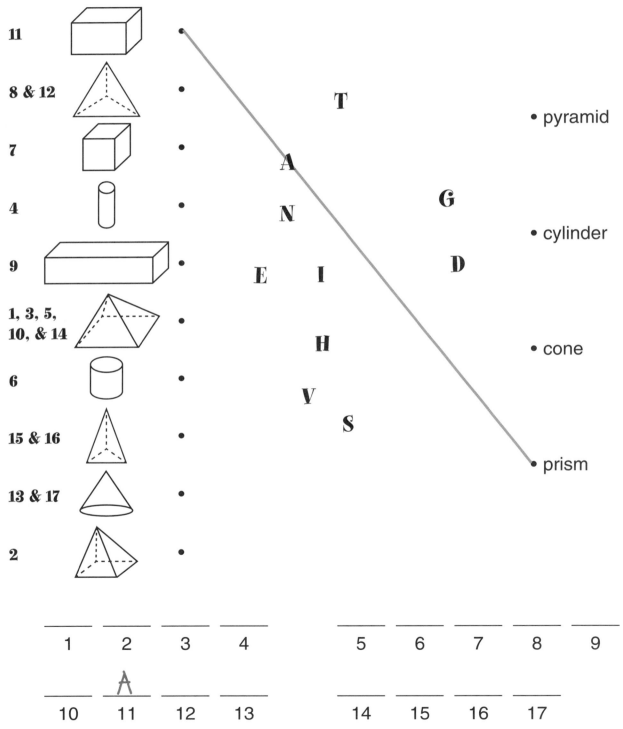

11

8 & 12

7

4

9

1, 3, 5, 10, & 14

6

15 & 16

13 & 17

2

T

A

N

G

D

E   I

H

V

S

• pyramid

• cylinder

• cone

• prism

___ ___ ___ ___   ___ ___ ___ ___ ___
 1   2   3   4   5   6   7   8   9

___ _A_ ___ ___   ___ ___ ___ ___
10 11 12 13   14 15 16 17

Draw, compare, and classify three-dimensional figures (spheres, prisms, cubes, cones, pyramids, and cylinders)

EMC 3017 • Basic Math Skills, Grade 4 • ©2003 by Evan-Moor Corp.

Draw the Figure

Name _____

Draw each of the following figures.

1. Sphere	**2.** Pyramid
3. Prism	**4.** Cylinder
5. Cone	**6.** Cube

7. Give two correct mathematical terms that could describe this shape.

_____

_____

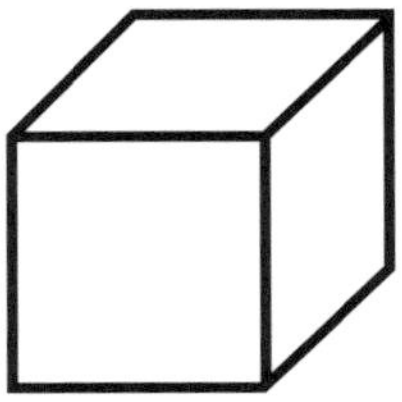

Draw, compare, and classify three-dimensional figures (spheres, prisms, cubes, cones, pyramids, and cylinders)

Identify Figures

Name _____

Complete the table below by writing **yes** or **no** in each box. Write **yes** if the given three-dimensional figure in the left column could be called that name. Write **no** if that would not be an appropriate term to use for the figure.

Figure	Sphere	Prism	Cube	Cone	Pyramid	Cylinder
1.						
2.						
3.						
4.						
5.						
6.						
7.						

Draw, compare, and classify three-dimensional figures (spheres, prisms, cubes, cones, pyramids, and cylinders)

EMC 3017 • Basic Math Skills, Grade 4 • ©2003 by Evan-Moor Corp.

Describing Figures

Name _____

Answer each question.

1. Brandon is talking to his grandpa on the phone and is trying to describe the shape of his new tent. What shape would you call this tent? How would you describe it?

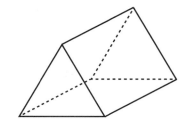

_____

_____

2. Tim has the box of cereal pictured below:

Tim is going to cut along the edges of the box. Then he will open up all the flaps and lay it flat on the table to create the net of the cereal box. Draw what the net will look like.

3. Julia is building a model of a pyramid and needs your help. She knows that she wants the base of the pyramid to be a square. What she doesn't know is what shape each of the other faces should be. Sketch a net of the pyramid, showing the base and the other faces connected to the base.

4. Angel is describing her can of three tennis balls to the class without them seeing what she is holding. Help her out with the names of the figures that she might use. Write a brief description that she could read to her class to help them guess what she's holding.

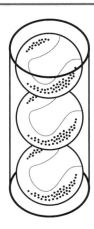

_____

_____

Draw, compare, and classify three-dimensional figures (spheres, prisms, cubes, cones, pyramids, and cylinders)

Geometry

Math Test

Name _____

Fill in the circle next to the correct answer.

For Numbers 1 through 4, identify the correct term for each figure.

1.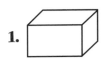

    Ⓐ pyramid   Ⓒ prism
    Ⓑ cube   Ⓓ cylinder

2.

    Ⓐ pyramid   Ⓒ prism
    Ⓑ cube   Ⓓ cylinder

3.

    Ⓐ pyramid   Ⓒ prism
    Ⓑ cube   Ⓓ cylinder

4.

    Ⓐ pyramid   Ⓒ prism
    Ⓑ cube   Ⓓ cylinder

5. All pyramids have _____.

    Ⓐ a triangular base
    Ⓑ a rectangular base
    Ⓒ triangular faces coming up from the base
    Ⓓ two parallel bases

6. All cylinders have _____.

    Ⓐ circular bases
    Ⓑ square bases
    Ⓒ triangular bases
    Ⓓ none of the above

7. All cubes have _____.

    Ⓐ six faces
    Ⓑ square bases
    Ⓒ congruent faces
    Ⓓ all of the above

8. All cones have _____.

    Ⓐ two square bases
    Ⓑ one circular base
    Ⓒ a triangular base
    Ⓓ two circular bases

9. List two real-world examples of where you might see a sphere.

_____

_____

10. Draw a picture of a triangular pyramid.

Draw, compare, and classify three-dimensional figures (spheres, prisms, cubes, cones, pyramids, and cylinders)

EMC 3017 • Basic Math Skills, Grade 4 • ©2003 by Evan-Moor Corp.

Tongue Twister

Name _____

Look at each white figure in the box. Then write the letter on the line above the congruent shape. The shape may be rotated or reflected. After completing the puzzle, read the tongue twister and try to say it quickly three times.

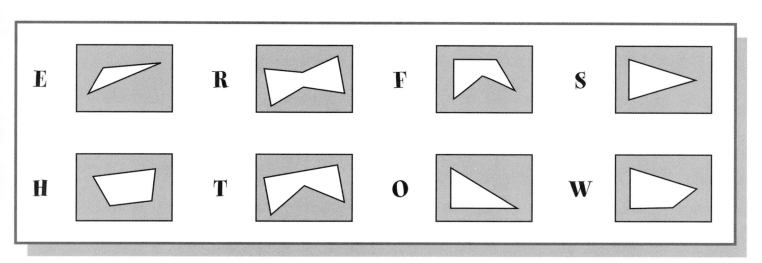

Identify congruent shapes using transformational geometry (rotations, translations, reflections)

Who Sleeps with His Shoes On?

To solve the riddle, draw a straight line between each figure on the left with its congruent figure on the right. Each line will go through one number and one letter. Write the letters in order to spell out the answer to the riddle.

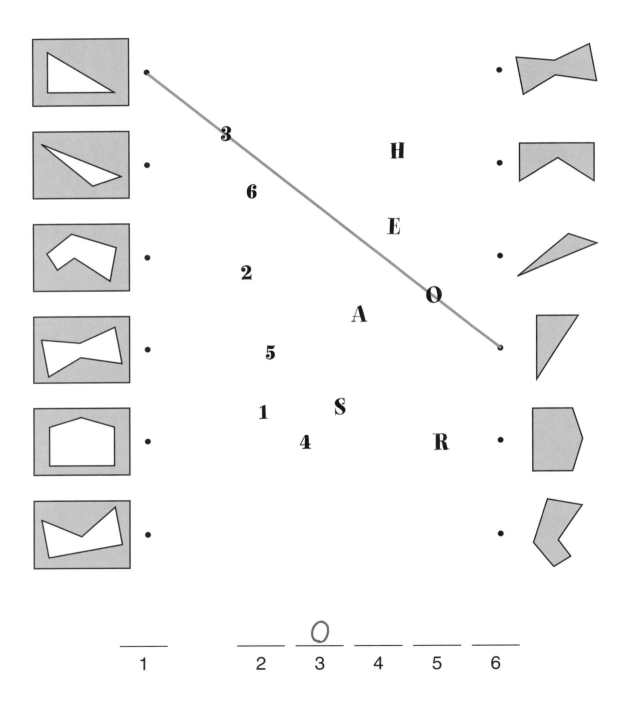

___ ___ $\underset{3}{O}$ ___ ___ ___
1   2   4   5   6

Identify congruent shapes using transformational geometry (rotations, translations, reflections)

Flip, Slide, or Turn

Name_____

Look at each shape on the left and write how the shape is transformed to the new position on the right. It could be **turned** (rotated), **slid** (translated), or **flipped** (reflected).

1.   _____

2.   _____

3.   _____

4.   _____

5.   _____

6.   _____

7.   _____

8.   _____

Identify congruent shapes using transformational geometry (rotations, translations, reflections)

Transformations

Name _____

Look at each shape on the left and write how the shape is transformed to the new position on the right. It could be **turned** (rotated), **slid** (translated), or **flipped** (reflected).

1.   _____

2.   _____

3.   _____

4.   _____

5.   _____

6.   _____

7.   _____

8.   _____

Identify congruent shapes using transformational geometry (rotations, translations, reflections)

EMC 3017 • Basic Math Skills, Grade 4 • ©2003 by Evan-Moor Corp.

Quilt Squares

Name _____

Figure A represents a quilt with nine squares. The top left square is the original square. On Figure B, write **slide**, **turn**, or **flip** to tell how the other squares have been transformed from the original.

Figure A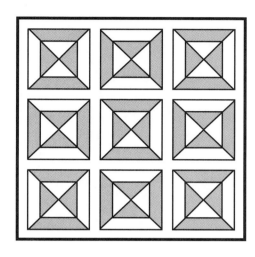

Figure B

1. original	2. _____	3. _____
4. _____	5. _____	6. _____
7. _____	8. _____	9. _____

Identify congruent shapes using transformational geometry (rotations, translations, reflections)

Math Test

Name _____

Fill in the circle next to the correct answer.

For Numbers 1 through 4, use these figures:

A   B   C   D

1. Which figure is congruent to the white region in this figure?

Ⓐ figure A Ⓒ figure C
Ⓑ figure B Ⓓ figure D

2. Which figure is congruent to the white region in this figure?

Ⓐ figure A Ⓒ figure C
Ⓑ figure B Ⓓ figure D

3. Which figure is congruent to the white region in this figure?

Ⓐ figure A Ⓒ figure C
Ⓑ figure B Ⓓ figure D

4. Which figure is congruent to the white region in this figure?

Ⓐ figure A Ⓒ figure C
Ⓑ figure B Ⓓ figure D

5. How are these figures transformed?

Ⓐ turned (rotated) Ⓒ slid (translated)
Ⓑ flipped (reflected) Ⓓ flipped or slid

6. How are these figures transformed?

Ⓐ turned (rotated) Ⓒ slid (translated)
Ⓑ flipped (reflected) Ⓓ flipped or slid

7. How are these figures transformed?

Ⓐ turned(rotated) Ⓒ slid (translated)
Ⓑ flipped (reflected) Ⓓ flipped and slid

8. How are these figures transformed?

Ⓐ turned (rotated) Ⓒ slid (translated)
Ⓑ flipped (reflected) Ⓓ flipped and slid

9. Draw the rainbow shape with a turn (rotation) to the right.

10. Draw the heart with a vertical flip (reflection).

Identify congruent shapes using transformational geometry (rotations, translations, reflections)

EMC 3017 • Basic Math Skills, Grade 4 • ©2003 by Evan-Moor Corp.

What Kind of Suit Does a Duck Wear?

Name _____

To solve the riddle, draw a line connecting the figure on the left with the number of lines of symmetry it has on the right. Write the letter that the line passes through in front of the figure. Read the answer from top to bottom.

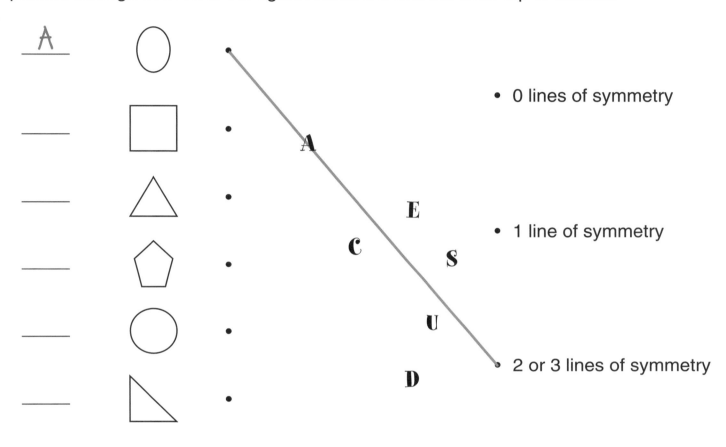

- 0 lines of symmetry

- 1 line of symmetry

- 2 or 3 lines of symmetry

- 4 lines of symmetry

- more than 4 lines of symmetry

Identify lines of symmetry in two-dimensional shapes

Geometry

Tongue Twister

Name_____

Look at each figure at the bottom of the page and determine how many lines of symmetry it has. Then look at the key and write the letter on each line above the figure. Read the tongue twister and try to say it quickly three times.

C 0 lines of symmetry	**R** 4 lines of symmetry
I 1 line of symmetry	**S** 5 lines of symmetry
O 2 lines of symmetry	**T** 6 lines of symmetry
P 3 lines of symmetry	**U** more than 6 lines of symmetry

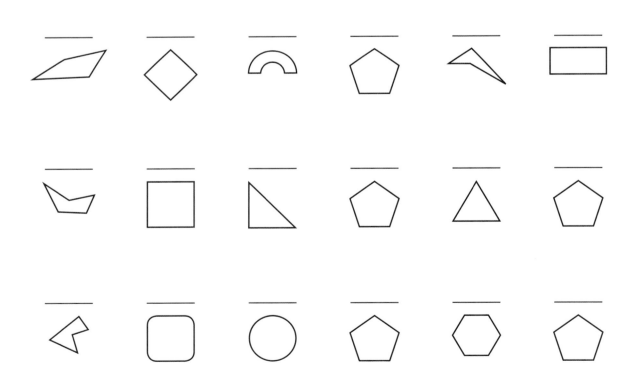

Identify lines of symmetry in two-dimensional shapes

EMC 3017 • Basic Math Skills, Grade 4 • ©2003 by Evan-Moor Corp.

Alphabet Symmetry

Name _____

The letters of the alphabet are written below. Determine how many lines of symmetry each letter has. If it doesn't have any lines of symmetry, write **0**.

A _____   K _____   U _____

B _____   L _____   V _____

C _____   M _____   W _____

D _____   N _____   X _____

E _____   O _____   Y _____

F _____   P _____   Z _____

G _____   Q _____

H _____   R _____   ABC's

I _____   S _____

J _____   T _____

Identify lines of symmetry in two-dimensional shapes

Draw Lines of Symmetry

Name _____

Draw lines of symmetry on the following figures. Then, next to each figure, write the number of lines of symmetry that figure has.

1. 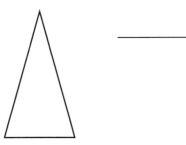 _____

2. 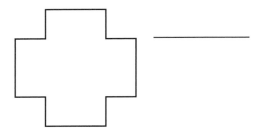 _____

3. 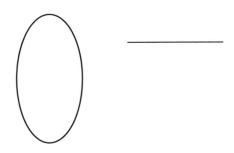 _____

4. 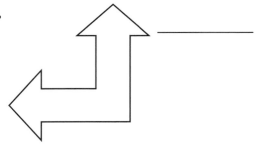 _____

5. 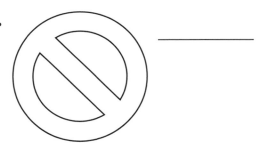 _____

6. 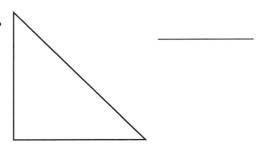 _____

7. 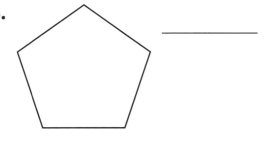 _____

8. 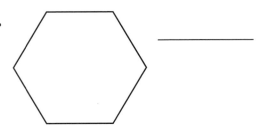 _____

Identify lines of symmetry in two-dimensional shapes

Using Symmetry

Name _____

Solve each problem.

1. Twins Sam and George share a bedroom that is rectangular in shape. They would like to divide the room into two equal parts that are symmetrical so they can each have the same amount of space. Divide the room for them by drawing a line of symmetry on this rectangle. Why did you decide to divide it this way?

_____

_____

_____

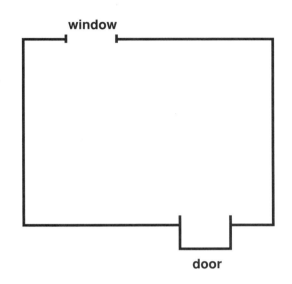

2. Susan and her sister made a cake. They want to divide it evenly between the two of them. Help Susan and her sister by drawing a line of symmetry, dividing the cake into two congruent pieces so they each have the same amount of cake.

3. A quilt square is shown. This is the beginning of the pattern. Draw at least three different lines of symmetry that could be used in designing the quilt.

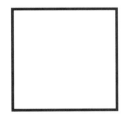

4. Juanita and Thomas were arguing about how many lines of symmetry there are in a pizza. Write a note to the two of them telling them how many lines of symmetry are in this round pizza.

_____

_____

_____

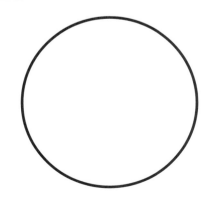

Identify lines of symmetry in two-dimensional shapes

Math Test

Name _____

For Numbers 1 through 8, fill in the circle next to the number of lines of symmetry each figure has.

1.

- Ⓐ 1
- Ⓑ 2
- Ⓒ 3
- Ⓓ 4

2.

- Ⓐ 1
- Ⓑ 2
- Ⓒ 3
- Ⓓ 4

3.

- Ⓐ 1
- Ⓑ 2
- Ⓒ 3
- Ⓓ 4

4.

- Ⓐ 1
- Ⓑ 2
- Ⓒ 3
- Ⓓ 4

5.

- Ⓐ 1
- Ⓑ 2
- Ⓒ 3
- Ⓓ 4

6.

- Ⓐ 1
- Ⓑ 2
- Ⓒ 3
- Ⓓ 4

7.

- Ⓐ 1
- Ⓑ 2
- Ⓒ 3
- Ⓓ 4

8

- Ⓐ 1
- Ⓑ 2
- Ⓒ 3
- Ⓓ 4

9. Draw a shape that has only one line of symmetry and draw the line of symmetry.

10. Draw a shape or figure that has more than 3 lines of symmetry and draw the lines of symmetry.

Identify lines of symmetry in two-dimensional shapes

Measurement

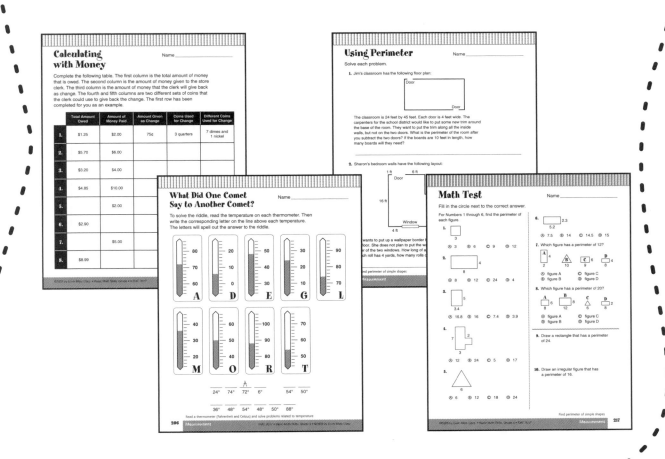

Tongue Twister

Write the letter for each set of coins on the line above the corresponding amount. Read the tongue twister and try to say it quickly three times.

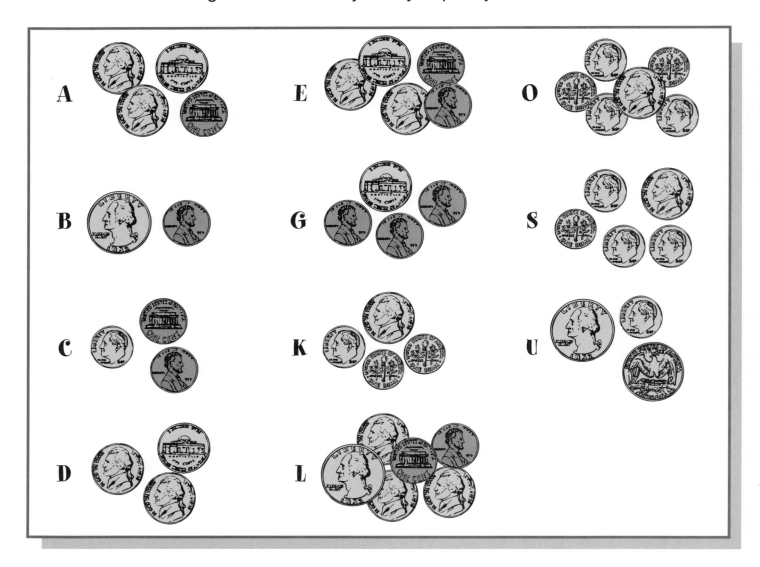

___	___	___	___	___		___	___	___	___
26¢	42¢	16¢	12¢	35¢		26¢	60¢	8¢	45¢

___	___	___	___	___		___	___	___	___	___
26¢	42¢	17¢	17¢	15¢		26¢	42¢	16¢	12¢	35¢

___	___	___	___	___
26¢	42¢	55¢	55¢	15¢

Count mixed coins and compute change

EMC 3017 • Basic Math Skills, Grade 4 • ©2003 by Evan-Moor Corp.

What Is As Big As
an Elephant and Weighs Nothing?

Name _____

Write the letter for each set of coins on the line above the corresponding amount. The letters will spell out the answer to the riddle.

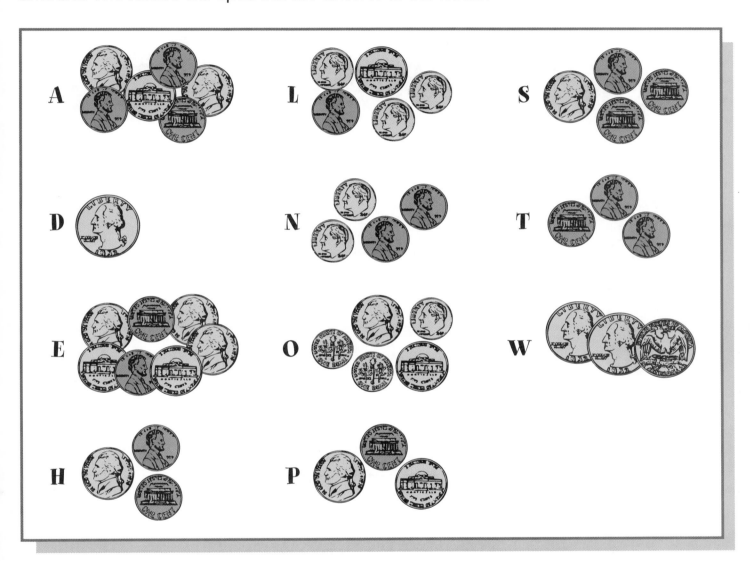

| 18¢ | 22¢ | | 27¢ | 36¢ | 27¢ | 11¢ | 7¢ | 18¢ | 22¢ | 3¢ | 8¢ |

| 8¢ | 7¢ | 18¢ | 25¢ | 40¢ | 75¢ |

Count mixed coins and compute change

Making Change

Name _____

Complete the following table. The first column is the total amount of money that is owed. The second column is the amount of money given to the store clerk. The third column is the amount of money that the clerk will give back as change. (Some boxes may have more than one possible answer.)

	Total Amount Owed	Amount of Money Paid	Amount of Money Given as Change
1.	$7.48	$10.00	
2.	$12.53	$15.00	
3.	$24.89	$25.00	
4.	$7.93	$15.00	
5.	$6.25		$3.75
6.		$20.00	$2.17
7.	$6.31		
8.			$4.21

Count mixed coins and compute change

EMC 3017 • Basic Math Skills, Grade 4 • ©2003 by Evan-Moor Corp.

Calculating with Money

Name _____

Complete the following table. The first column is the total amount of money that is owed. The second column is the amount of money given to the store clerk. The third column is the amount of money that the clerk will give back as change. The fourth and fifth columns are two different sets of coins that the clerk could use to give back the change. The first row has been completed for you as an example.

	Total Amount Owed	Amount of Money Paid	Amount Given as Change	Coins Used for Change	Different Coins Used for Change
1.	$1.25	$2.00	75¢	3 quarters	7 dimes and 1 nickel
2.	$5.70	$6.00			
3.	$3.20	$4.00			
4.	$4.85	$10.00			
5.		$2.00		3 dimes and 1 nickel	
6.	$2.90			2 one-dollar bills and 1 dime	
7.		$5.00		1 dime, 1 nickel, and 3 pennies	
8.	$8.99			1 ten-dollar bill, 1 one-dollar bill, and 1 penny	

Count mixed coins and compute change

Using Money

Name _____

Solve each problem.

1. Gerald is buying some candy for $1.38. If he gives the clerk $2.00, how much change should he receive? What are two combinations of coins that the clerk could use to give Gerald his change? What is the fewest number of coins the clerk could use?

_____

_____

2. Tabitha is buying some CDs for her birthday. The total bill is $28.58. If she gives the clerk $30.00, how much change should she receive? If the clerk wants to use as few bills and coins as possible, what bills and coins should he select?

_____

3. In the General Store, there are many different candies to select from. Towers are 20¢, Smoths are 28¢, Grints are 37¢, Milts are 40¢, Jinxs are 43¢, and Poxes are 55¢. Robby bought the Smoths and Jinxs. He paid an additional 4¢ in tax. If he gave the clerk $5.00, what change did he receive?

_____

4. In the General Store listed in #3, Sally bought two different items and paid an additional 5¢ in tax. If she paid $1.00 and got 12¢ back in change, what two items could she have purchased? Explain your thinking and how you solved the problem.

_____

_____

5. Samantha has 58¢ in her pocket. What are four different combinations of coins that she could have that each total 58¢?

_____

Count mixed coins and compute change

EMC 3017 • Basic Math Skills, Grade 4 • ©2003 by Evan-Moor Corp.

Math Test

Name _____

Fill in the circle next to the correct answer.

For Numbers 1 through 4, find the value of each set of coins.

1.

- Ⓐ 75¢
- Ⓑ 95¢
- Ⓒ 20¢
- Ⓓ 65¢

2.

- Ⓐ 48¢
- Ⓑ 45¢
- Ⓒ 47¢
- Ⓓ 46¢

3.

- Ⓐ 22¢
- Ⓑ 12¢
- Ⓒ 20¢
- Ⓓ 30¢

4.

- Ⓐ 46¢
- Ⓑ 36¢
- Ⓒ 41¢
- Ⓓ 31¢

5. Jack owed $2.74 and paid $3.00. How much change should he get?

- Ⓐ $1.26
- Ⓑ $1.16
- Ⓒ 26¢
- Ⓓ 16¢

6. Jill owed $3.29 and paid $5.00. How much change should she get?

- Ⓐ $1.71
- Ⓑ $2.71
- Ⓒ $1.81
- Ⓓ $2.81

7. Which set of coins total 50¢?

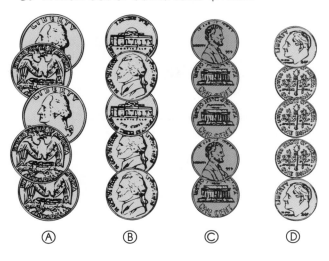

Ⓐ　　Ⓑ　　Ⓒ　　all of these Ⓓ

8. Which set of coins total $1.25?

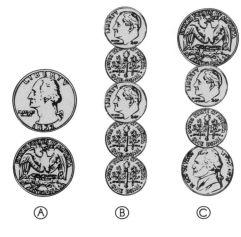

Ⓐ　　Ⓑ　　Ⓒ　　Ⓓ

9. What are the fewest coins you can use to make 74¢?

_____

10. What are two different sets of coins that each total 27¢?

_____

Count mixed coins and compute change

What Does a Cat Call a Boo-Boo?

Name _____

To find the answer to the riddle, put the following metric units of measurement in order from smallest to largest. Then write the letters following each unit of measure in the same order and they will spell out the answer.

hectometer	**I**	centimeter	**M**
meter	**O**	kilometer	**E**
millimeter	**A**	dekameter	**W**
decimeter	**E**		

smallest

_____   _____

_____   _____

_____   _____

_____   _____

_____   _____

_____   _____

largest

Identify and order metric measurements

EMC 3017 • Basic Math Skills, Grade 4 • ©2003 by Evan-Moor Corp.

Riddle

To find the answer to the riddle, put the following metric units of measurement in order from smallest to largest. Then write the letters following each unit of measurement in the same order and they will spell out the answer.

kiloliter	**E**	milliliter	**A**
liter	**A**	deciliter	**E**
centiliter	**B**	dekaliter	**G**
hectoliter	**L**		

What do you get when you cross a bee and a seagull?

smallest

_____   _____

_____   _____

_____   _____

_____   _____

_____   _____

_____   _____

_____

largest

Identify and order metric measurements

Sort the Units

Name _____

Below are three groups of metric units of measure that are all mixed up.
Write the names of the measurement units in the correct circle.

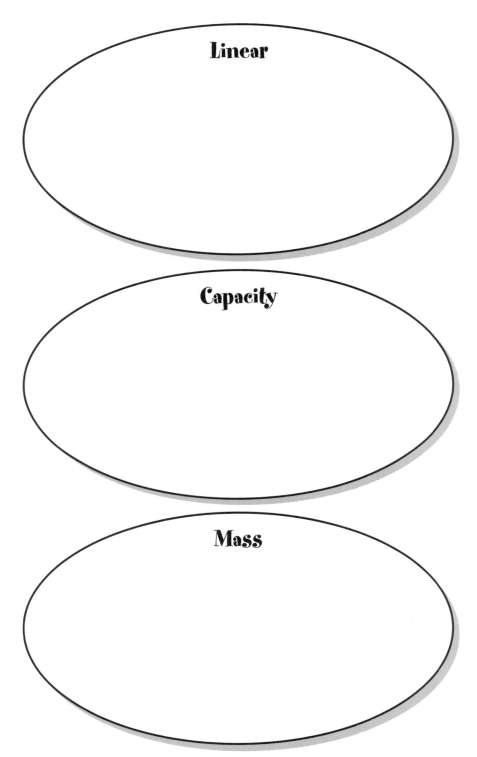

decimeter

centiliter

centigram

kiloliter

liter

millimeter

deciliter

kilometer

meter

milligram

gram

decigram

kilogram

milliliter

centimeter

Linear

Capacity

Mass

Identify and order metric measurements

EMC 3017 • Basic Math Skills, Grade 4 • ©2003 by Evan-Moor Corp.

Sort and Order

Below are three groups of metric units of measure that are all mixed up. First, identify the linear units, the capacity units, and the mass units. Then, within each of these groups, list them in order from smallest to largest under the appropriate heading.

liter	decimeter	milligram
millimeter	centiliter	kiloliter
deciliter	centigram	kilogram
meter	kilometer	milliliter
decigram	gram	centimeter

Linear	Capacity	Mass
_____	_____	_____
_____	_____	_____
_____	_____	_____
_____	_____	_____

Identify and order metric measurements

Using Metric Measures

Name _____

Solve each problem.

1. Mrs. Johnson needs your help. She has several measuring instruments, but the labels all came off. She has one that measures length, and it is a little longer than a yardstick. Another one measures weight similar to a few pennies. A third one measures capacity and is slightly larger than a half-gallon pitcher.

Help her label each with an appropriate unit of measure.

_____

_____

_____

2. Charlie has several pieces of string and needs help putting them in order. They are the following lengths:

      1 meter
      1 millimeter
      1 centimeter
      1 kilometer
      1 decimeter

List them in order from smallest to largest.

_____

_____

_____

_____

_____

3. George can't keep track of which units are used for measuring distance and which are used for measuring mass. He has this list in front of him:

      dekagram
      meter
      decigram
      decimeter
      centigram
      kilometer
      meter
      milligram

Write a note to George and help him decide which are used for distance and which are used for mass. Include in this note a hint or two that will help him keep this straight in the future.

_____

_____

_____

_____

Identify and order metric measurements

Math Test

Name _____

Fill in the circle next to the correct answer.

1. Which of the following is used to measure weight?

Ⓐ kiloliter
Ⓑ decimeter
Ⓒ milligram
Ⓓ kilometer

2. Which of the following is used to measure capacity?

Ⓐ liter
Ⓑ gram
Ⓒ meter
Ⓓ yard

3. Which of the following is used to measure length?

Ⓐ milliliter
Ⓑ kilogram
Ⓒ decimeter
Ⓓ centigram

4. Which of these is longer than a meter?

Ⓐ millimeter
Ⓑ kilometer
Ⓒ decimeter
Ⓓ centimeter

5. Which of these is heavier than a gram?

Ⓐ kilogram
Ⓑ milligram
Ⓒ decigram
Ⓓ centigram

6. Which of these is more than a liter?

Ⓐ milliliter
Ⓑ deciliter
Ⓒ kiloliter
Ⓓ centiliter

7. Which of these is about the length of a yardstick?

Ⓐ 1 kilometer
Ⓑ 1 centimeter
Ⓒ 1 millimeter
Ⓓ 1 meter

8. Which of these is about the capacity of a pitcher of water?

Ⓐ 1 liter
Ⓑ 1 kiloliter
Ⓒ 1 centiliter
Ⓓ 1 milliliter

9. List these measures of capacity in order from smallest to largest:

kiloliter, liter, milliliter, deciliter, centiliter

_____   _____

_____   _____

_____

10. Which of these does NOT belong in this group?

kilometer, meter, millimeter, meteor, centimeter

_____

Identify and order metric measurements

Comparing Measures

Name

At each question mark, circle the larger measure. Then follow the path with the larger measure through the maze.

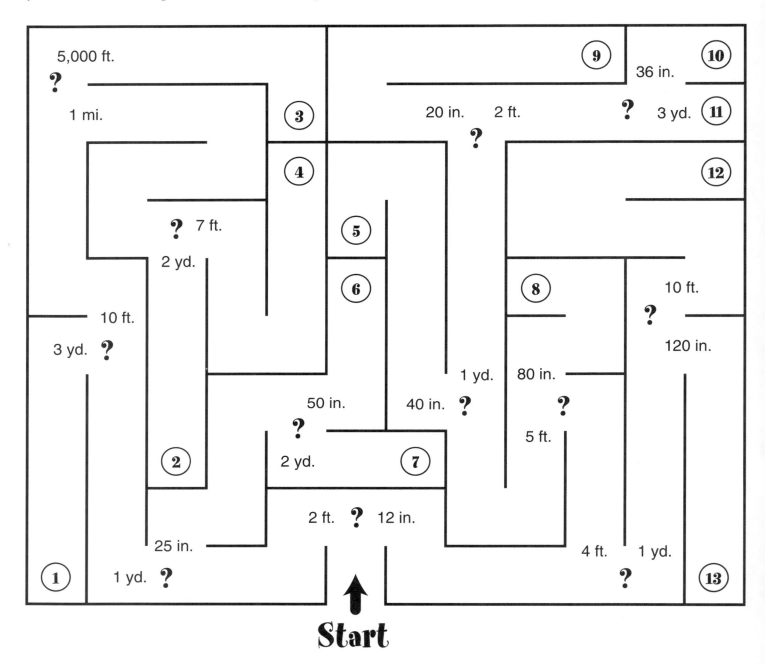

What number was at the end of your path? _____

Compare and use customary and metric units of linear measurement

EMC 3017 • Basic Math Skills, Grade 4 • ©2003 by Evan-Moor Corp.

Secret Message

Name _____

Write the symbol < or > in each blank to make a true statement.
Then circle the letter under that symbol. The circled letters will spell
out a secret message for you when read from top to bottom.

	<	>
200 centimeters _____ 3 meters	Y	S
1 meter _____ 500 millimeters	A	O
20 centimeters _____ 20 millimeters	I	U
500 millimeters _____ 1 meter	A	E
11 decimeters _____ 1 meter	S	R
1 kilometer _____ 2,000 meters	E	U
5 millimeters _____ 1 centimeter	A	Y
2 meters _____ 15 decimeters	R	S
10 decimeter _____ 2 meters	T	D
100 centimeters ____ 100 millimeters	U	A
150 centimeters _____ 2 meters	R	V

What is the Secret Message?

_____

Compare and use customary and metric units of linear measurement

Measure It

Name _____

You will need an inch ruler for this page. Measure each object to the nearest quarter inch (in.).

Object	Length
1.	_____ in.
2.	_____ in.
3.	_____ in.
4.	_____ in.
5.	_____ in.
6.	_____ in.

Compare and use customary and metric units of linear measurement

EMC 3017 • Basic Math Skills, Grade 4 • ©2003 by Evan-Moor Corp.

Use a Metric Ruler

Name_____

You will need a centimeter ruler for this page. Measure each object to the nearest half centimeter (cm).

Object	Length
1.	_____ cm
2.	_____ cm
3.	_____ cm
4.	_____ cm
5.	_____ cm
6.	_____ cm

Compare and use customary and metric units of linear measurement

Using Linear Measurement

Name _____

Solve each problem.

1. Frankie got to choose the piece of licorice that he wanted from his teacher. One piece is 18 centimeters in length, and the other one is 3 decimeters in length. Which one should he choose in order to get the longer piece? Why?

   _____

   _____

2. The lumber store is selling boards of varying length, each for $2.00. One is 3 meters in length, while another one is 240 centimeters in length. If we want the longer one, which one should we select? Why?

   _____

   _____

3. At the fabric store, there were two pieces of cloth that were each $3. Alex didn't care what color of fabric he got, so he wanted the longer piece. The purple fabric was 60 inches. The green fabric was 2 yards. Which one should Alex select and why?

   _____

   _____

4. Amber and her dad were putting in a sprinkler system, and they could buy two different rolls of pipe for the same price. The first roll had $\frac{1}{2}$ kilometer of pipe, while the second roll had 420 meters of pipe. Which roll gives Amber and her dad the longer piece of pipe? Why?

   _____

Compare and use customary and metric units of linear measurement

EMC 3017 • Basic Math Skills, Grade 4 • ©2003 by Evan-Moor Corp.

Math Test

Fill in the circle next to the correct answer.

For Numbers 1 through 5, use a ruler to measure each line to the nearest half centimeter.

1. |————————|

- Ⓐ 5 cm
- Ⓑ 7 cm
- Ⓒ 3 cm
- Ⓓ 1 cm

2. |—————|

- Ⓐ 2.5 cm
- Ⓑ 5 cm
- Ⓒ 1.5 cm
- Ⓓ 3 cm

3. |————|

- Ⓐ 1 cm
- Ⓑ 2 cm
- Ⓒ 3 cm
- Ⓓ 4 cm

4. |———|

- Ⓐ 4 cm
- Ⓑ 3.5 cm
- Ⓒ 3 cm
- Ⓓ 1.5 cm

5. |—————|

- Ⓐ 3 cm
- Ⓑ 4 cm
- Ⓒ 2 cm
- Ⓓ 1 cm

6. Which of these is longer than a foot?

- Ⓐ 15 inches
- Ⓑ 8 inches
- Ⓒ 1 inch
- Ⓓ 10 inches

7. Which of these is equal to a yard?

- Ⓐ 24 inches
- Ⓑ 2 feet
- Ⓒ 30 inches
- Ⓓ 3 feet

8. Which of these is NOT a true sentence?

- Ⓐ 1 mile > 5,000 feet
- Ⓑ 8 yards < 20 feet
- Ⓒ 2 feet = 24 inches
- Ⓓ 2 yards < 100 inches

9. Which is longer, 3 yards of string or 16 feet? Justify your answer.

_____

_____

_____

_____

10. Which is shorter, 2 meters of tape or 250 centimeters? Justify your answer.

_____

_____

_____

_____

Compare and use customary and metric units of linear measurement

Tongue Twister

Draw a straight line from the measurement on the left to the equivalent measurement on the right. Each line will go through one or more numbers. At the bottom of the page, write the corresponding letter on the line above each number. The letters will spell out a tongue twister. Try to say it fast three times.

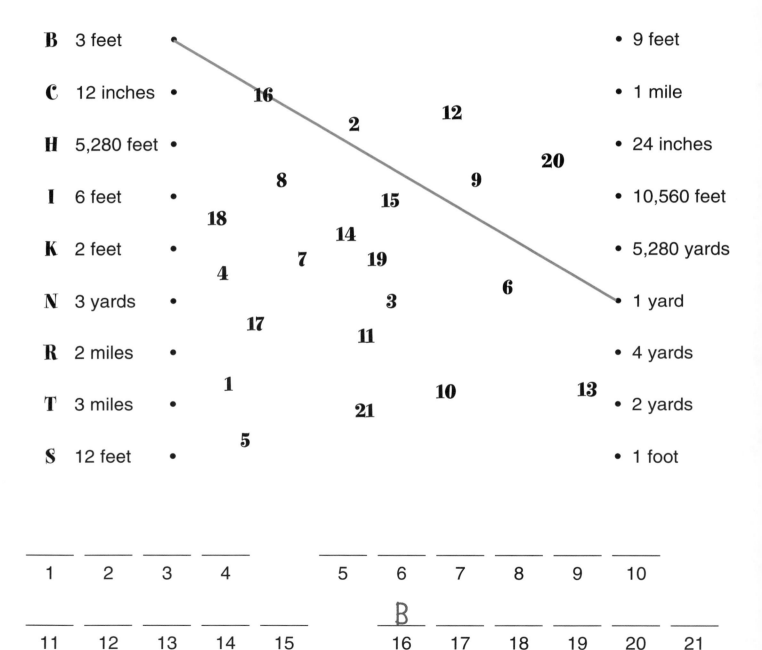

B 3 feet

C 12 inches

H 5,280 feet

I 6 feet

K 2 feet

N 3 yards

R 2 miles

T 3 miles

S 12 feet

• 9 feet

• 1 mile

• 24 inches

• 10,560 feet

• 5,280 yards

• 1 yard

• 4 yards

• 2 yards

• 1 foot

16   2   12   20   8   9   15   18   14   19   7   4   3   6   17   11   1   10   13   21   5

___ ___ ___ ___   ___ ___ ___ ___ ___ ___
 1   2   3   4   5   6   7   8   9   10

___ ___ ___ ___ ___   _B_ ___ ___ ___ ___ ___
11 12 13 14 15   16 17 18 19 20 21

Find conversions between units within a system of linear measurement

Tongue Twister

Name _____

Draw a straight line from the measurement on the left to the equivalent measurement on the right. Each line will go through one or more numbers. At the bottom of the page, write the corresponding letter on the line above each number. The letters will spell out a tongue twister. Try to say it fast three times.

E 1 meter

G 1 centimeter

H 2 meters

I 1 dekameter

N 1 kilometer

O 2 kilometers

P 5 centimeters

S 2 centimeters

T 1 decimeter

U 30 millimeters

11 16 21 2 10 9 13 18 3 23 12 15 1 5 6 17 22 14 4 7 19 20 8

• 2,000 meters

• 1,000 meters

• 50 millimeters

• 10 centimeters

• 20 millimeters

• 100 centimeters

• 10 meters

• 2,000 millimeters

• 3 centimeters

• 10 millimeters

E					
1	2	3	4	5	6

				E				
7	8	9	10	11	12	13	14

15	16	17	18	19	20	21	22	23

Find conversions between units within a system of linear measurement

Order the Units

Name _____

1. Write the following units of metric measure in order from largest to smallest.

largest

decimeter   _____

meter   _____

dekameter   _____

centimeter   _____

millimeter   _____

kilometer   _____

hectometer   _____

smallest

Use the list you have just completed to answer these questions.

2. 1 meter = _____ centimeters

3. 1 meter = _____ decimeters

4. 1 kilometer = _____ meters

5. 1 meter = _____ millimeters

6. 1 hectometer = _____ meters

7. 1 dekameter = _____ meters

Find conversions between units within a system of linear measurement

Equivalent Measures

Name _____

1. Write the following units of measure in order from largest to smallest.

largest

foot   _____

mile   _____

yard   _____

inch   _____

smallest

Complete each of the following to make a true statement.

2. 1 yard = _____ feet

3. 1 foot = _____ inches

4. 1 mile = _____ feet

5. 1 yard = _____ inches

6. 2 feet = _____ inches

7. 7 yards = _____ feet

8. 2 miles = _____ feet

9. 5 feet = _____ inches

10. 10 yards = _____ inches

1 mile
? yards
? feet
? inches

Find conversions between units within a system of linear measurement

Using Conversions

Name _____

Solve each problem.

1. James was building a tree house and needed a board that was at least
   28 inches long. His mom said she had a board that was 3 feet long. Is it
   long enough? Justify your answer.

   _____

   _____

2. Hillary was driving through the city of Denver, Colorado, when she saw
   a sign referring to it as being the "Mile High City." What is the elevation of
   Denver in feet?

   _____

3. A roll of transparent tape is approximately 20 meters long. Is there enough
   tape to go across each face of a cube twice if the cube is 25 centimeters
   across each face? Justify your answer.

   _____

   _____

4. Jordi is always getting mixed up about which is larger, the decimeter or
   the dekameter. Write a note to Jordi telling him some way that he can keep
   them straight.

   _____

   _____

   _____

Find conversions between units within a system of linear measurement

EMC 3017 • Basic Math Skills, Grade 4 • ©2003 by Evan-Moor Corp.

Math Test

Name _____

Fill in the circle next to the correct answer.

1. 3 feet equals _____.

ⓐ 1 yard
ⓑ 1 inch
ⓒ 12 inches
ⓓ 9 yards

2. 12 inches equals _____.

ⓐ 1 mile
ⓑ 1 yard
ⓒ 1 foot
ⓓ 1 meter

3. 1 mile equals _____.

ⓐ 24 feet
ⓑ 40 feet
ⓒ 5,000 feet
ⓓ 5,280 feet

4. 6 feet equals _____.

ⓐ 60 inches
ⓑ 3 yards
ⓒ 72 inches
ⓓ 4 yards

5. 1 meter equals _____.

ⓐ 1,000 decimeters
ⓑ 1,000 centimeters
ⓒ 1,000 kilometers
ⓓ 1,000 millimeters

6. 100 centimeters equals _____.

ⓐ 1 millimeter
ⓑ 1 centimeter
ⓒ 1 meter
ⓓ 1 kilometer

7. 1 kilometer equals _____.

ⓐ 1,000 centimeters
ⓑ 1,000 decimeters
ⓒ 1,000 millimeters
ⓓ 1,000 meters

8. 1,000 millimeters equals _____.

ⓐ 1 meter
ⓑ 1 decimeter
ⓒ 1 centimeter
ⓓ 1 kilometer

9. What are two units of measure that are equivalent to 1 meter?

_____

_____

10. What are two units of measure that are equivalent to 3 feet?

_____

_____

Find conversions between units within a system of linear measurement

Tongue Twister

Name _____

Match each measurement on the left with an equivalent measurement on the right and connect these with a straight line. Each line will pass through a number and a letter. At the bottom of the page, write the letter above each corresponding number. Read the tongue twister and try to say it quickly three times.

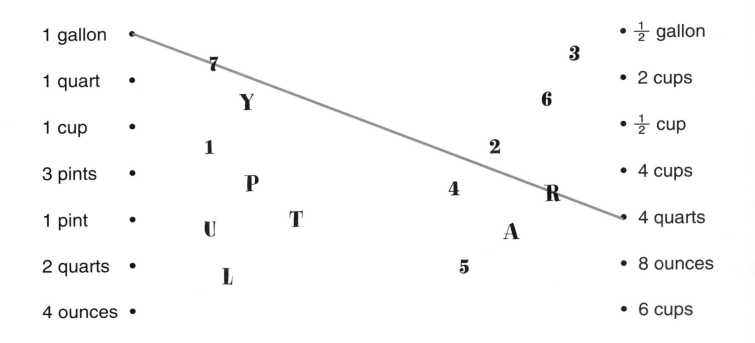

1 gallon •

1 quart •

1 cup •

3 pints •

1 pint •

2 quarts •

4 ounces •

7   **Y**   **1**   **P**   **U**   **T**   **L**   **4**   **5**   **2**   **A**   **R**   **6**   **3**

• ½ gallon

• 2 cups

• ½ cup

• 4 cups

• 4 quarts

• 8 ounces

• 6 cups

___ _R_ ___ ___ ___   ___ ___ ___ _R_ ___ ___
5   7   3   4   2   6   4   3   7   1   4

Identify and compare customary and metric units of capacity

Tongue Twister

Match each measurement on the left with an equivalent measurement on the right and connect these with a straight line. Each line will pass through a number and a letter. At the bottom of the page, write the letter above each corresponding number. Read the tongue twister and try to say it quickly three times.

A   1 liter ·   · 200 centiliters

D   3 hectoliters ·   · 20 milliliters

E   2 liters ·   · 100 liters

H   2 centiliters ·   · 30 milliliters

I   3 liters ·   · 10 deciliters

N   3 deciliters ·   · 10 liters

O   2 kiloliters ·   · 30 centiliters

P   3 centiliters ·   · 300 liters

R   1 dekaliter ·   · 3,000 milliliters

T   1 kiloliter ·   · 1,000 liters

W   1 hectoliter ·   · 200 dekaliters

15   12   13   1   3   9   14   6   21   8   23   22   4   20   17   2   7   18   5   16   19   11   10

___ ___   ___ ___ ___ ___   ___ ___
 1   2   3   4   5   6   7   8

A
___ ___   ___ ___ ___
 9   10   11 12 13

___ ___ ___ ___ ___ ___ ___   ___ ___ ___
14 15 16 17 18 19 20   21 22 23

Identify and compare customary and metric units of capacity

Compare the Measurements

Name _____

Complete each sentence with **<**, **>**, or **=**.

1. 1 gallon _____ 1 quart

2. 1 cup _____ 1 gallon

3. 1 pint _____ 1 cup

4. 8 ounces _____ 1 cup

5. 16 ounces _____ 1 quart

6. 1 gallon _____ 1 ounce

7. 2 quarts _____ 8 cups

8. 4 cups _____ 1 gallon

9. 1 gallon _____ 4 pints

10. 1 pint _____ 2 cups

Identify and compare customary and metric units of capacity

Compare Metric Measures

Name _____

Complete each sentence with <, >, or =.

1. 1 liter _____ 1 milliliter

2. 1 centiliter _____ 1 milliliter

3. 1 kiloliter _____ 1 liter

4. 1 hectoliter _____ 1 centiliter

5. 1 deciliter _____ 1 kiloliter

6. 1 milliliter _____ 1 centiliter

7. 1 centiliter _____ 1 liter

8. 1 dekaliter _____ 1 milliliter

9. 1 deciliter _____ 1 liter

10. 1 hectoliter _____ 1 liter

Identify and compare customary and metric units of capacity

Using Capacity

Name _____

Solve each problem.

1. Eric was looking in the refrigerator and saw two pitchers of punch. He wanted to combine them into a single 2-quart pitcher, but didn't know if the pitcher was big enough. The first small pitcher holds 1 quart, and it was half full. The other pitcher holds 2 quarts, and it was about three-fourths full. Can Eric pour the remaining punch from the smaller pitcher into the larger one without overflowing the pitcher?

_____

2. Use the following table of conversions to complete this task:

> 1 cup = 8 ounces
> 1 pint = 2 cups
> 1 quart = 2 pints
> 1 gallon = 4 quarts

Julie is doing some baking. Her recipe calls for 2 pints of one ingredient, 3 cups of another ingredient, 4 ounces of another, and $1\frac{1}{2}$ cups of another ingredient. Once she combines all of these ingredients, will they fit in her 2-quart mixing bowl?

_____

3. Heidi has 20 dekaliters of oil in one barrel and 150 liters of oil in another barrel. Which barrel has more oil?

_____

4. Patricia uses 5 milliliters of dye for 2 liters of water. If she is mixing up 10 liters of water, how many milliliters of dye does she need?

_____

Identify and compare customary and metric units of capacity

EMC 3017 • Basic Math Skills, Grade 4 • ©2003 by Evan-Moor Corp.

Math Test

Fill in the circle next to the correct answer.

1. 1 quart = _____

    Ⓐ 4 cups

    Ⓑ 2 pints

    Ⓒ $\frac{1}{4}$ gallon

    Ⓓ all of the above

2. 1 cup = _____

    Ⓐ $\frac{1}{2}$ pint

    Ⓑ 16 ounces

    Ⓒ $\frac{1}{2}$ quart

    Ⓓ none of the above

3. 1 liter = _____

    Ⓐ 10 centiliters

    Ⓑ 100 milliliters

    Ⓒ 10 deciliters

    Ⓓ 10 hectoliters

4. 1 centiliter = _____

    Ⓐ $\frac{1}{100}$ liter

    Ⓑ 1 milliliter

    Ⓒ 10 liters

    Ⓓ 10 kiloliters

5. 1 quart < _____

    Ⓐ 2 cups

    Ⓑ 1 ounce

    Ⓒ 1 pint

    Ⓓ 1 gallon

6. 1 cup > _____

    Ⓐ 4 ounces

    Ⓑ 1 pint

    Ⓒ 2 quarts

    Ⓓ 1 gallon

7. 1 liter < _____

    Ⓐ 1 centiliter

    Ⓑ 1 hectoliter

    Ⓒ 10 milliliters

    Ⓓ 1 deciliter

8. 1 deciliter > _____

    Ⓐ 1 liter

    Ⓑ 2 dekaliters

    Ⓒ 1 centiliter

    Ⓓ 1 kiloliter

---

9. Jared wants to put 2 quarts of punch into 4-ounce popsicle holders. How many popsicles will he be able to make from the 2 quarts of punch?

_____

10. Nancy has 25 milliliters of soap in a bottle. In another bottle, she has 8 centiliters of soap. Can she put them together in a 1-deciliter bottle? Justify your answer.

_____

_____

Identify and compare customary and metric units of capacity

What Did One Comet Say to Another Comet?

Name _____

To solve the riddle, read the temperature on each thermometer. Then write the corresponding letter on the line above each temperature. The letters will spell out the answer to the riddle. Be sure to notice the scale used on each thermometer.

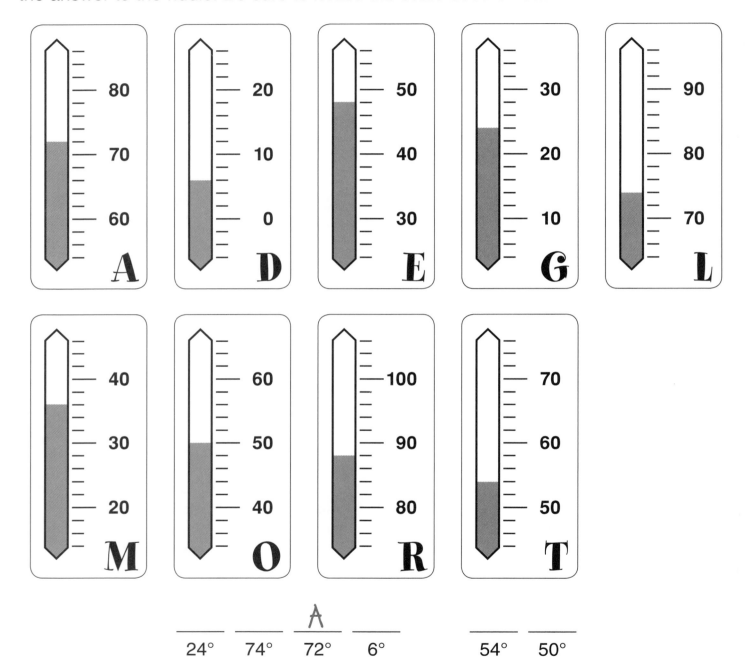

____ ____ Å ____   ____ ____
24° 74° 72° 6°   54° 50°

____ ____ ____ ____ ____ ____
36° 48° 54° 48° 50° 88°

Riddle

Name _____

To solve the riddle, read the temperature on each thermometer. Then write the corresponding letter on the line above each temperature. The letters will spell out the answer to the riddle. Be sure to notice the scale used on each thermometer.

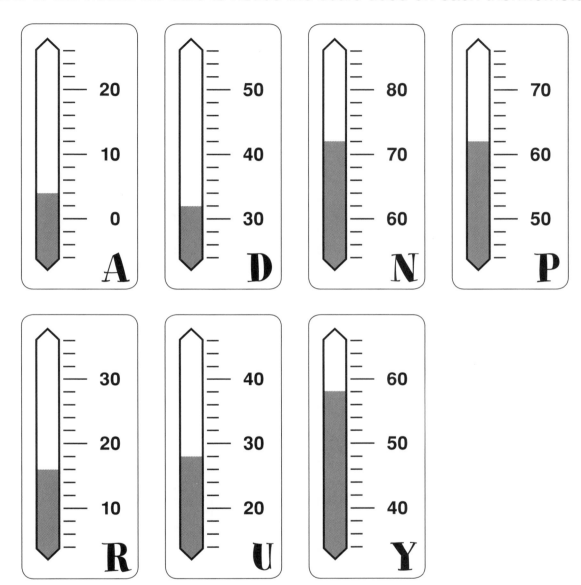

What is the best thing to do when an elephant charges?

___ A̲ ___   A̲ ___ ___   ___ ___ ___
62° 4° 58°   4° 72° 32°   16° 28° 72°

Read a thermometer (Fahrenheit and Celsius) and solve problems related to temperature

What's the Temperature?

Name _____

Write the temperature shown on each thermometer. Be sure to notice the scale used on each thermometer.

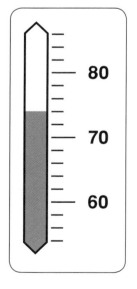
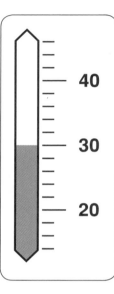
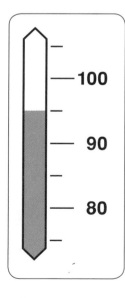
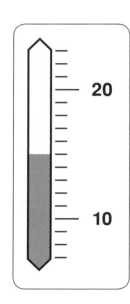
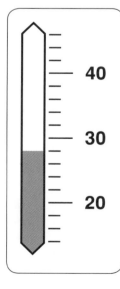
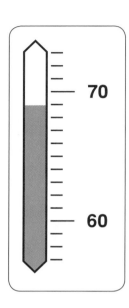
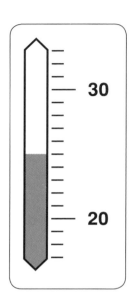

1. _____   2. _____   3. _____   4. _____   5. _____

6. _____   7. _____   8. _____   9. _____   10. _____

Read a thermometer (Fahrenheit and Celsius) and solve problems related to temperature

Temperature

Name _____

Color each thermometer to show the temperature listed. Be sure to notice the scale used on each thermometer.

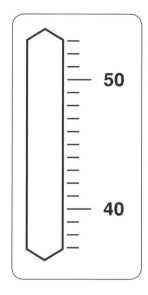

1. 48°

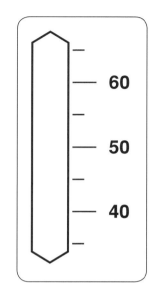

2. 55°

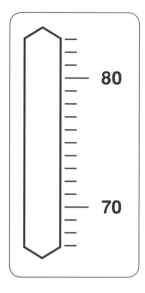

3. 72°

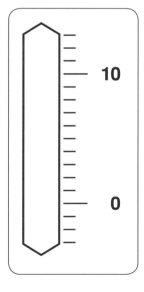

4. 4°

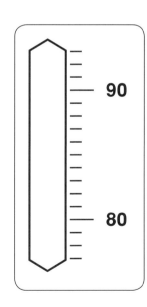

5. 81°

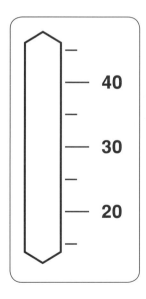

6. 35°

Read a thermometer (Fahrenheit and Celsius) and solve problems related to temperature

Using Temperature

Name _____

Solve each problem.

1. Mr. Smith's class was given the task of recording the outside temperature throughout the day. Shirley took the first temperature reading at 8:00 A.M., right as school started. What temperature does the thermometer show?

_____

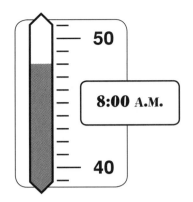

2. Rhonda took the next reading at 12:00 noon. What temperature does the thermometer show?

_____

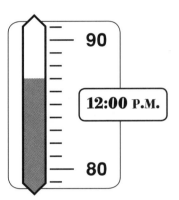

3. Sonia took the third reading of the day at 5:00 P.M. What temperature does the thermometer show?

_____

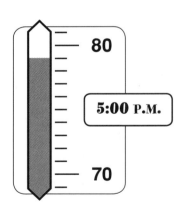

4. How much did the temperature rise from 8:00 A.M. until 12:00 noon?

_____

5. How much hotter was the temperature at 5:00 P.M. compared to 8:00 A.M.?

_____

Read a thermometer (Fahrenheit and Celsius) and solve problems related to temperature

EMC 3017 • Basic Math Skills, Grade 4 • ©2003 by Evan-Moor Corp.

Math Test

Name _____

Fill in the circle next to the correct answer.

For Numbers 1 through 4, read the thermometer.

1.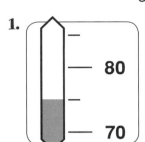
Ⓐ 75°
Ⓑ 70°
Ⓒ 85°
Ⓓ 80°

2.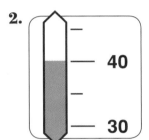
Ⓐ 45°
Ⓑ 42°
Ⓒ 40°
Ⓓ 30°

3.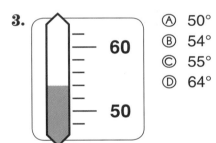
Ⓐ 50°
Ⓑ 54°
Ⓒ 55°
Ⓓ 64°

4.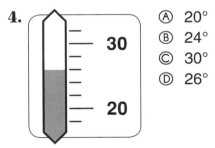
Ⓐ 20°
Ⓑ 24°
Ⓒ 30°
Ⓓ 26°

5. The temperature at 8:00 A.M. was 45° and at 12:00 noon it was 76°. How much did the temperature rise?

Ⓐ 31° Ⓒ 36°
Ⓑ 29° Ⓓ 35°

6. The temperature at 7:00 A.M. was 37° and at 3:00 P.M. it was 52°. How much did the temperature rise?

Ⓐ 25° Ⓒ 17°
Ⓑ 20° Ⓓ 15°

7. The temperature at 3:00 P.M. was 45° and at 9:00 P.M. it was 29°. How much did the temperature go down?

Ⓐ 14° Ⓒ 24°
Ⓑ 16° Ⓓ 20°

8. The temperature at 1:00 P.M. was 59° and at 9:00 P.M. it was 45°. How much did the temperature go down?

Ⓐ 20° Ⓒ 14°
Ⓑ 10° Ⓓ 4°

9. Label the thermometer to show 46°.

10. Label the thermometer to show a temperature 28° higher than the thermometer above.

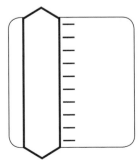

Read a thermometer (Fahrenheit and Celsius) and solve problems related to temperature

Measurement

Tongue Twister

Name_____

Determine the perimeter of each figure below. Then write the corresponding letter on the line above the figure. Read the tongue twister and try to say it quickly three times.

say it quick!

Frank
fries freshhhh
f-i-s-h f-i-l-l-e-t-s

A	perimeter of 24	L	perimeter of 20
E	perimeter of 16	R	perimeter of 32
G	perimeter of 15	U	perimeter of 30

A

___ ___ ___ ___ ___ ___

6

8

5
3

5

8
4

2
8

___ ___ ___ ___ ___

6
10

6
9

13
3

8

6
4

___ ___ ___ ___ ___

7
9

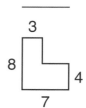
3
8   4
7

5

4

7
4
5

Find perimeter of simple shapes

Measurement

EMC 3017 • Basic Math Skills, Grade 4 • ©2003 by Evan-Moor Corp.

What Is a Giraffe's Favorite Kind of Joke?

Name _____

To solve the riddle, look at each figure below and determine its perimeter. Then write the corresponding letter on the line above the figure. The letters will spell out the answer to the riddle.

A perimeter of 24		**S** perimeter of 36	
L perimeter of 20		**T** perimeter of 40	
O perimeter of 18		**Y** perimeter of 30	
R perimeter of 28			

A
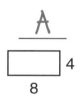
4
8

_____
15
5

_____

8

_____
6
4

_____
7 1
2

_____
6
12

_____
12
4
4
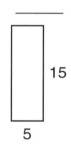

_____
5
4

_____
2
8 4
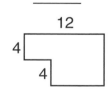

_____
10

Find perimeter of simple shapes

Find the Perimeter

Name _____

Calculate the perimeter of each shape.

1.  11   23   _____

2.   13   _____

3. 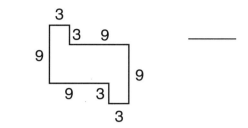 _____

4.   10.2   3.1   _____

---

5. Using a ruler, draw a figure that has a perimeter of 24 centimeters.

6. Draw a different figure that has a perimeter of 8 inches.

7. Draw another figure that has a perimeter of 9 inches.

EMC 3017 • Basic Math Skills, Grade 4 • ©2003 by Evan-Moor Corp.

Polygon Perimeters

Calculate the perimeter of each shape.

1. 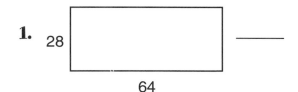 _____

2.  _____

3. 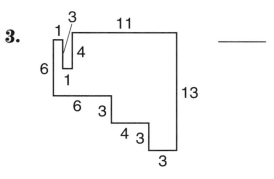 _____

4.  _____

---

5. Using a ruler, draw a figure that
   has a perimeter 16 centimeters.

6. Draw a different figure that has
   a perimeter of 12 inches.

7. Draw another figure that has a
   perimeter of 15 inches.

Find perimeter of simple shapes

Using Perimeter

Name _____

Solve each problem.

1. Jim's classroom has the following floor plan:

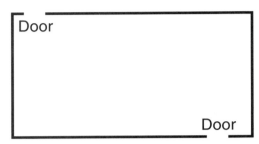

The classroom is 24 feet by 45 feet. Each door is 4 feet wide. The carpenters for the school district would like to put some new trim around the base of the room. They want to put the trim along all the inside walls, but not on the two doors. What is the perimeter of the room after you subtract the two doors? If the boards are 10 feet in length, how many boards will they need?

_____

2. Sharon's bedroom walls have the following layout:

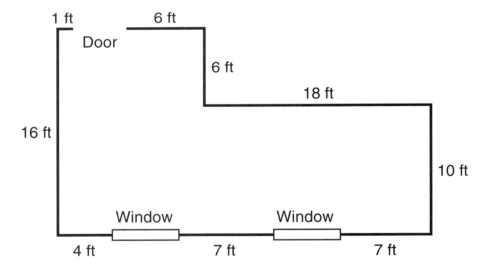

She wants to put up a wallpaper border halfway between her ceiling and her floor. She does not plan to put the wallpaper border across the door or either of the two windows. How long of a wallpaper border does she need? If each roll has 4 yards, how many rolls does she need to buy?

_____

Find perimeter of simple shapes

Math Test

Name _____

Fill in the circle next to the correct answer.

For Numbers 1 through 6, find the perimeter of each figure.

1.

3

Ⓐ 3　　Ⓑ 6　　Ⓒ 9　　Ⓓ 12

2.

4

8

Ⓐ 8　　Ⓑ 12　　Ⓒ 24　　Ⓓ 4

3.

5

3.4

Ⓐ 16.8　　Ⓑ 16　　Ⓒ 7.4　　Ⓓ 3.9

4.

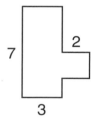

7 　 2

3

Ⓐ 12　　Ⓑ 24　　Ⓒ 5　　Ⓓ 17

5.

6

Ⓐ 6　　Ⓑ 12　　Ⓒ 18　　Ⓓ 24

6.

2.3

5.2

Ⓐ 7.5　　Ⓑ 14　　Ⓒ 14.5　　Ⓓ 15

7. Which figure has a perimeter of 12?

A 4　　**B** 10　　**C** 6　9　　**D** 4　8

2

Ⓐ figure A　　Ⓒ figure C
Ⓑ figure B　　Ⓓ figure D

8. Which figure has a perimeter of 20?

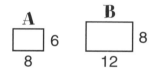

A 6　8　　**B** 8　12　　**C** 6　　**D** 2　8

Ⓐ figure A　　Ⓒ figure C
Ⓑ figure B　　Ⓓ figure D

9. Draw a rectangle that has a perimeter of 24.

10. Draw an irregular figure that has a perimeter of 16.

Find perimeter of simple shapes

Measurement　　**217**

Tongue Twister

Name _____

Find the area of each figure. Then write the corresponding letter on the each line above the area. Read the tongue twister and try to say it quickly three times.

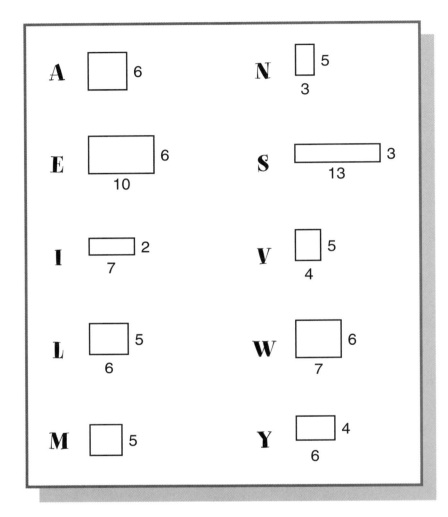

____ ____ ____ ____ ____   ____ ____ ____ ____ ____
39   60   20   60   15   39   14   30   30   24

____ ____ ____ ____ ____   ____ ____ ____ ____
39   42   36   15   39   39   42   36   25

Compute area of squares and rectangles

EMC 3017 • Basic Math Skills, Grade 4 • ©2003 by Evan-Moor Corp.

Riddle

Name _____

Find the area of each figure. Then write the corresponding letter on the line above the area. The letters will spell out the answer to the riddle.

A — 7 × 3

O — 5 × 5

H — 6 × 5

M — 7 × 6

E — 7 × 2

S — 4 × 5

C — 4 × 4

P — 10 × 6

I — 6 × 6

N — 4 × 1

F — 9 × 7

U — 8 × 8

D — 3 × 5

R — 6 × 4

K — 13 × 3

Why was Cinderella such a bad basketball player?

___ ___ ___   ___ ___ ___   ___
20   30   14   30   21   15   21

___ ___ ___ ___ ___ ___ ___   ___ ___ ___
60   64   42   60   39   36   4   63   25   24

___   ___ ___ ___ ___ ___
21   16   25   21   16   30

Compute area of squares and rectangles

Find the Area

Name _____

What is the area of each figure?

1.

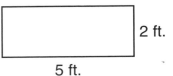

2 ft.

5 ft.

_____ square feet

2.

2 cm

_____ square centimeters

3.

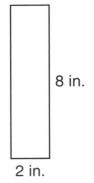

8 in.

2 in.

_____ square inches

4.

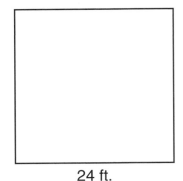

24 ft.

_____ square feet

5.

15 m

30 m

_____ square meters

6.

30 mm

90 mm

_____ square millimeters

Compute area of squares and rectangles

What Is the Area?

Name_____

What is the area of each figure?

1.

8

_____

2.

4

8

_____

3.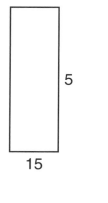

5

15

_____

4.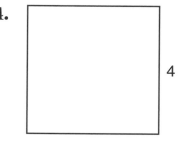

4

_____

5.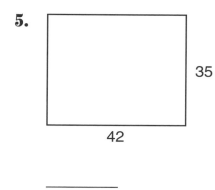

35

42

_____

6.

28

64

_____

Compute area of squares and rectangles

Measurement

Two Ways

Name _____

Can you find the area of the following figure using at least two different ways? Explain the steps for each procedure you develop.

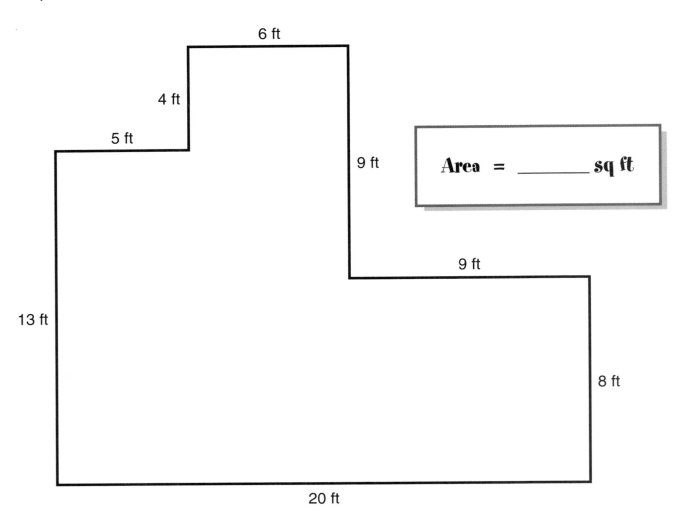

Procedure 1

_____

_____

Procedure 2

_____

_____

Compute area of squares and rectangles

EMC 3017 • Basic Math Skills, Grade 4 • ©2003 by Evan-Moor Corp.

Math Test

Name _____

Fill in the circle next to the correct answer.

1. What is the area of a square that has a side length of 3?

   Ⓐ 6   Ⓒ 9

   Ⓑ 3   Ⓓ 12

2. What is the area of a rectangle that is 8 by 4?

   Ⓐ 32   Ⓒ 12

   Ⓑ 16   Ⓓ 24

3. What is the area of a rectangle that is 7 by 2?

   Ⓐ 16   Ⓒ 9

   Ⓑ 14   Ⓓ 18

4. What is the area of a square that has a side length of 20?

   Ⓐ 20   Ⓒ 40

   Ⓑ 80   Ⓓ 400

5. What is the area of a rectangle that is 5 by 4?

   Ⓐ 18   Ⓒ 20

   Ⓑ 4   Ⓓ 9

6. What is the area of a square that has a side length of 35?

   Ⓐ 1,225   Ⓒ 70

   Ⓑ 35   Ⓓ 14

For Numbers 7 and 8, use these figures.

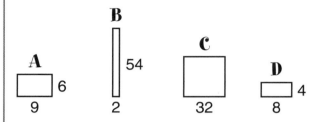

7. Which figure has an area of 54?

   Ⓐ figure A   Ⓒ figure C

   Ⓑ figure B   Ⓓ figure D

8. Which figure has an area of 32?

   Ⓐ figure A   Ⓒ figure C

   Ⓑ figure B   Ⓓ figure D

9. Draw a rectangle with an area of 24 square units.

10. Draw a rectangle with different dimensions that still has an area of 24 square units.

Compute area of squares and rectangles

What's Brown, Quacks, and Is Full of Words?

Name _____

To solve the riddle, look at each clockface below and determine what time it represents. Write the letter from the clock in front of the corresponding time. The letters will spell out the solution to the riddle when read from top to bottom.

_____ 9:30

_____ 8:00

_____ 4:45

_____ 2:30

_____ 1:00

_____ 5:20

_____ 8:40

_____ 12:40

_____ 5:30

_____ 9:30

_____ 7:15

_____ 11:50

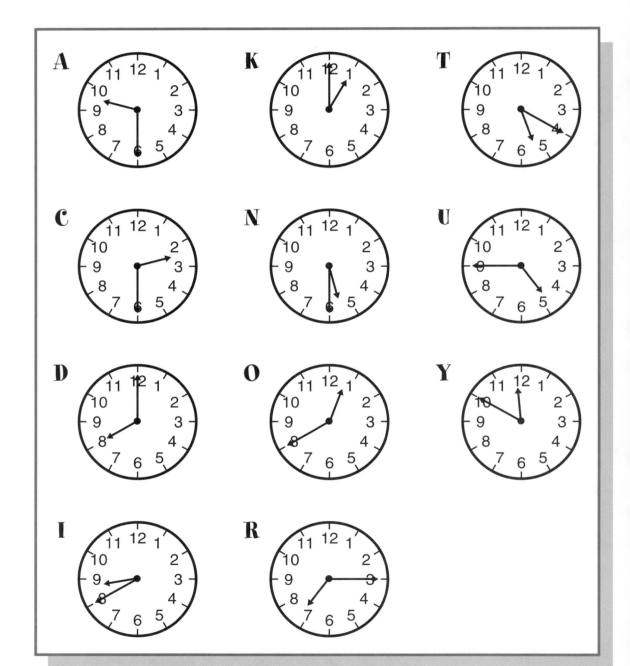

Tell time and calculate elapsed time (including A.M. and P.M.)

EMC 3017 • Basic Math Skills, Grade 4 • ©2003 by Evan-Moor Corp.

Tongue Twister

Name _____

Look at each clockface below and determine what time it represents. Write the letter from the clock above the corresponding time(s). The letters will spell out the tongue twister. Try to say it fast three times.

___	___	___		___	___	___	___
5:20	2:30	5:30		5:20	2:30	12:40	5:30

___	___	___	___		___	___
5:20	2:30	5:30	12:40		2:30	4:45

___	___	___	___	___
5:20	2:30	8:00	7:15	12:40

Tell time and calculate elapsed time (including P.M. and A.M.)

What Time Is It?

Name _____

Below each clock, write the time that is represented.

1.

_____

4.

_____

2.

_____

5.

_____

3.

_____

6.

_____

Tell time and calculate elapsed time (including A.M. and P.M.)

EMC 3017 • Basic Math Skills, Grade 4 • ©2003 by Evan-Moor Corp.

Write the Time

Name _____

Under each clock, write the time that is represented.

1.

_____

4.

_____

7.

_____

2.

_____

5.
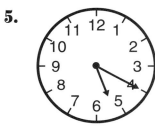
_____

8.
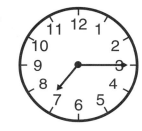
_____

3.

_____

6.

_____

9.

_____

Tell time and calculate elapsed time (including P.M. and A.M.)

Birthday Party

Name _____

The clocks below are in correct sequence for the Saturday that Jimmy had his birthday party. Below each clock, write the time that it represents.

House is clean for party

_____

First guest arrives

_____

Party begins

_____

Presents are opened

_____

Cake is eaten

_____

Party is over

_____

Answer the following questions.

1. How long was Jimmy's birthday party?

_____

2. How long was it between the time the party started and when the presents were opened?

_____

3. Which clock(s) do you think were during the A.M. time period?

_____

4. How long was the house clean before the first guest arrived?

_____

5. How long after presents were opened was the cake eaten?

_____

Tell time and calculate elapsed time (including A.M. and P.M.)

EMC 3017 • Basic Math Skills, Grade 4 • ©2003 by Evan-Moor Corp.

Math Test

Name_____

Fill in the circle next to t[...]

For Numbers 1 through 6, fir[...] these clocks to answer Numbers 7 and 8.
clock shows.

1.

Ⓑ 6:00
Ⓒ 3:00
Ⓓ 4:00

clock 1   **clock 2**   **clock 3**   **clock 4**

2.

Ⓐ 3:35
Ⓑ 7:03
Ⓒ 7:00
Ⓓ 7:15

7. Which clock shows 7:15?

Ⓐ clock 1   Ⓒ clock 3
Ⓑ clock 2   Ⓓ clock 4

3.

Ⓐ 11:45
Ⓑ 12:45
Ⓒ 9:00
Ⓓ 8:55

8. Which clock shows 2:30?

Ⓐ clock 1   Ⓒ clock 3
Ⓑ clock 2   Ⓓ clock 4

4.

Ⓐ 2:35
Ⓑ 7:10
Ⓒ 1:35
Ⓓ 7:00

9. Helen woke up at 4:45 A.M. Draw the hands on the clock to show 4:45 A.M. She was so tired that she went to bed at 7:40 P.M. Draw the hands on the clock to show 7:40 P.M.

5.

Ⓐ 2:40
Ⓑ 8:10
Ⓒ 2:10
Ⓓ 8:40

   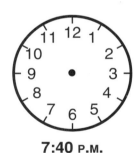

4:45 A.M.   **7:40 P.M.**

10. Given the information in Number 9, how long was Helen awake?

6.

Ⓐ 6:00
Ⓑ 4:55
Ⓒ 12:00
Ⓓ 12:55

_____

Tell time and calculate elapsed time (including P.M. and A.M.)

Measurement

Data Analysis and Probability

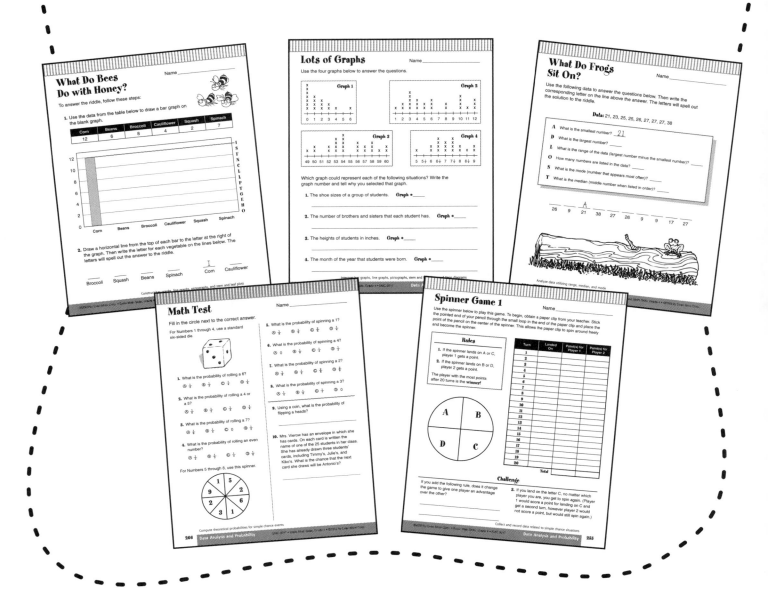

EMC 3017 • Basic Math Skills, Grade 4 • ©2003 by Evan-Moor Corp.

What Do Bees Do with Honey?

Name _____

To answer the riddle, follow these steps:

1. Use the data from the table below to construct a bar graph on the blank graph.

Corn	Beans	Broccoli	Cauliflower	Squash	Spinach
12	6	8	4	2	7

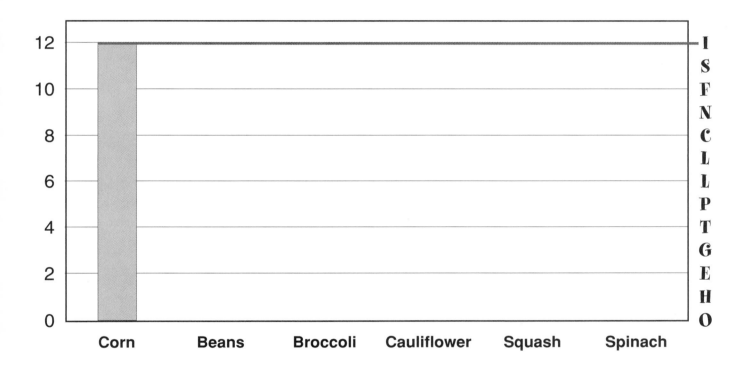

2. Draw a horizontal line from the top of each bar to the letter at the right of the graph. Then write the letter for each vegetable on the lines below. The letters will spell out the answer to the riddle.

____   ____   ____   ____   _I_   ____

Broccoli   Squash   Beans   Spinach   Corn   Cauliflower

Construct bar graphs, line graphs, pictographs, and stem and leaf plots

Riddle

To answer the riddle, follow these steps:

1. The table below represents the number of students that selected each flavor as their favorite soda. Use the table to construct a bar graph to represent the information on the graph.

Grape	Orange	Pineapple	Cherry	Cream Soda	Lemon-Lime
6	2	4	9	11	3

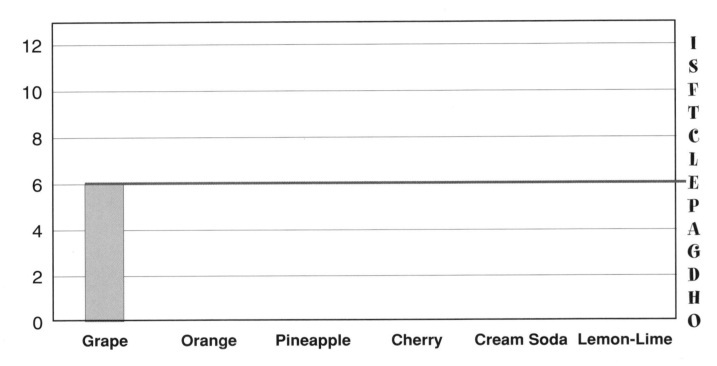

2. Draw a horizontal line from the top of each bar to the letter at the right of the graph. Then write the letter for each flavor on the lines below. The letters will spell out the answer to the riddle.

What is sweet, black, and makes history lessons interesting?

____   ____   ____   _E_   ____

Orange   Pineapple   Cherry   Grape   Cream Soda

Construct bar graphs, line graphs, pictographs, and stem and leaf plots

Make a Line Graph

Name_____

Two students recorded the following data for morning temperatures last week:

Monday–68 degrees, Tuesday–70 degrees, Wednesday–70 degrees,
Thursday–69 degrees, Friday–71 degrees, Saturday–72 degrees,
Sunday–64 degrees.

Create a table for the data and then create a line graph that accurately represents the data. Remember to include a title, a scale, and labels for your graph.

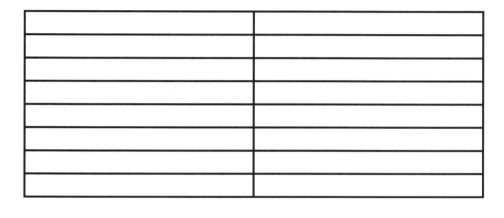

Construct bar graphs, line graphs, pictographs, and stem and leaf plots

Stem and Leaf Plots

Name _____

1. Sandra's scores for the first four spelling tests were 84, 92, 96, and 100. She made this stem and leaf plot for her scores.

Stem	Leaves
8	4
9	2 6
10	0

- For 84, she put an 8 in the tens column and a 4 in the ones column.

- For 92 and 96, she put a 9 in the tens column and a 2 and 6 in the ones column.

- For 100, she put a 10 in the tens column and a 0 in the ones column.

Her next 4 scores were 86, 88, 98, and 100. Add these scores to her stem and leaf plot.

2. George's spelling test scores were 60, 64, 76, 78, 84, 88, 90, 92, 98, and 100. In the space below, create a new stem and leaf plot for George's scores.

Stem	Leaves

Construct bar graphs, line graphs, pictographs, and stem and leaf plots

Data Analysis and Probability   EMC 3017 • Basic Math Skills, Grade 4 • ©2003 by Evan-Moor Corp.

Using a Graph

Name _____

Answer each question.

1. Sally kept track of the number of books she read from January through April. She created this graph to represent that information.

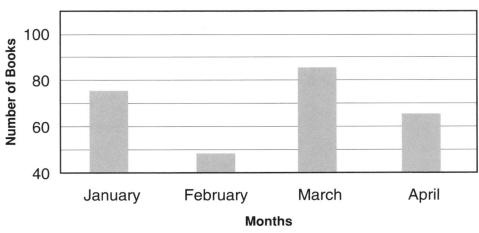

Number of Books Sally Read

After looking over the graph, Juanita commented that Sally read almost five times as many books in March as she did in February. Sally disagreed with Juanita's observation. What do you think Sally pointed out to Juanita to help clear up her misunderstanding?

_____

2. What are some other things that people can do when they create graphs that might give misleading information?

_____

3. Survey your classmates about the age of one of their parents or guardians. As you gather the information, record it in a table. Then create a stem and leaf plot to represent this information.

Construct bar graphs, line graphs, pictographs, and stem and leaf plots

Data Analysis and Probability

Math Test

Name _____

Fill in the circle next to the correct answer.

Use this graph for Numbers 1 through 4.

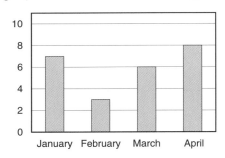

1. What type of graph is this?
   - Ⓐ bar
   - Ⓒ stem and leaf
   - Ⓑ line
   - Ⓓ pictograph

2. What is the title of the graph?
   - Ⓐ Month
   - Ⓒ January
   - Ⓑ 0–10
   - Ⓓ Teeth Lost in Room 2b

3. What do the numbers represent?
   - Ⓐ number of children
   - Ⓑ number of months
   - Ⓒ number of teeth lost
   - Ⓓ number of classes

4. How many teeth were lost during the month of March?
   - Ⓐ 5
   - Ⓑ 4
   - Ⓒ 6
   - Ⓓ 8

Use this stem and leaf plot for Numbers 5 through 8.

Math Test Scores

Stem	Leaves
4	8
5	
6	6
7	2 6
8	2 4 8
9	2 4 6 8 8 8
10	0 0

5. How many test scores are represented?
   - Ⓐ 7
   - Ⓑ 15
   - Ⓒ 22
   - Ⓓ 100

6. What was John's lowest math test score?
   - Ⓐ 4
   - Ⓑ 8
   - Ⓒ 6
   - Ⓓ 48

7. How many 100s did John get?
   - Ⓐ 1
   - Ⓑ 2
   - Ⓒ 3
   - Ⓓ 0

8. What test score did John get the most often?
   - Ⓐ 98
   - Ⓑ 100
   - Ⓒ 72
   - Ⓓ 50

9. Use the data below to create a pictograph about Mr. Call's class and each student's favorite kind of apple.

   Granny Smith: ЖHT III
   Red Delicious: ЖHT I
   Golden Delicious: ЖHT ЖHT III

10. Approximate the high temperatures over the last week and create a line graph to represent the data.

Construct bar graphs, line graphs, pictographs, and stem and leaf plots

Data Analysis and Probability　EMC 3017 • Basic Math Skills, Grade 4 • ©2003 by Evan-Moor Corp.

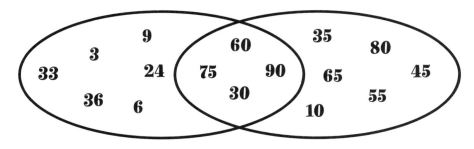

Riddle

Name _____

To answer the riddle, answer each question below the Venn diagram.
Then write the corresponding letter on the line in front of the clue. The
letters will spell out the answer to the riddle from top to bottom.

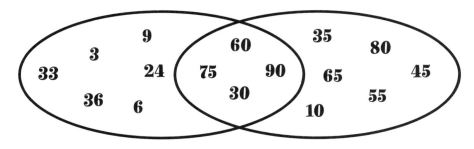

What do a cobra, a car, and a snowsuit have in common?

____A____ What do all the numbers in the left circle have in common?

_____ What do all the numbers in the right circle have in common?

_____ What do all the numbers in the intersection have in common?

_____ What is another number that could be added to the left circle?

_____ What is another number that could be added to the right circle?

C They are all multiples of 2.	**S** They are all multiples of 10.	**M** 26	
A They are all multiples of 3.	**O** They are all multiples of 15.	**N** 32	
H They are all multiples of 5.	**O** 21	**D** 40	

Challenge

List three other numbers that could be included
in the intersection of the Venn diagram.   _____ _____ _____

Interpret bar graphs, line graphs, pictographs, stem and leaf plots, and Venn diagrams

Logical Reasoning

Name _____

Use the information below to label each bar with the appropriate name.

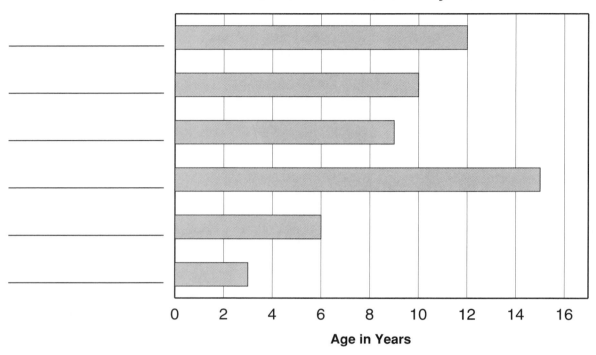

Number of Books Sally Read

Age in Years

1. Six children are named Andra, Andrew, Juan, Lisa, Marta, and Tim.

2. Lisa is the youngest.

3. Juan is the oldest.

4. Marta is one year older than Andra.

5. Andrew is twice as old as Tim.

How old am I?

Interpret bar graphs, line graphs, pictographs, stem and leaf plots, and Venn diagrams

   EMC 3017 • Basic Math Skills, Grade 4 • ©2003 by Evan-Moor Corp.

Analyzing Data

Name _____

Use the following graph to answer the questions.

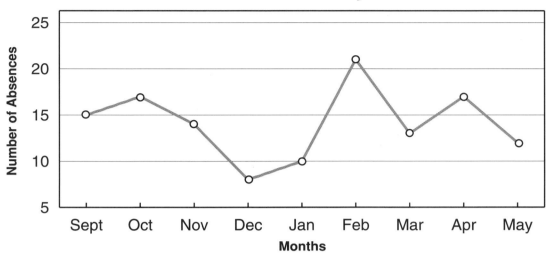

Total Absences in Mr. Layden's Class

1. What does this graph represent?

   _____

   _____

   _____

2. Why doesn't the graph include all the months, such as July?

   _____

3. What month has the fewest absences?

   _____

4. What month has the most absences?

   _____

5. What is the range of the absences for these months?

   _____

6. What might be one explanation for fewer absences in the month of December?

   _____

   _____

   _____

   _____

Interpret bar graphs, line graphs, pictographs, stem and leaf plots, and Venn diagrams

Pizza Time

Name _____

The following graphs represent the same data. They both represent the number of students in Mrs. Timm's class that ate pizza and the number of slices each student ate. The first is a bar graph and the second is a line plot. Use these graphs to answer the questions.

Pizza Eaten at Class Party

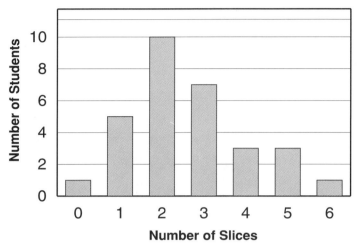

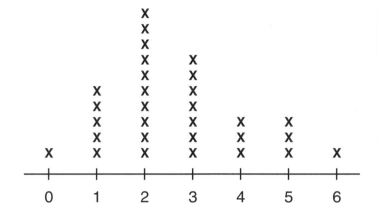

1. How many students ate one slice of pizza?

_____

2. How many slices did all the students in Mrs. Timm's class eat?

_____

3. What do the numbers across the bottom of the line plot represent?

_____

4. What does each X represent on the line plot?

_____

5. How do these two graphs compare?

_____

6. What is the largest number of slices of pizza eaten by one student?

_____

7. Which graph do you think is easier to read and why?

_____

_____

_____

_____

Interpret bar graphs, line graphs, pictographs, stem and leaf plots, and Venn diagrams

EMC 3017 • Basic Math Skills, Grade 4 • ©2003 by Evan-Moor Corp.

Lots of Graphs

Name _____

Use the four graphs below to answer the questions.

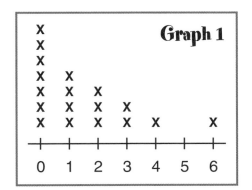

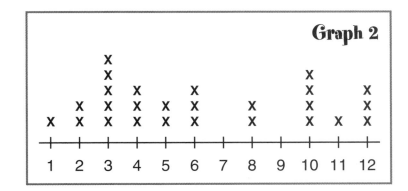

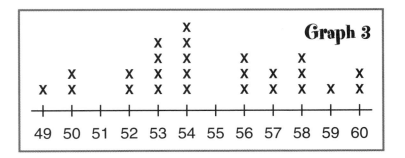

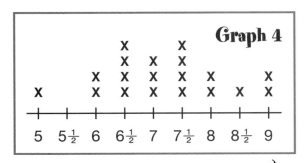

Which graph could represent each of the following situations? Write the graph number and tell why you selected that graph.

1. The shoe sizes of a group of students.   **Graph #_____**

_____

2. The number of brothers and sisters that each student has.   **Graph #_____**

_____

3. The heights of students in inches.   **Graph #_____**

_____

4. The month of the year that students were born.   **Graph #_____**

_____

Interpret bar graphs, line graphs, pictographs, stem and leaf plots, and Venn diagrams

Math Test

Name _____

Fill in the circle next to the correct answer.

Use this bar graph to answer Numbers 1 through 4.

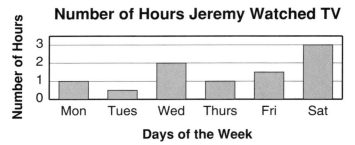

Number of Hours Jeremy Watched TV

Days of the Week

1. How many hours in all did Jeremy watch TV during the six days on the graph?

   Ⓐ 2　　Ⓑ 4　　Ⓒ 6　　Ⓓ 9

2. On what day did he watch the least amount of TV?

   Ⓐ Monday　　　Ⓒ Wednesday
   Ⓑ Tuesday　　　Ⓓ Saturday

3. How much more TV did he watch on Wednesday compared to Tuesday?

   Ⓐ twice as much　　Ⓒ $1\frac{1}{2}$ hours more
   Ⓑ half as much　　　Ⓓ 3 hours more

4. On which day did he watch the most TV?

   Ⓐ Wednesday　　Ⓒ Friday
   Ⓑ Thursday　　　Ⓓ Saturday

Use this line graph to answer Numbers 5 through 8.

Outside Temperature

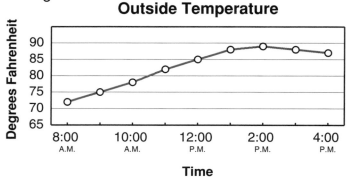

Time

5. What was the outside temperature at 9:00 A.M.?

   Ⓐ 60°　　Ⓑ 75°　　Ⓒ 72°　　Ⓓ 70°

6. About what was the temperature at 10:30 A.M.?

   Ⓐ 70°　　Ⓑ 78°　　Ⓒ 80°　　Ⓓ 82°

7. How much cooler was the temperature at 8:00 compared to 12:00?

   Ⓐ 10° cooler　　　Ⓒ 20° cooler
   Ⓑ 5° cooler　　　Ⓓ 13° cooler

8. At what time was the hottest temperature?

   Ⓐ 2:00 P.M.　　　Ⓒ 11:00 A.M.
   Ⓑ 8:00 A.M.　　　Ⓓ 4:00 P.M.

Use this bar graph to answer Numbers 9 and 10.

Number of Cans Collected for Food Drive

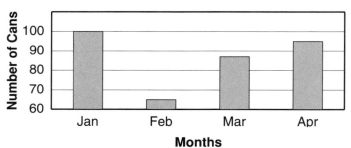

Months

9. How many cans of food were collected in March?

   _____

10. Why does it look like almost no cans were collected during the month of February?

   _____

Interpret bar graphs, line graphs, pictographs, stem and leaf plots, and Venn diagrams

Asking Questions

Name _____

Good survey questions are clear and unbiased. Cut out the puzzle pieces with good survey questions. Put those pieces together to form a rectangle.

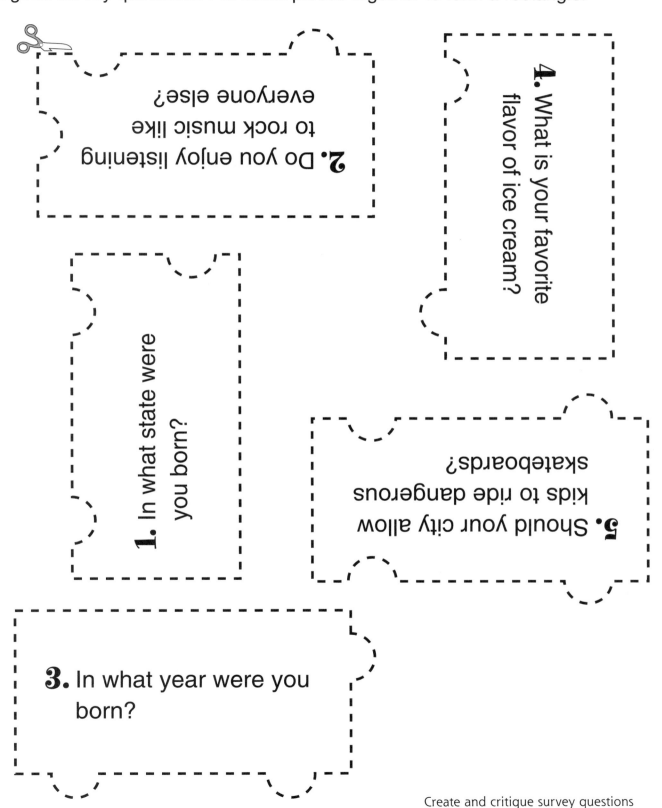

2. Do you enjoy listening to rock music like everyone else?

4. What is your favorite flavor of ice cream?

1. In what state were you born?

5. Should your city allow kids to ride dangerous skateboards?

3. In what year were you born?

Create and critique survey questions

Make Your Own Puzzle

Name _____

1. Write a good survey question on each of these puzzle pieces.

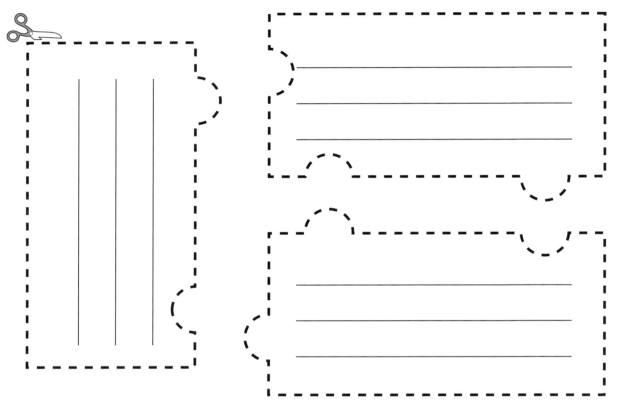

2. Write a biased or unclear survey question on each of these puzzle pieces.

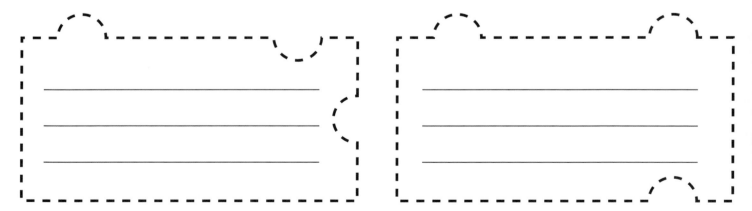

3. Cut out all the puzzle pieces and give them to a friend. Have your friend identify the good survey questions and put those pieces together to make a rectangle.

Create and critique survey questions

Data Analysis and Probability   EMC 3017 • Basic Math Skills, Grade 4 • ©2003 by Evan-Moor Corp.

Writing Survey Questions

Name_____

When writing survey questions, we must watch out for our own feelings and biases. We don't want them to come through in the questions that we ask. Circle the words in each question below that are biased, and then write a similar question that could be asked without the bias.

1. What is your favorite soda? Is it grape like mine?

   _____

2. Do you like the best football team in the world, the Denver Broncos?

   _____

3. Do you agree with most people that girls are more athletic than boys?

   _____

4. Should kids be allowed to endanger others by riding their bikes on the sidewalks?

   _____

5. Do you like the wonderful band Hi Rocks?

   _____

6. Should your city's water be supplied with the dangerous chemical fluoride?

   _____

Create and critique survey questions

What Is Wrong?

Name _____

What is wrong with each of the following survey questions?

1. What is your favorite soda pop? Is it grape, orange, Coke, or Pepsi?

_____

2. I love my black Labrador dog that I have. What is your favorite kind of dog?

_____

3. Do you have brothers, or are you an only child?

_____

4. Do you go to the movies a lot?

_____

5. Do you watch TV more than the average kid?

_____

6. Are dogs better than cats?

_____

7. Is your bedroom in your house bigger than your friends'?

_____

8. If you found $20, would you not give it back to the owner?

_____

Create and critique survey questions

Data Analysis and Probability   EMC 3017 • Basic Math Skills, Grade 4 • ©2003 by Evan-Moor Corp.

Collecting Data

Name _____

Select a topic that you would like to gather information about. Write five questions that you would ask each of your participants to gain information about your topic. (Remember to write clear questions that are free of your opinions or biases.)

Topic

_____

Question 1

_____

_____

Question 2

_____

_____

Question 3

_____

_____

Question 4

_____

_____

Question 5

_____

_____

Create and critique survey questions

Math Test

Name _____

Fill in the circle next to the correct answer.

1. Which of the following is a well-written question (clear and free from bias)?

   Ⓐ In what year were you born?
   Ⓑ Are you intelligent?
   Ⓒ Do you have cats or pets?
   Ⓓ Do you like the best team in the world, the Chargers?

2. Which of the following demonstrates a biased question?

   Ⓐ What is your favorite flavor of ice cream?
   Ⓑ Do you like my favorite teacher, Mrs. Jones?
   Ⓒ Do you like chocolate?
   Ⓓ What is your favorite color?

3. Which of the following questions is vaguely written?

   Ⓐ Do you have any pets?
   Ⓑ What is your last name?
   Ⓒ Do you recycle aluminum cans?
   Ⓓ Are you shorter?

4. What could be confusing about asking someone what his or her middle name is?

   Ⓐ They use their middle name instead of their first name.
   Ⓑ They don't have one.
   Ⓒ They have more than one.
   Ⓓ all of the above

5. What is vague about asking someone if they drink milk a lot?

   Ⓐ The term "a lot" is not clear.
   Ⓑ Some people don't like milk.
   Ⓒ Some people drink milk every day.
   Ⓓ Everyone likes milk and drinks it a lot.

6. What is biased about asking someone if our city should add the dangerous chemical fluoride to our drinking water?

   Ⓐ Not everyone likes water.
   Ⓑ The chemical fluoride is in our toothpaste.
   Ⓒ The word **dangerous** makes them think that way just from hearing the question.
   Ⓓ Some people don't use water.

7. What is the confusion about asking someone if they live with their mom or dad?

   Ⓐ Some children might live with their grandparents.
   Ⓑ Some children live with a guardian.
   Ⓒ Some children live with both their mom and dad.
   Ⓓ all of the above

8. Which of the following is the clearest question?

   Ⓐ Do you like snakes or lizards?
   Ⓑ Do you like chocolate or strawberry milk?
   Ⓒ What is your favorite flavor of gum?
   Ⓓ What is your favorite car or sport?

9. Make up a topic that you wish to create a survey about.

   _____

10. Write three clear questions for the survey on the topic you selected above.

   _____

   _____

   _____

Create and critique survey questions

Tongue Twister

Name _____

Use the following data to answer the questions below. Then write the corresponding letter on the line above the answer. The letters will spell out a tongue twister. Try to say it fast three times.

Data: 13, 35, 52, 56, 58, 64, 64, 74, 92

A How many numbers are listed in the data? __9__

B What is the smallest number? _____

E What is the largest number? _____

I What is the range of the data (largest number minus the smallest number)? _____

L What is the mode (number that appears most often)? _____

M What is the median (middle number when listed in order)? _____

S When listed from smallest to largest, what is the second number? _____

T When listed from smallest to largest, what is the third number? _____

V When listed from smallest to largest, what is the eighth number? _____

```
___  ___  ___      ___  A   ___  ___
 64   92   52       64   9    58   92

___  A   ___  ___  ___         ___  ___  ___  ___
 64   9   58   13   35          64   79   74   92
```

Analyze data utilizing range, median, and mode

Data Analysis and Probability

What Do Frogs Sit On?

Name _____

Use the following data to answer the questions below. Then write the corresponding letter on the line above the answer. The letters will spell out the solution to the riddle.

Data: 21, 23, 25, 25, 26, 27, 27, 27, 38

A   What is the smallest number? __21__

D   What is the largest number? _____

L   What is the range of the data (largest number minus the smallest number)? _____

O   How many numbers are listed in the data? _____

S   What is the mode (number that appears most often)? _____

T   What is the median (middle number when listed in order)? _____

____ ____ _A_ ____ ____ ____ ____ ____ ____ ____
26   9   21   38   27   26   9   9   17   27

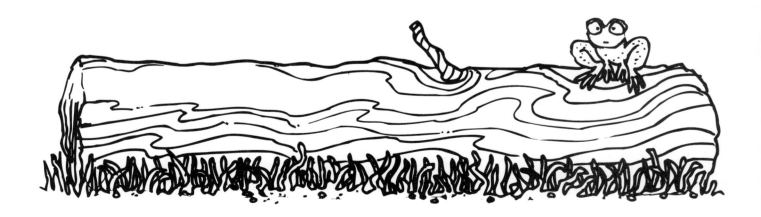

Analyze data utilizing range, median, and mode

Data Analysis and Probability   EMC 3017 • Basic Math Skills, Grade 4 • ©2003 by Evan-Moor Corp.

Food Drive

Name _____

Mr. Higdon made a stem and leaf plot to show the number of cans of food that were collected by some classes during the food drive.

Stem	Leaves
4	2
5	1 3
6	5
7	2 3 4 6 6
8	2 2 2 4 4 4 5 6 8
9	2 4 4 4 5 6 6 7 7 8 8 8 8 9 9
10	0 0 0 1 5 7

Use the stem and leaf plot to answer the questions.

1. What was the fewest number of cans that a class collected for the food drive? _____

2. What was the largest number of cans that a class collected? _____

3. What is the mode (number that appears most often)? _____

4. How many classrooms in the school participated in the food drive? _____

5. What is the median (middle number when listed in order)? _____

6. What is the range (largest number minus the smallest number)? _____

Analyze data utilizing range, median, and mode

Using Data

Name _____

A number of adults were surveyed outside the city shopping center. One of the questions asked their age. Here are the results of that question:

> **19, 33, 53, 27, 33, 18, 45**

1. What is the smallest number?

_____

2. What is the largest number?

_____

3. What is the range (largest number minus the smallest number)?

_____

4. What is the mode (number that appears most often)?

_____

5. What is the median (middle number when the list is in order)?

_____

A number of students were asked how many hours of sleep they had during the last seven days. Here are their results:

> **40, 56, 55, 49, 60, 56, 42**

6. What is the smallest number?

_____

7. What is the largest number?

_____

8. What is the range (largest number minus the smallest number)?

_____

9. What is the mode (number that appears most often)?

_____

10. What is the median (middle number when the list is in order)?

_____

Analyze data utilizing range, median, and mode

EMC 3017 • Basic Math Skills, Grade 4 • ©2003 by Evan-Moor Corp.

Analyze the Data

Name_____

Use this list of data to answer the questions below.

> **13, 15, 16, 16, 17, 18, 18, 18, 19, 19, 21, 24, 25, 29**

1. What one number could you add to the list so that the data would have a range of 60?

   _____

2. What is one of the two numbers you could add to the list above so that the data would have a second mode?

   _____

3. What two numbers could you add to the list of data that would increase the median value?

   _____   _____

4. Can you add two numbers less than 29 and still accomplish what you did in #3?

   _____

5. What effect would adding an 18 to the list of data have on the median, mode, or range?

   _____

Analyze data utilizing range, median, and mode

Math Test

Name _____

Fill in the circle next to the correct answer.

For Numbers 1 through 4, use this data.

25, 28, 29, 30, 31, 31, 35

1. What is the largest number?

- Ⓐ 27
- Ⓑ 31
- Ⓒ 32
- Ⓓ 35

2. What is the range?

- Ⓐ 10
- Ⓑ 12
- Ⓒ 25
- Ⓓ 32

3. What is the mode (number that appears most often)?

- Ⓐ 30
- Ⓑ 31
- Ⓒ 32
- Ⓓ 35

4. What is the median (middle number when listed in order)?

- Ⓐ 29
- Ⓑ 30
- Ⓒ 31
- Ⓓ 32

For Numbers 5 through 8, use this stem and leaf plot.

Stem (tens)	Leaves (ones)
8	2 4
9	8 8 8
10	0

5. How many test scores are represented?

- Ⓐ 6
- Ⓒ 25
- Ⓑ 5
- Ⓓ 15

6. What is the lowest test score?

- Ⓐ 0
- Ⓒ 82
- Ⓑ 24
- Ⓓ 8

7. What is the highest test score?

- Ⓐ 65
- Ⓒ 100
- Ⓑ 99
- Ⓓ 888

8. What is the mode (number that appears most often)?

- Ⓐ 84
- Ⓒ 96
- Ⓑ 100
- Ⓓ 98

9. List five numbers that would have a median value of 95.

_____ _____ _____ _____ _____

10. List three numbers that would have a mode of 16.

_____ _____ _____

Analyze data utilizing range, median, and mode

Data Analysis and Probability   EMC 3017 • Basic Math Skills, Grade 4 • ©2003 by Evan-Moor Corp.

Spinner Game 1

Name _____

Use the spinner below to play this game. To begin, obtain a paper clip from your teacher. Stick the pointed end of your pencil through the small loop in the end of the paper clip and place the point of the pencil on the center of the spinner. This allows the paper clip to spin around freely and become the spinner.

Rules

1. If the spinner lands on A or C, player 1 gets a point.
2. If the spinner lands on B or D, player 2 gets a point.

The player with the most points after 20 turns is the **winner!**

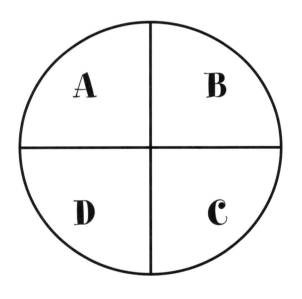

Turn	Landed On	Point(s) for Player 1	Point(s) for Player 2
1			
2			
3			
4			
5			
6			
7			
8			
9			
10			
11			
12			
13			
14			
15			
16			
17			
18			
19			
20			
Total			

Challenge

If you add the following rule, does it change the game to give one player an advantage over the other?

_____

_____

3. If you land on the letter C, no matter which player you are, you get to spin again. (Player 1 would score a point for landing on C and get a second turn; however, player 2 would not score a point, but would still spin again.)

Collect and record data related to simple chance situations

Spinner Game 2

Name _____

Use the spinner below to play this game. To begin, obtain a paper clip from your teacher. Stick the pointed end of your pencil through the small loop in the end of the paper clip and place the point of the pencil on the center of the spinner. This allows the paper clip to spin around freely and become the spinner.

Rules

1. If the spinner lands on a vowel, player 1 gets a point.

2. If the spinner lands on a consonant, player 2 gets a point.

Keep track of 20 turns and see who has the most points.

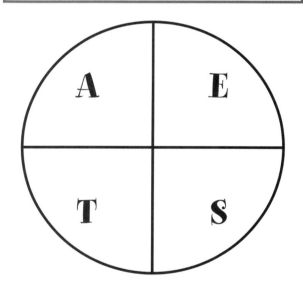

Turn	Landed On	Point(s) for Player 1	Point(s) for Player 2
1			
2			
3			
4			
5			
6			
7			
8			
9			
10			
11			
12			
13			
14			
15			
16			
17			
18			
19			
20			
	Total		

Challenge

If you add the following rules, does it change the game to give one player an advantage over the other?

_____

_____

3. If player 1 lands on A or E, he or she gets two points.

4. If player 2 lands on T, he or she gets one point.

5. If player 2 lands on S, he or she gets three points.

Collect and record data related to simple chance situations

Flip a Coin

Name _____

Use a coin for the following experiment.

Flip the coin 4 times and use tally marks to record your outcomes
in this table.

Heads	
Tails	

Now flip the coin 30 times and use tally marks to record your outcomes
in this table.

Heads	
Tails	

Answer these questions:

1. Did your experiments come out to half of the turns being heads and
half being tails?

_____

2. If you were off by one or two in the first experiment, how is that
different from being off by one or two in the second experiment?

_____

3. The second experiment has a sample of 30, while the first experiment
has a sample of 4. What is important about the size of the sample you
are taking?

_____

Collect and record data related to simple chance situations

Use the Spinner

Name _____

Use the spinner below to play this game. To begin, obtain a paper clip from your teacher. Stick the pointed end of your pencil through the small loop in the end of the paper clip and place the point of the pencil on the center of the spinner. This allows the paper clip to spin around freely and become the spinner.

Spin the spinner 20 times, and keep track of your turns on the chart.

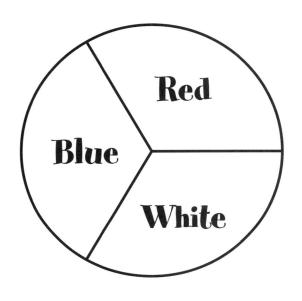

Turn Number	Red	White	Blue
1			
2			
3			
4			
5			
6			
7			
8			
9			
10			
11			
12			
13			
14			
15			
16			
17			
18			
19			
20			

1. How many times did the spinner land on red? _____

2. How many times did the spinner land on white? _____

3. How many times did the spinner land on blue? _____

4. Do you think these results are the same as your classmates'? Why or why not?

_____

Collect and record data related to simple chance situations

Create a Spinner

Name _____

Use these four rules to draw the spinners requested in each of the problems below.

Rules

1. The spinner has three regions, labeled A, B, and C.
2. Player 1 gets a point if either player lands on A during any turn.
3. Player 2 gets a point if either player lands on B or C during any turn.
4. Each player will spin the spinner 10 times.

Problems

1. Create a spinner that would give the two players equal chances of winning using the four rules.

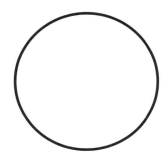

---

2. Create a spinner that would give player 1 the advantage using the four rules.

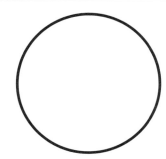

---

3. Create a spinner that would give player 2 the advantage using the four rules.

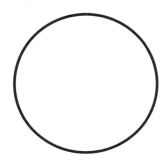

Collect and record data related to simple chance situations

Note: This assessment does not follow the multiple-choice format.

Name _____

Math Test

1. Use a standard six-sided die and roll it 30 times, recording your results in this table:

Number on Die	Tally Marks Showing Frequency	Total Frequency
1		
2		
3		
4		
5		
6		

2. Draw a spinner that satisfies all the following conditions:

- The spinner has four regions.

- The regions are numbered 2, 3, 4, and 5.

- Regions 2 and 5 are the same size.

- The chances of getting an even number are larger than the chances of getting an odd number.

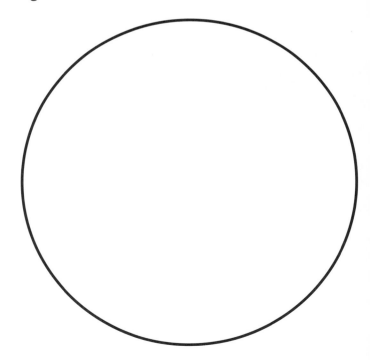

Collect and record data related to simple chance situations

Tongue Twister

Name _____

Look at each of the figures below and find the probability. Look for that value at the bottom of the page and write the corresponding letter on the line above the value. The letters will spell out a tongue twister. Try to say it fast three times.

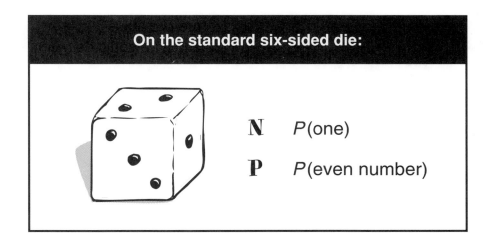

On the standard six-sided die:

N P(one)

P P(even number)

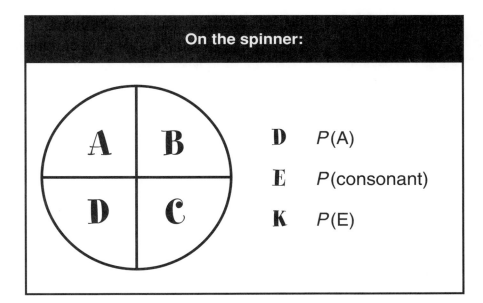

On the spinner:

D P(A)

E P(consonant)

K P(E)

___	N	___	___		___	___	___	___	,
0	$\frac{1}{6}$	$\frac{3}{4}$	0.75		$\frac{1}{4}$	0.75	$\frac{3}{4}$	$\frac{3}{6}$	

___	___	___	___		___	N	___	___	.
0.25	0.75	$\frac{3}{4}$	$\frac{1}{2}$		0	$\frac{1}{6}$	$\frac{3}{4}$	0.75	

Compute theoretical probabilities for simple chance events

What Kind of Nut Has No Shell?

Name _____

To solve the riddle, look at each of the figures below and compute the probability. Look for that value at the bottom of the page and write the corresponding letter on the line above the value. The letters will spell out the solution to the riddle.

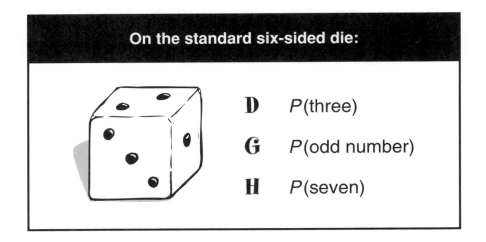

On the standard six-sided die:

D P(three)

G P(odd number)

H P(seven)

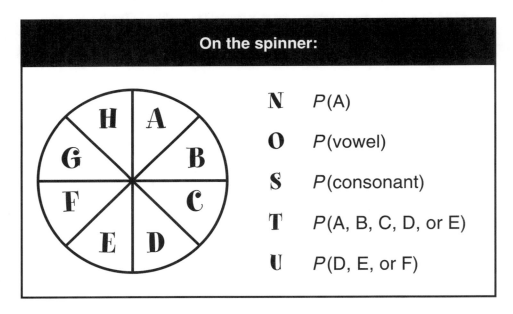

On the spinner:

N P(A)

O P(vowel)

S P(consonant)

T P(A, B, C, D, or E)

U P(D, E, or F)

<u> D </u>   ___   ___   ___   ___   ___   ___   ___   ___

$\frac{1}{6}$ $\frac{2}{8}$ $\frac{3}{8}$ $\frac{1}{2}$ 0 $\frac{1}{8}$ $\frac{3}{8}$ $\frac{5}{8}$ $\frac{6}{8}$

Skill practice copy here

Find the Probability

Name _____

Determine the probability of each event.

When rolling a standard six-sided die, what is the probability of getting...?

1. a 3 _____

2. a 5 _____

3. a 1 or a 2 _____

4. an odd number _____

5. an even number _____

6. a 7 _____

When you are flipping a coin, what is the probability of getting...?

7. heads _____

8. tails _____

When you are spinning this spinner, what is the probability of getting...?

9. red _____

10. blue _____

11. orange _____

12. blue or white _____

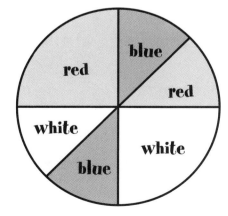

Compute theoretical probabilities for simple chance events

Data Analysis and Probability

Probability

Name _____

Determine the probability of each event.

When rolling a standard six-sided die, what is the probability of getting...?

1. a 1 _____

2. a 4 _____

3. a 5 or a 6 _____

4. an odd number _____

5. an even number _____

6. a 0 _____

If you had a bag with three blue marbles and five red marbles inside, what is the probability of drawing...?

7. a red marble _____

8. a blue marble _____

9. a black marble _____

When you are spinning this spinner, what is the probability of getting...?

10. white _____

11. blue _____

12. red _____

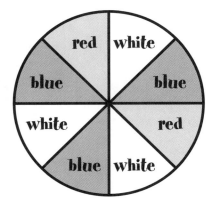

Compute theoretical probabilities for simple chance events

Data Analysis and Probability   EMC 3017 • Basic Math Skills, Grade 4 • ©2003 by Evan-Moor Corp.

Using Probability

Name _____

Solve each problem.

1. Ryan and Beth are arguing about the spinner. Ryan says that the white and blue have the same chance of being spun because they each have three sections on the spinner. However, Beth thinks that the white sections are larger so that they have a better chance of being spun. Who is correct? Tell why.

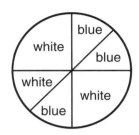

_____

2. In Mr. Call's class, there are 28 students. Mr. Call has each student's name written on a popsicle stick and placed in a jar. Occasionally, Mr. Call will reach into the jar and pull out a stick and ask that person to answer the next question. What are the chances that Michael will have his name pulled out of the jar the first time?

_____

3. In the jar described in #2, Mr. Call has called three students so far. Each time he calls on someone, he keeps that stick out of the jar so that person doesn't get called on again. What is Toby's chance of being drawn as the fourth student?

_____

4. Raymond and Julia are debating if the spinner to the right is a fair spinner. Fairness is defined as the two players having the same chances of winning. The rules for this spinner state that if the spinner lands on an even number, then Player A gets to move one space. If the spinner lands on an odd number, then Player B gets to move one space. Do you think that this is a fair spinner? Why or why not?

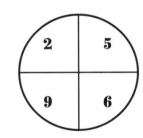

_____

5. Using the same spinner in #4, the rules now say that Player A gets to move if the spinner lands on an even number and he moves the number of spaces the spinner lands on. Player B gets to move if the spinner lands on an odd number and he moves the number of spaces the spinner lands on. Is this a fair game? Why or why not?

_____

Compute theoretical probabilities for simple chance events

Math Test

Name _____

Fill in the circle next to the correct answer.

For Numbers 1 through 4, use a standard six-sided die.

1. What is the probability of rolling a 6?

Ⓐ $\frac{1}{2}$ Ⓑ $\frac{1}{3}$ Ⓒ $\frac{1}{4}$ Ⓓ $\frac{1}{6}$

2. What is the probability of rolling a 4 or a 5?

Ⓐ $\frac{1}{6}$ Ⓑ $\frac{1}{2}$ Ⓒ $\frac{1}{3}$ Ⓓ $\frac{1}{4}$

3. What is the probability of rolling a 7?

Ⓐ $\frac{1}{6}$ Ⓑ $\frac{1}{4}$ Ⓒ 0   Ⓓ $\frac{1}{2}$

4. What is the probability of rolling an even number?

Ⓐ $\frac{1}{2}$ Ⓑ $\frac{1}{3}$ Ⓒ $\frac{1}{4}$ Ⓓ $\frac{1}{6}$

For Numbers 5 through 8, use this spinner.

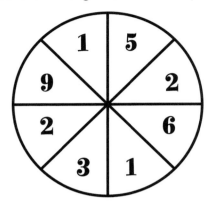

5. What is the probability of spinning a 1?

Ⓐ $\frac{1}{8}$ Ⓑ $\frac{1}{6}$ Ⓒ $\frac{2}{6}$ Ⓓ $\frac{1}{4}$

6. What is the probability of spinning a 4?

Ⓐ 0   Ⓑ $\frac{1}{8}$ Ⓒ $\frac{1}{4}$ Ⓓ $\frac{1}{2}$

7. What is the probability of spinning a 2?

Ⓐ $\frac{1}{8}$ Ⓑ $\frac{1}{2}$ Ⓒ $\frac{2}{8}$ Ⓓ $\frac{2}{6}$

8. What is the probability of spinning a 3?

Ⓐ $\frac{1}{4}$ Ⓑ $\frac{1}{8}$ Ⓒ $\frac{1}{7}$ Ⓓ 0

9. Using a coin, what is the probability of flipping a heads?

_____

10. Mrs. Vierow has an envelope in which she has cards. On each card is written the name of one of the 25 students in her class. She has already drawn three students' cards, including Timmy's, Julie's, and Kiko's. What is the chance that the next card she draws will be Antonio's?

_____

Compute theoretical probabilities for simple chance events

Data Analysis and Probability   EMC 3017 • Basic Math Skills, Grade 4 • ©2003 by Evan-Moor Corp.

How Many Combinations?

Name _____

Draw all the possible outfits that Daniel could wear given the following choices for shirts and pants. Each outfit must consist of one shirt and one pair of pants.

Three possible shirts:		Four possible pairs of pants:	
red	blue	blue jeans	white pants
	white	black jeans	red pants

Use counting techniques, tree charts, and organized lists to determine all possible combinations of items

What's an Astronaut's Favorite Meal of the Day?

Name _____

To solve this riddle, utilize the counting principle to solve the questions below. The **counting principle** says that if one event can happen in 2 different ways and a second event can happen in 4 different ways, then the two can occur together in 8 (2 times 4) different ways. For example, if Sally has 4 different pairs of pants and 3 different colored shirts, then she can create 12 unique outfits with those pants and shirts (4 times 3).

After you have solved each question, look for the answer at the bottom of the page and write the corresponding letter on the line above the answer. The letters will spell out the solution to the riddle.

A The number of outfits if Jim has three shirts and four pairs of pants

C The number of outfits if Alex has five shirts and four pairs of pants

H The number of cards that can be made with four different colors of paper and four different colors of markers

L The number of one-scoop ice-cream cones with four flavors of ice cream and two types of cones

N The number of ice-cream sundaes that can be made with five flavors of ice cream and 5 toppings

U The number of ways Sally can wear her hair with three different styles and five different-colored hair clips

____ ____ ____ ____ ____ ____
8   12   15   25   20   16

Use counting techniques, tree charts, and organized lists to determine all possible combinations of items

Data Analysis and Probability   EMC 3017 • Basic Math Skills, Grade 4 • ©2003 by Evan-Moor Corp.

Tree Diagrams

Name_____

Draw a **tree diagram** for each of the following situations and tell how many combinations there are for each. Here is an example of a tree diagram to help demonstrate the number of outfits that could be created from three pairs of pants (red, blue, and green) and two shirts (white and black). Each "branch" lists one possible outfit. For example, the top branch shows the outfit with red pants and white shirt. There are a total of six different outfits on this tree diagram.

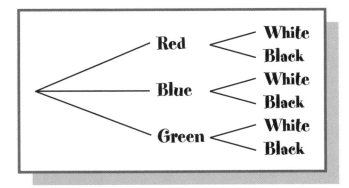

1. Two types of ice-cream cones (sugar and plain) and three flavors of ice cream (chocolate, vanilla, and swirl)

2. Three colors of balloons (red, blue, and purple) and three colors of ribbon (white, green, and yellow)

3. Three sizes of drinks (small, medium, and large) and four flavors of drinks (grape, orange, root beer, and lemon-lime)

Use counting techniques, tree charts, and organized lists to determine all possible combinations of items

Counting Techniques

Name _____

1. Draw a tree diagram to represent the six possible outcomes on a standard six-sided die.

2. Make an organized list to represent the possible combinations of a game in which the players use a spinner and a die. The spinner has three sections with the letters A, B, and C in them. The die is a standard six-sided die.

3. Henry was getting ready in the morning and noticed that he had four shirts in his closet (red, blue, green, and plaid) as well as three pairs of shorts (denim, white, and black). How many different combinations of one shirt and one pair of shorts can Henry wear?

_____

4. In some games, such as Monopoly, there are advantages to rolling doubles. If a game has two dice, what are all the possible combinations of the two dice? What is the probability of rolling doubles (when both dice show the same number)?

_____

Use counting techniques, tree charts, and organized lists to determine all possible combinations of items

EMC 3017 • Basic Math Skills, Grade 4 • ©2003 by Evan-Moor Corp.

How Many?

Name _____

There are six possible combinations from a car dealership if there are three colors (red, blue, and green) and two types of vehicles (vans and trucks).

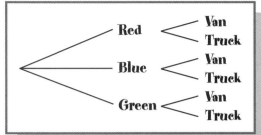

1. Add one more trait to make eight possible combinations. Draw the new tree diagram.

2. Add one more trait to make nine possible combinations. Draw the new tree diagram.

3. Add two more traits to make twelve possible combinations. Draw the new tree diagram below or use another sheet of paper.

Use counting techniques, tree charts, and organized lists to determine all possible combinations of items

Data Analysis and Probability

Math Test

Name _____

Fill in the circle next to the correct answer.

For Numbers 1 through 4, use this tree diagram.

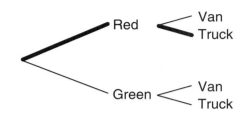

Red — Van / Truck

Green — Van / Truck

1. What are the two traits?

- Ⓐ color and type of vehicle
- Ⓑ red and green
- Ⓒ van and truck
- Ⓓ color and size

2. What does the dark set of lines represent?

- Ⓐ a red van   Ⓒ a red truck
- Ⓑ a green truck   Ⓓ a green van

3. How many combinations are there of the two colors and two types of vehicles?

- Ⓐ 1   Ⓑ 2   Ⓒ 3   Ⓓ 4

4. If you added a third color to the diagram, how many different combinations would there be for the three colors and the two types of vehicles?

- Ⓐ 4   Ⓑ 6   Ⓒ 8   Ⓓ 10

For Numbers 5 through 8, use the organized list.

Shirt	Pants
Red	Blue jeans
Red	White slacks
Red	Black jeans
Red	Faded blue jeans
Blue	Blue jeans
Blue	White slacks
Blue	Black jeans
Blue	Faded blue jeans

5. What does the table represent?

- Ⓐ flavors of ice cream
- Ⓑ shirts and pants that could be worn
- Ⓒ colors of cars
- Ⓓ colors of socks

6. How many shirts does the organized list represent?

- Ⓐ 1   Ⓑ 2   Ⓒ 3   Ⓓ 4

7. How many pairs of pants does the organized list represent?

- Ⓐ 1   Ⓑ 2   Ⓒ 3   Ⓓ 4

8. How many combinations are represented in the list?

- Ⓐ 2   Ⓑ 4   Ⓒ 6   Ⓓ 8

9. If Shirley is rolling two dice (one red and one green), how many possible sums could she get?

_____

10. Johnny is spinning this spinner two times. Show all the possible sums he could get with the two spins.

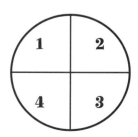

_____

Use counting techniques, tree charts, and organized lists to determine all possible combinations of items

Data Analysis and Probability   EMC 3017 • Basic Math Skills, Grade 4 • ©2003 by Evan-Moor Corp.

Resources

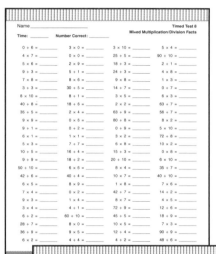

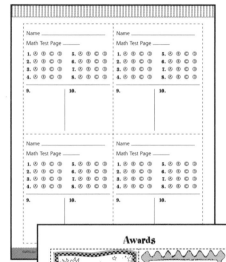

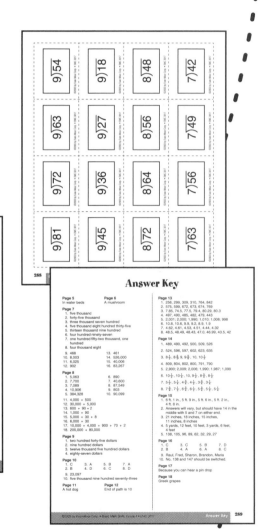

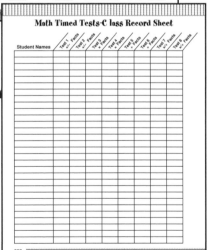

Name _____

Time: _____   Number Correct: _____

6 + 4 = _____	4 – 2 = _____	3 – 1 = _____	11 – 9 = _____
8 + 3 = _____	10 – 7 = _____	5 + 3 = _____	4 – 4 = _____
9 – 4 = _____	14 – 4 = _____	15 – 8 = _____	1 + 7 = _____
8 + 2 = _____	7 + 8 = _____	6 + 0 = _____	0 + 10 = _____
9 + 3 = _____	16 – 7 = _____	5 – 1 = _____	0 – 0 = _____
2 + 9 = _____	7 + 9 = _____	3 + 5 = _____	12 – 5 = _____
11 – 5 = _____	9 – 6 = _____	9 – 3 = _____	9 – 1 = _____
18 – 9 = _____	2 + 6 = _____	8 – 5 = _____	9 + 7 = _____
12 – 9 = _____	1 + 10 = _____	3 – 3 = _____	5 + 2 = _____
3 + 2 = _____	10 – 3 = _____	10 + 8 = _____	7 – 1 = _____
1 + 5 = _____	19 – 10 = _____	1 + 6 = _____	2 + 4 = _____
8 – 3 = _____	8 + 8 = _____	4 – 1 = _____	11 – 7 = _____
7 + 5 = _____	10 + 6 = _____	5 – 0 = _____	1 + 8 = _____
9 – 2 = _____	2 + 3 = _____	4 + 8 = _____	12 – 8 = _____
8 – 0 = _____	5 – 3 = _____	10 – 0 = _____	4 + 6 = _____
10 + 3 = _____	7 – 7 = _____	4 + 10 = _____	17 – 9 = _____
12 – 7 = _____	8 – 1 = _____	19 – 9 = _____	8 + 4 = _____
4 + 1 = _____	18 – 8 = _____	8 + 6 = _____	11 – 1 = _____
9 + 5 = _____	4 + 5 = _____	9 – 5 = _____	5 – 4 = _____
3 + 9 = _____	2 + 2 = _____	5 + 10 = _____	6 + 7 = _____
7 – 6 = _____	7 – 4 = _____	7 – 3 = _____	3 + 0 = _____
10 – 10 = _____	12 – 3 = _____	14 – 6 = _____	9 – 7 = _____
5 + 6 = _____	15 – 9 = _____	7 + 7 = _____	1 + 9 = _____
0 + 8 = _____	5 + 8 = _____	9 + 10 = _____	11 – 6 = _____
10 + 10 = _____	10 + 0 = _____	5 – 2 = _____	16 – 6 = _____

Name _____

Time: _____   Number Correct: _____

3 + 7 = _____	13 − 7 = _____	10 − 6 = _____	10 − 1 = _____
6 + 10 = _____	17 − 10 = _____	1 + 0 = _____	10 + 4 = _____
15 − 10 = _____	8 + 10 = _____	1 − 0 = _____	6 + 5 = _____
7 − 5 = _____	2 + 8 = _____	6 − 1 = _____	10 − 5 = _____
0 + 4 = _____	5 + 4 = _____	2 + 7 = _____	17 − 8 = _____
3 − 2 = _____	6 − 3 = _____	6 + 2 = _____	4 + 4 = _____
7 + 2 = _____	1 + 2 = _____	12 − 4 = _____	13 − 3 = _____
15 − 7 = _____	10 − 9 = _____	2 − 2 = _____	9 + 2 = _____
0 + 1 = _____	13 − 6 = _____	13 − 10 = _____	15 − 5 = _____
8 − 4 = _____	18 − 10 = _____	11 − 10 = _____	1 + 4 = _____
0 + 9 = _____	6 + 6 = _____	6 − 6 = _____	10 − 8 = _____
4 − 3 = _____	4 + 3 = _____	11 − 3 = _____	16 − 10 = _____
6 − 2 = _____	6 − 4 = _____	7 + 3 = _____	2 + 1 = _____
3 + 4 = _____	9 − 9 = _____	3 + 8 = _____	7 + 10 = _____
5 + 0 = _____	0 + 0 = _____	10 + 1 = _____	6 − 0 = _____
6 + 9 = _____	4 + 9 = _____	9 + 8 = _____	9 + 4 = _____
10 − 4 = _____	8 + 1 = _____	14 − 5 = _____	15 − 6 = _____
7 + 6 = _____	5 + 9 = _____	12 − 2 = _____	14 − 9 = _____
10 − 2 = _____	7 − 2 = _____	3 + 6 = _____	10 + 5 = _____
9 + 9 = _____	9 − 8 = _____	2 − 1 = _____	6 + 8 = _____
7 + 0 = _____	0 + 7 = _____	14 − 10 = _____	13 − 5 = _____
2 + 10 = _____	9 + 0 = _____	3 + 10 = _____	2 + 0 = _____
6 − 5 = _____	8 − 2 = _____	5 + 5 = _____	13 − 9 = _____
0 + 6 = _____	16 − 9 = _____	14 − 8 = _____	0 + 5 = _____
3 − 0 = _____	5 + 7 = _____	3 + 1 = _____	11 − 4 = _____

Time: _____   Number Correct: _____

5 × 6 = _____	10 × 10 = _____	4 × 4 = _____	0 × 4 = _____
9 × 0 = _____	8 × 3 = _____	1 × 2 = _____	7 × 0 = _____
3 × 9 = _____	5 × 9 = _____	0 × 10 = _____	6 × 6 = _____
6 × 7 = _____	2 × 1 = _____	7 × 6 = _____	9 × 7 = _____
4 × 6 = _____	0 × 5 = _____	6 × 4 = _____	8 × 10 = _____
3 × 2 = _____	5 × 4 = _____	3 × 6 = _____	5 × 5 = _____
7 × 4 = _____	10 × 2 = _____	2 × 10 = _____	7 × 9 = _____
9 × 5 = _____	1 × 6 = _____	0 × 6 = _____	10 × 4 = _____
3 × 8 = _____	0 × 2 = _____	3 × 0 = _____	6 × 9 = _____
6 × 2 = _____	7 × 1 = _____	7 × 7 = _____	2 × 0 = _____
2 × 3 = _____	8 × 5 = _____	9 × 6 = _____	2 × 9 = _____
4 × 5 = _____	9 × 8 = _____	10 × 8 = _____	6 × 3 = _____
8 × 6 = _____	1 × 9 = _____	8 × 1 = _____	10 × 0 = _____
2 × 7 = _____	10 × 6 = _____	4 × 3 = _____	3 × 10 = _____
5 × 1 = _____	3 × 5 = _____	6 × 8 = _____	1 × 3 = _____
7 × 10 = _____	4 × 10 = _____	7 × 2 = _____	5 × 2 = _____
1 × 0 = _____	1 × 4 = _____	3 × 4 = _____	9 × 1 = _____
4 × 8 = _____	5 × 7 = _____	0 × 1 = _____	6 × 10 = _____
7 × 3 = _____	8 × 9 = _____	4 × 0 = _____	8 × 7 = _____
2 × 5 = _____	6 × 1 = _____	10 × 5 = _____	9 × 4 = _____
0 × 8 = _____	3 × 3 = _____	5 × 8 = _____	8 × 8 = _____
7 × 5 = _____	6 × 0 = _____	6 × 5 = _____	0 × 9 = _____
4 × 2 = _____	3 × 7 = _____	8 × 4 = _____	2 × 4 = _____
2 × 6 = _____	5 × 10 = _____	2 × 8 = _____	9 × 9 = _____
7 × 8 = _____	9 × 3 = _____	2 × 2 = _____	4 × 1 = _____

EMC 3017 • Basic Math Skills, Grade 4 • ©2003 by Evan-Moor Corp.

Time: _____ **Number Correct:** _____

8 × 6 = _____	0 × 0 = _____	8 × 1 = _____	5 × 6 = _____
9 × 1 = _____	2 × 1 = _____	5 × 1 = _____	6 × 10 = _____
8 × 5 = _____	6 × 8 = _____	2 × 6 = _____	8 × 7 = _____
7 × 7 = _____	8 × 3 = _____	1 × 7 = _____	9 × 9 = _____
4 × 6 = _____	4 × 2 = _____	3 × 9 = _____	10 × 2 = _____
6 × 3 = _____	1 × 9 = _____	4 × 8 = _____	5 × 4 = _____
2 × 8 = _____	4 × 4 = _____	6 × 7 = _____	2 × 2 = _____
6 × 6 = _____	5 × 7 = _____	7 × 5 = _____	1 × 4 = _____
1 × 0 = _____	7 × 1 = _____	9 × 6 = _____	1 × 1 = _____
10 × 3 = _____	9 × 4 = _____	10 × 4 = _____	2 × 0 = _____
3 × 1 = _____	10 × 8 = _____	10 × 10 = _____	6 × 2 = _____
0 × 3 = _____	0 × 5 = _____	2 × 3 = _____	6 × 5 = _____
1 × 5 = _____	1 × 3 = _____	1 × 6 = _____	8 × 0 = _____
5 × 3 = _____	4 × 0 = _____	0 × 9 = _____	9 × 5 = _____
8 × 2 = _____	5 × 5 = _____	4 × 5 = _____	9 × 8 = _____
9 × 10 = _____	6 × 4 = _____	5 × 2 = _____	3 × 10 = _____
5 × 8 = _____	7 × 2 = _____	8 × 4 = _____	9 × 0 = _____
2 × 4 = _____	8 × 9 = _____	9 × 7 = _____	4 × 1 = _____
6 × 0 = _____	4 × 7 = _____	9 × 2 = _____	3 × 8 = _____
2 × 7 = _____	3 × 6 = _____	10 × 1 = _____	10 × 0 = _____
4 × 10 = _____	3 × 3 = _____	2 × 5 = _____	10 × 5 = _____
7 × 4 = _____	2 × 9 = _____	1 × 8 = _____	6 × 9 = _____
3 × 2 = _____	1 × 10 = _____	0 × 10 = _____	7 × 6 = _____
0 × 7 = _____	5 × 9 = _____	3 × 5 = _____	2 × 10 = _____
10 × 6 = _____	7 × 10 = _____	4 × 3 = _____	7 × 3 = _____

Time: _____   Number Correct: _____

20 ÷ 5 = _____	2 ÷ 2 = _____	4 ÷ 2 = _____	50 ÷ 5 = _____
18 ÷ 3 = _____	0 ÷ 9 = _____	56 ÷ 8 = _____	35 ÷ 5 = _____
28 ÷ 4 = _____	9 ÷ 9 = _____	80 ÷ 8 = _____	54 ÷ 9 = _____
16 ÷ 2 = _____	4 ÷ 1 = _____	27 ÷ 3 = _____	28 ÷ 7 = _____
9 ÷ 1 = _____	12 ÷ 2 = _____	7 ÷ 1 = _____	24 ÷ 8 = _____
14 ÷ 7 = _____	20 ÷ 2 = _____	10 ÷ 5 = _____	6 ÷ 6 = _____
32 ÷ 8 = _____	36 ÷ 4 = _____	7 ÷ 7 = _____	60 ÷ 10 = _____
27 ÷ 9 = _____	30 ÷ 5 = _____	90 ÷ 10 = _____	24 ÷ 4 = _____
10 ÷ 2 = _____	24 ÷ 6 = _____	45 ÷ 5 = _____	8 ÷ 1 = _____
9 ÷ 3 = _____	15 ÷ 5 = _____	48 ÷ 6 = _____	18 ÷ 2 = _____
4 ÷ 4 = _____	0 ÷ 3 = _____	35 ÷ 7 = _____	21 ÷ 3 = _____
12 ÷ 6 = _____	20 ÷ 10 = _____	36 ÷ 6 = _____	72 ÷ 8 = _____
21 ÷ 7 = _____	40 ÷ 8 = _____	49 ÷ 7 = _____	40 ÷ 4 = _____
20 ÷ 4 = _____	63 ÷ 9 = _____	25 ÷ 5 = _____	8 ÷ 4 = _____
14 ÷ 2 = _____	81 ÷ 9 = _____	45 ÷ 9 = _____	3 ÷ 3 = _____
40 ÷ 5 = _____	24 ÷ 3 = _____	70 ÷ 10 = _____	0 ÷ 10 = _____
63 ÷ 7 = _____	12 ÷ 3 = _____	64 ÷ 8 = _____	18 ÷ 6 = _____
60 ÷ 6 = _____	5 ÷ 5 = _____	54 ÷ 6 = _____	8 ÷ 2 = _____
0 ÷ 7 = _____	16 ÷ 8 = _____	0 ÷ 1 = _____	15 ÷ 3 = _____
30 ÷ 3 = _____	0 ÷ 5 = _____	6 ÷ 2 = _____	36 ÷ 9 = _____
48 ÷ 8 = _____	50 ÷ 10 = _____	6 ÷ 1 = _____	70 ÷ 10 = _____
72 ÷ 9 = _____	56 ÷ 7 = _____	12 ÷ 4 = _____	2 ÷ 1 = _____
100 ÷ 10 = _____	42 ÷ 7 = _____	18 ÷ 9 = _____	30 ÷ 10 = _____
42 ÷ 6 = _____	30 ÷ 6 = _____	40 ÷ 10 = _____	90 ÷ 9 = _____
6 ÷ 3 = _____	16 ÷ 4 = _____	32 ÷ 4 = _____	8 ÷ 8 = _____

Name_____

Time:_____   Number Correct:_____

18 ÷ 2 = _____	6 ÷ 2 = _____	36 ÷ 6 = _____	9 ÷ 3 = _____
40 ÷ 5 = _____	16 ÷ 4 = _____	32 ÷ 8 = _____	8 ÷ 4 = _____
6 ÷ 6 = _____	12 ÷ 2 = _____	10 ÷ 2 = _____	8 ÷ 8 = _____
14 ÷ 7 = _____	54 ÷ 6 = _____	32 ÷ 4 = _____	0 ÷ 6 = _____
15 ÷ 3 = _____	27 ÷ 3 = _____	9 ÷ 1 = _____	35 ÷ 7 = _____
64 ÷ 8 = _____	40 ÷ 4 = _____	30 ÷ 3 = _____	80 ÷ 10 = _____
60 ÷ 6 = _____	100 ÷ 10 = _____	56 ÷ 7 = _____	24 ÷ 3 = _____
30 ÷ 10 = _____	0 ÷ 5 = _____	16 ÷ 8 = _____	20 ÷ 2 = _____
0 ÷ 8 = _____	24 ÷ 8 = _____	7 ÷ 7 = _____	20 ÷ 4 = _____
4 ÷ 1 = _____	36 ÷ 9 = _____	40 ÷ 10 = _____	12 ÷ 6 = _____
6 ÷ 3 = _____	42 ÷ 7 = _____	72 ÷ 9 = _____	27 ÷ 9 = _____
15 ÷ 5 = _____	56 ÷ 8 = _____	45 ÷ 5 = _____	45 ÷ 9 = _____
21 ÷ 3 = _____	28 ÷ 4 = _____	90 ÷ 9 = _____	18 ÷ 3 = _____
16 ÷ 2 = _____	2 ÷ 2 = _____	12 ÷ 4 = _____	63 ÷ 7 = _____
10 ÷ 1 = _____	10 ÷ 5 = _____	20 ÷ 5 = _____	80 ÷ 8 = _____
28 ÷ 7 = _____	18 ÷ 9 = _____	21 ÷ 7 = _____	20 ÷ 10 = _____
25 ÷ 5 = _____	40 ÷ 8 = _____	9 ÷ 9 = _____	0 ÷ 4 = _____
54 ÷ 9 = _____	35 ÷ 5 = _____	30 ÷ 5 = _____	18 ÷ 6 = _____
42 ÷ 6 = _____	7 ÷ 1 = _____	14 ÷ 2 = _____	8 ÷ 2 = _____
24 ÷ 4 = _____	70 ÷ 7 = _____	48 ÷ 6 = _____	48 ÷ 8 = _____
81 ÷ 9 = _____	30 ÷ 6 = _____	36 ÷ 4 = _____	49 ÷ 7 = _____
70 ÷ 10 = _____	50 ÷ 10 = _____	50 ÷ 5 = _____	6 ÷ 1 = _____
0 ÷ 10 = _____	2 ÷ 1 = _____	72 ÷ 8 = _____	90 ÷ 10 = _____
4 ÷ 4 = _____	0 ÷ 3 = _____	5 ÷ 1 = _____	5 ÷ 5 = _____
0 ÷ 1 = _____	24 ÷ 6 = _____	12 ÷ 3 = _____	63 ÷ 9 = _____

$8 \times 8 =$ ____	$6 \times 7 =$ ____	$70 \div 10 =$ ____	$5 \times 5 =$ ____
$5 \times 1 =$ ____	$10 \div 1 =$ ____	$1 \times 2 =$ ____	$50 \div 5 =$ ____
$24 \div 6 =$ ____	$80 \div 10 =$ ____	$0 \div 4 =$ ____	$1 \times 6 =$ ____
$5 \times 2 =$ ____	$16 \div 8 =$ ____	$8 \div 8 =$ ____	$0 \times 4 =$ ____
$20 \div 4 =$ ____	$8 \times 5 =$ ____	$8 \times 3 =$ ____	$2 \times 10 =$ ____
$16 \div 2 =$ ____	$10 \times 3 =$ ____	$9 \times 6 =$ ____	$5 \times 7 =$ ____
$9 \times 1 =$ ____	$2 \div 2 =$ ____	$7 \times 5 =$ ____	$30 \div 6 =$ ____
$70 \div 7 =$ ____	$4 \times 4 =$ ____	$6 \times 9 =$ ____	$81 \div 9 =$ ____
$6 \div 3 =$ ____	$54 \div 6 =$ ____	$3 \div 1 =$ ____	$36 \div 4 =$ ____
$3 \times 7 =$ ____	$100 \div 10 =$ ____	$21 \div 3 =$ ____	$10 \times 8 =$ ____
$5 \times 9 =$ ____	$7 \times 2 =$ ____	$5 \times 0 =$ ____	$6 \div 1 =$ ____
$6 \times 4 =$ ____	$0 \times 7 =$ ____	$20 \div 2 =$ ____	$24 \div 8 =$ ____
$49 \div 7 =$ ____	$0 \div 1 =$ ____	$2 \times 1 =$ ____	$21 \div 7 =$ ____
$30 \div 3 =$ ____	$15 \div 5 =$ ____	$8 \div 4 =$ ____	$7 \times 7 =$ ____
$10 \times 9 =$ ____	$10 \times 6 =$ ____	$3 \times 9 =$ ____	$9 \times 2 =$ ____
$6 \div 6 =$ ____	$12 \div 2 =$ ____	$64 \div 8 =$ ____	$30 \div 10 =$ ____
$4 \times 6 =$ ____	$3 \times 1 =$ ____	$54 \div 9 =$ ____	$8 \times 1 =$ ____
$8 \div 2 =$ ____	$2 \times 8 =$ ____	$9 \times 4 =$ ____	$10 \times 4 =$ ____
$28 \div 4 =$ ____	$7 \times 10 =$ ____	$2 \times 6 =$ ____	$7 \div 1 =$ ____
$0 \times 1 =$ ____	$0 \div 10 =$ ____	$4 \times 3 =$ ____	$32 \div 4 =$ ____
$2 \times 3 =$ ____	$32 \div 8 =$ ____	$12 \div 3 =$ ____	$5 \times 8 =$ ____
$7 \times 0 =$ ____	$10 \times 10 =$ ____	$27 \div 3 =$ ____	$0 \times 9 =$ ____
$45 \div 9 =$ ____	$36 \div 6 =$ ____	$9 \times 7 =$ ____	$4 \times 1 =$ ____
$40 \div 5 =$ ____	$10 \times 0 =$ ____	$5 \div 5 =$ ____	$24 \div 4 =$ ____
$1 \times 9 =$ ____	$4 \times 10 =$ ____	$10 \div 2 =$ ____	$20 \div 5 =$ ____

Name _____

Time: _____   Number Correct: _____

0 ÷ 6 = _____	3 × 0 = _____	3 × 10 = _____	5 × 4 = _____
4 × 7 = _____	0 × 0 = _____	25 ÷ 5 = _____	90 ÷ 10 = _____
5 × 6 = _____	2 × 9 = _____	18 ÷ 3 = _____	2 ÷ 1 = _____
9 ÷ 3 = _____	5 ÷ 1 = _____	24 ÷ 3 = _____	4 × 8 = _____
7 × 8 = _____	8 × 6 = _____	9 × 8 = _____	1 × 3 = _____
3 ÷ 3 = _____	30 ÷ 5 = _____	14 ÷ 7 = _____	0 ÷ 7 = _____
8 × 10 = _____	8 ÷ 1 = _____	3 × 5 = _____	6 × 3 = _____
40 ÷ 8 = _____	18 ÷ 6 = _____	2 × 2 = _____	63 ÷ 7 = _____
35 ÷ 5 = _____	2 × 4 = _____	63 ÷ 9 = _____	56 ÷ 7 = _____
9 × 9 = _____	0 × 6 = _____	80 ÷ 8 = _____	8 × 2 = _____
9 ÷ 1 = _____	0 ÷ 2 = _____	0 ÷ 9 = _____	5 × 10 = _____
6 × 1 = _____	1 × 1 = _____	3 × 2 = _____	72 ÷ 8 = _____
5 × 3 = _____	7 ÷ 7 = _____	6 × 8 = _____	10 × 2 = _____
10 ÷ 5 = _____	16 ÷ 4 = _____	15 ÷ 3 = _____	0 × 8 = _____
9 ÷ 9 = _____	18 ÷ 2 = _____	20 ÷ 10 = _____	6 × 10 = _____
50 ÷ 10 = _____	6 × 6 = _____	8 × 4 = _____	35 ÷ 7 = _____
42 ÷ 6 = _____	40 ÷ 4 = _____	10 × 7 = _____	40 ÷ 10 = _____
6 × 5 = _____	8 × 9 = _____	1 × 8 = _____	7 × 6 = _____
7 × 4 = _____	0 × 2 = _____	42 ÷ 7 = _____	14 ÷ 2 = _____
9 × 3 = _____	1 × 4 = _____	8 × 7 = _____	4 × 5 = _____
3 × 4 = _____	4 ÷ 1 = _____	72 ÷ 9 = _____	12 ÷ 6 = _____
6 ÷ 2 = _____	60 ÷ 10 = _____	45 ÷ 5 = _____	18 ÷ 9 = _____
28 ÷ 7 = _____	8 × 0 = _____	10 × 5 = _____	7 × 3 = _____
36 ÷ 9 = _____	9 × 5 = _____	12 ÷ 4 = _____	90 ÷ 9 = _____
6 × 2 = _____	4 ÷ 4 = _____	4 ÷ 2 = _____	48 ÷ 6 = _____

Math Timed Tests–Class Record Sheet

Student Names	Test 1 +/− Facts	Test 2 +/− Facts	Test 3 × Facts	Test 4 × Facts	Test 5 ÷ Facts	Test 6 ÷ Facts	Test 7 ×/÷ Facts	Test 8 ×/÷ Facts

Name _____

Math Test Page _____

1. Ⓐ Ⓑ Ⓒ Ⓓ   5. Ⓐ Ⓑ Ⓒ Ⓓ
2. Ⓐ Ⓑ Ⓒ Ⓓ   6. Ⓐ Ⓑ Ⓒ Ⓓ
3. Ⓐ Ⓑ Ⓒ Ⓓ   7. Ⓐ Ⓑ Ⓒ Ⓓ
4. Ⓐ Ⓑ Ⓒ Ⓓ   8. Ⓐ Ⓑ Ⓒ Ⓓ

9.   10.

Name _____

Math Test Page _____

1. Ⓐ Ⓑ Ⓒ Ⓓ   5. Ⓐ Ⓑ Ⓒ Ⓓ
2. Ⓐ Ⓑ Ⓒ Ⓓ   6. Ⓐ Ⓑ Ⓒ Ⓓ
3. Ⓐ Ⓑ Ⓒ Ⓓ   7. Ⓐ Ⓑ Ⓒ Ⓓ
4. Ⓐ Ⓑ Ⓒ Ⓓ   8. Ⓐ Ⓑ Ⓒ Ⓓ

9.   10.

Name _____

Math Test Page _____

1. Ⓐ Ⓑ Ⓒ Ⓓ   5. Ⓐ Ⓑ Ⓒ Ⓓ
2. Ⓐ Ⓑ Ⓒ Ⓓ   6. Ⓐ Ⓑ Ⓒ Ⓓ
3. Ⓐ Ⓑ Ⓒ Ⓓ   7. Ⓐ Ⓑ Ⓒ Ⓓ
4. Ⓐ Ⓑ Ⓒ Ⓓ   8. Ⓐ Ⓑ Ⓒ Ⓓ

9.   10.

Name _____

Math Test Page _____

1. Ⓐ Ⓑ Ⓒ Ⓓ   5. Ⓐ Ⓑ Ⓒ Ⓓ
2. Ⓐ Ⓑ Ⓒ Ⓓ   6. Ⓐ Ⓑ Ⓒ Ⓓ
3. Ⓐ Ⓑ Ⓒ Ⓓ   7. Ⓐ Ⓑ Ⓒ Ⓓ
4. Ⓐ Ⓑ Ⓒ Ⓓ   8. Ⓐ Ⓑ Ⓒ Ⓓ

9.   10.

Awards

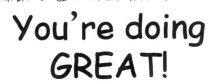

You're doing
GREAT!
Keep up
the good work!

10×7	9×7	8×7	6×6
10×8	9×8	8×8	7×6
10×9	9×9	9×5	7×7
10×10	10×6	9×6	8×6

12×9	12×5	11×11	11×7
12×10	12×6	12×2	11×8
12×11	12×7	12×3	11×9
12×12	12×8	12×4	11×10

$6\overline{)36}$	$6\overline{)42}$	$6\overline{)48}$	$6\overline{)54}$
$5\overline{)30}$	$5\overline{)35}$	$5\overline{)40}$	$5\overline{)45}$
$4\overline{)24}$	$4\overline{)28}$	$4\overline{)32}$	$4\overline{)36}$
$3\overline{)18}$	$3\overline{)21}$	$3\overline{)24}$	$3\overline{)27}$

$9\overline{)54}$	$9\overline{)63}$	$9\overline{)72}$	$9\overline{)81}$
$9\overline{)18}$	$9\overline{)27}$	$9\overline{)36}$	$9\overline{)45}$
$8\overline{)48}$	$8\overline{)56}$	$8\overline{)64}$	$8\overline{)72}$
$7\overline{)42}$	$7\overline{)49}$	$7\overline{)56}$	$7\overline{)63}$

EMC 3017 • Basic Math Skills, Grade 4 • ©2003 by Evan-Moor Corp.

Answer Key

©2003 by Evan-Moor Corp.

Page 5
In water beds

Page 6
A mushroom

Page 7
1. five thousand
2. forty-five thousand
3. three thousand seven hundred
4. five thousand eight hundred thirty-five
5. thirteen thousand nine hundred
6. four hundred ninety-seven
7. one hundred fifty-two thousand one hundred
8. four thousand eight

9. 468
10. 8,003
11. 6,025
12. 902
13. 461
14. 526,000
15. 40,006
16. 83,267

Page 8
1. 5,063
2. 7,700
3. 7,089
4. 10,906
5. 384,328
6. 890
7. 40,600
8. 87,549
9. 803
10. 90,099

11. 4,000 + 500
12. 30,000 + 5,000
13. 600 + 90 + 2
14. 1,000 + 90
15. 5,000 + 30 + 8
16. 6,000 + 30
17. 10,000 + 4,000 + 900 + 70 + 2
18. 200,000 + 80,000

Page 9
1. two hundred forty-five dollars
2. nine hundred dollars
3. twelve thousand five hundred dollars
4. eighty-seven dollars

Page 10
1. C
2. B
3. A
4. D
5. B
6. C
7. A
8. D

9. 23,097
10. five thousand nine hundred seventy-three

Page 11
A hot dog

Page 12
End of path is 10

Page 13
1. 256, 299, 309, 310, 764, 842
2. 575, 599, 672, 673, 674, 769
3. 7.85, 74.5, 77.5, 79.4, 80.29, 80.3
4. 497, 490, 485, 482, 479, 443
5. 2,001; 2,000; 1,990; 1,010; 1,008; 998
6. 10.8, 10.6, 9.9, 9.2, 8.9, 1.9
7. 4.62, 4.61, 4.53, 4.51, 4.44, 4.32
8. 48.5, 48.49, 48.43, 47.0, 46.99, 43.5, 42

Page 14
1. 489, 490, 492, 500, 509, 526
2. 524, 596, 597, 602, 623, 635
3. $8\frac{1}{2}$, $8\frac{2}{3}$, 9, $9\frac{5}{8}$, 10, $10\frac{1}{2}$
4. 809, 804, 802, 800, 791, 790
5. 2,900; 2,009; 2,006; 1,990; 1,987; 1,098
6. $10\frac{1}{2}$, $10\frac{1}{4}$, 10, $9\frac{1}{2}$, $8\frac{3}{4}$, $8\frac{1}{2}$
7. $5\frac{1}{2}$, $5\frac{1}{4}$, $4\frac{3}{4}$, $4\frac{1}{2}$, $3\frac{3}{4}$, $3\frac{1}{4}$
8. $7\frac{3}{4}$, $7\frac{1}{2}$, $6\frac{3}{4}$, $6\frac{1}{2}$, $5\frac{3}{4}$, $5\frac{1}{2}$, $5\frac{1}{4}$

Page 15
1. 6 ft. 1 in., 5 ft. 9 in., 5 ft. 6 in., 5 ft. 2 in., 4 ft. 8 in.
2. Answers will vary, but should have 14 in the middle with 5 and 7 on either end.
3. 21 inches, 18 inches, 15 inches, 11 inches, 8 inches
4. 5 yards, 12 feet, 10 feet, 3 yards, 6 feet, 4 feet
5. 108, 105, 96, 89, 62, 32, 29, 27

Page 16
1. C
2. B
3. C
4. A
5. B
6. A
7. D
8. C

9. Raul, Fred, Sharon, Brandon, Maria
10. No, 138 and 147 should be switched.

Page 17
Because you can hear a pin drop

Page 18
Greek grapes

Page 19

1. ten thousands
2. hundred thousands
3. ones
4. hundreds
5. millions
6. hundred thousands
7. tens
8. thousands
9. millions
10. ten thousands

11. 1
12. 6
13. 9
14. 5
15. 0

Page 20

1. 6,500
2. 7,240
3. 29,000
4. 590,000
5. 300,000
6. 190,750
7. 83,800
8. 731,000

9. 70,000
10. 288,000
11. 380,720
12. 381,000
13. 380,000
14. 400,000
15. 380,700

Page 21

1. $20 + $20 + $20 + $10 + $30 = $100
2. Jane is correct because when there is a 3 in the ones place, you should round down to 25,800.
3. Roberto is always rounding down. He should look at the digit to the right of the hundreds place (the tens place value). If that number is 5 or more, he should round up.
4. correct

Page 22

1. A
2. C
3. C
4. D
5. B
6. D
7. D
8. A

9. correct
10. Shirley, your answer is not correct. When you look at the thousands place value, there is a 4, which means you do not need to round up. So the correct answer should be 1,870,000.

Page 23
They are two tired

Page 24
Aluminum linoleum

Page 25

1. 1,478
2. 1,171
3. 486
4. 1,714
5. 2,044
6. 2,597
7. 2,256
8. 2,031
9. 2,145
10. 2,621

Page 26

1. 1,840
2. 3,095
3. 1,490
4. 1,842
5. 3,043
6. 1,932
7. 1,796
8. 1,095
9. 1,942
10. 3,118

Page 27

1. $51
2. $406
3. $252
4. $752
5. $154

Page 28

1. D
2. A
3. B
4. B
5. A
6. D
7. C
8. D

9. Answers will vary, but must use the given numbers.
10. $746

Page 29

1. 25 (512 − 487)
2. 751 (875 − 124)
3. You will get the largest difference if you subtract the largest number possible from the smallest number.
4. 26 (623 − 597)
5. You will get the smallest difference with 2 numbers that are closest in value.
6. 741 (976 − 235)

Page 30
To tie up the game

Page 31

1. 29
2. 242
3. 233
4. 122
5. 483
6. 490
7. 190
8. 468
9. 247
10. 99
11. 703
12. 520
13. 200
14. 99
15. 263
16. 138
17. 25
18. 500
19. 99
20. 41

Page 32

1. 400
2. 90
3. 282
4. 57
5. 146
6. 104
7. 7
8. 1
9. 100
10. 99
11. 195
12. 273
13. 235
14. 170
15. 497
16. 401
17. 101
18. 701
19. 310
20. 585

Page 33

1. $444
2. Yes, with 23 additional seats.
3. $573
4. No, he is $23 short.
5. Yes, they have 267 miles to go.

Page 34

1. B
2. A
3. B
4. C
5. D
6. C
7. A
8. B

9. Yes, because he has 149 tickets left.
10. $47; 145 − 98 = 47

Page 35
They only eat weak knights

Page 36
Tiny orangutan tongues

 EMC 3017 • Basic Math Skills, Grade 4 • ©2003 by Evan-Moor Corp.

Page 37

×	6	1	4	9	2	7	3	10	5	8
7	42	7	28	63	14	49	21	70	35	56
2	12	2	8	18	4	14	6	20	10	16
9	54	9	36	81	18	63	27	90	45	72
4	24	4	16	36	8	28	12	40	20	32
5	30	5	20	45	10	35	15	50	25	40
1	6	1	4	9	2	7	3	10	5	8
3	18	3	12	27	6	21	9	30	15	24
8	48	8	32	72	16	56	24	80	40	64
10	60	10	40	90	20	70	30	100	50	80
6	36	6	24	54	12	42	18	60	30	48

Page 38

1. 30   16   7
2. 14   72   56
3. 32   42   18
4. 54   9   28
5. 6   70   45
6. 50   64   5
7. 18   36   40
8. 81   16   90
9. 4   24   21
10. 49   4   48
11. 40   60   100
12. 2   35   27
13. 8   63
14 36   16

Page 39

1. 27 baseball cards
2. 40 frogs
3. No, he only has 18 cupcakes, so he is 3 short.
4. 20 quarters
5 Yes, she will have 56 marbles.
6. 21 steps

Page 40

1. B   3. C   5. C   7. D
2. A   4. D   6. B   8. C

9. Yes, because he has 54 muffins.
10. 30 pieces of gum

Page 41

He needed a web site

Page 42

Six thick thistle sticks

Page 43

×	2	12	10	6	8	5	7	1	11	4	9	3
1	2	12	10	6	8	5	7	1	11	4	9	3
6	12	72	60	36	48	30	42	6	66	24	54	18
12	24	144	120	72	96	60	84	12	132	48	108	36
4	8	48	40	24	32	20	28	4	44	16	36	12
7	14	84	70	42	56	35	49	7	77	28	63	21
10	20	120	100	60	80	50	70	10	110	40	90	30
3	6	36	30	18	24	15	21	3	33	12	27	9
8	16	96	80	48	64	40	56	8	88	32	72	24
11	22	132	110	66	88	55	77	11	121	44	99	33
9	18	108	90	54	72	45	63	9	99	36	81	27
5	10	60	50	30	40	25	35	5	55	20	45	15
2	4	24	20	12	16	10	14	2	22	8	18	6

Page 44

1. 60   16   77
2. 14   72   56
3. 32   42   22
4. 54   9   28
5. 11   70   45
6. 50   64   5
7. 108   108   40
8. 81   16   90
9. 44   24   21
10. 49   24   48
11. 0   60   100
12. 12   35   144
13. 88   63
14. 36   16

Page 45

1. 72 eggs
2. 60 stamps
3. 24 slices
4. No, she only has 66 plants.
5. 48

Page 46

1. B   3. D   5. C   7. D
2. A   4. B   6. D   8. B

9. Yes, he has 30 pieces of gum for 25 students.
10. 48 cookies

Page 47

When it is ajar

Page 48

1. 3,072   3. 4,025   5. 46,310
2. 35,364   4. 21,170

Page 49

1. 1,875   8. 60,080   15. 11,800
2. 4,368   9. 58,469   16. 8,466
3. 2,356   10. 10,276   17. 9,853
4. 9,344   11. 7,560   18. 11,152
5. 15,418   12. 275   19. 3,996
6. 27,156   13. 1,344   20. 7,560
7. 23,016   14. 2,144

Page 50

1. 3,213   8. 5,412   15. 28,548
2. 3,526   9. 15,730   16. 53,088
3. 516   10. 21,150   17. 8,148
4. 16,080   11. 1,316   18. 22,428
5. 6,876   12. 4,422   19. 22,632
6. 32,670   13. 2,968   20. 1,890
7. 15,402   14. 18,240

Page 51

1. $12,300
2. 6,500 sheets of paper
3. 6,321 pages
4. 6,419 pages
5. 12,180 sheets of newspaper

Page 52
1. B   3. A   5. C   7. A
2. C   4. D   6. A   8. D
9. 360 buttons
10. No, they'll only have $17,370, $1,630 short.

Page 53
a monkey

Page 54

Page 55
1. 18 ÷ 3 = 6 and 18 ÷ 6 = 3
2. 24 ÷ 4 = 6 and 24 ÷ 6 = 4
3. 15 ÷ 3 = 5 and 15 ÷ 5 = 3
4. Pictures will vary, but should be in a 2 by 4 array.
5. Pictures will vary, but should be in a 3 by 4 array.

Page 56
1. 16 ÷ 4 = 4 and 16 ÷ 4 = 4 (only one answer)
2. 27 ÷ 3 = 9 and 27 ÷ 9 = 3
3. 9 ÷ 3 = 3 and 9 ÷ 3 = 3 (only one answer)
4. Pictures will vary, but should show a 6 by 3 array.
5. Pictures will vary, but should show a 3 by 3 array.

Page 57
1. 3 candy bars; pictures will vary.
2. $5 each; pictures will vary.
3. 5 pieces of candy; pictures will vary.
4. 7 pages; 12 more stickers for 10 pages; pictures will vary.

Page 58
1. A   3. D   5. C   7. A
2. C   4. A   6. D   8. C
9. Pictures will vary, but should show 21 objects divided into groups of 7.
10. Pictures will vary, but should show that each person will get 3 pieces of gum.

Page 59
Traffic jam

Page 60
A lighthouse

Page 61
1. 3   2   1
2. 6   9   3
3. 3   9   3
4. 7   1   5
5. 7   0   7
6. 7   8   3
7. 3   5   6
8. 3   6   2
9. 2   6   5
10. 9   2   9
11. 4   3   4
12. 8   4   9
13. 6   2
14. 7   0

Page 62
1. 7   3   3
2. 3   9   3
3. 6   4   6
4. 3   0   4
5. 7   8   4
6. 9   1   4
7. 5   3   7
8. 4   3   1
9. 1   8   0
10. 2   5   3
11. 9   2   8
12. 1   2   8
13. 6   2
14. 0   6

Page 63
1. 8 cookies each
2. groups of 2, 3, 4, 6, 8 and 12
3. 6 balloons
4. 9 signatures per page
5. 2 cupcakes each; 1 + 5 + 3 + 3 = 12, 24 ÷ 12 = 2

Page 64
1. C   3. B   5. D   7. B
2. A   4. D   6. C   8. D
9. Answers will vary.   10. 9 tickets

Page 65
Baboon bamboo

Page 66
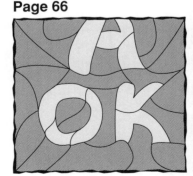

EMC 3017 • Basic Math Skills, Grade 4 • ©2003 by Evan-Moor Corp.

Page 67

1. 9 R3   4. 4 R1   7. 7   10. 2R1
2. 9 R4   5. 12   8. 8 R1
3. 7 R2   6. 7 R6   9. 8 R4

11. Answers will vary.   12. Answers will vary.

Page 68

1. 6 R8   4. 4 R3   7. 3 R4   10. 1 R7
2. 5 R2   5. 21   8. 9 R5
3. 5 R1   6. 6 R1   9. 7 R3

11. Answers will vary.   12. Answers will vary.

Page 69

1. Answers will vary. For example, break the cookies each in half.
2. Answers will vary. Exchange the dime for 2 nickels.
3. Answers will vary. Give the extra balloon back to the teacher.
4. Answers will vary. Each person gets 4 minutes.
5. 10 banners with 6 inches left over
6. 7 plates with 1 left to snack on
7. Each person gets 7 markers and there will be 6 leftover.

Page 70

1. A   3. D   5. A   7. A
2. B   4. B   6. D   8. C

9. Answers will vary.
10. 19 with 2 extras; maybe they could each keep one

Page 71

Odd numbers: 215, 413, 721, 429, 89, 555, 315
Even numbers: 724, 616

Page 72

Prime numbers: 11, 31, and 7
Composite numbers: 49, 8, 12, 25, and 16

Page 73

1. odd   7. even   13. even   19. odd
2. even   8. even   14. even   20. even
3. odd   9. odd   15. even   21. even
4. odd   10. odd   16. odd   22. even
5. odd   11. even   17. odd   23. odd
6. odd   12. odd   18. odd   24. even

Page 74

```
X O O X O X O X X
O X O X X O O X O
X X O X X X X O X
O X X X X O X X X
O X O X X O X X X
X X O X X X X O X
O X X X X O X X X
O X O X X X X O X
X X O X X X X O X
X X X X X X O X X
```

Page 75

1. Lengths are 5 and 7. Answers will vary for the second part. One solution is to cut 2 lengths of 7. Cut each of those off using the 5, leaving a length of 2 for each. Lay the two 2s end to end and compare with the 5 stick. The difference is 1.
2. Lengths are 7, 11, and 13. Answers will vary for the second part. One solution is to cut 2 lengths of 11. Cut each of those off using the 7, leaving a length of 4 for each. Lay the two 4s end to end and this gives you the 8.
3. Yes, the sum of two odd numbers is always even.
4. Yes, the sum of two even numbers is always even.
5. Yes, the sum of one even and one odd number is always odd.

Page 76

1. C   3. D   5. D   7. A
2. C   4. A   6. D   8. C

9. Answers will vary, but must be five even numbers greater than 45.
10. 11, 13, 17, 19, 23, and 29

Page 77
He was playing catch her (catcher)

Page 78
Beep repaired (Be prepared)

Page 79

1. Circled in red: 5 10 15 20 25 30 35 40 45 50 55 60 65 70 75 80 90 95 100
2. Crossed out in blue: 3 6 9 12 15 18 21 24 27 30 33 36 39 42 45 48 51 54 57 60 63 66 69 72 75 78 81 84 87 90 93 96 99
3. 2 4 6 8 10 12 14 18 20 22 24 26 28 30 32 34 36 38 40 42 44 46 48 50 52 54 56 58 60 62 64 66 68 70 72 74 76 78 80 82 84 86 88 90 92 94 96 98 100

Page 80

1. 1, 2, 4, 8
2. 1, 2, 3, 4, 6, 12
3. 1, 3, 5, 15
4. 1, 3, 7, 21
5. 1, 2, 3, 4, 6, 8, 12, 24
6. 1, 3, 9
7. 1, 2, 4, 8, 16, 32
8. 1, 7
9. 1, 2, 3, 6
10. 1, 2, 4, 8, 16
11. 1, 5, 7, 35
12. 1, 2, 4, 5, 8, 10, 20, 40
13. 1, 5, 25
14. 1, 3, 5, 9, 15, 45
15. 1, 2, 3, 6, 7, 14, 21, 42
16. 1, 31
17. 1, 2, 11, 22
18. 1, 2, 3, 6, 9, 18
19. 1, 5
20. 1, 2, 5, 10

Page 81
1. 1, 2, 3, 4, 6, 8, 12, or 24 stacks
2. Answers will vary, but should be multiples of 3 (6, 9, 12, 15, 18, etc.).
3. 1 row of 12, 2 rows of 6, 3 rows of 4, 4 rows of 3, 6 rows of 2, or 12 rows of 1. Answers will vary on the second part.
4. 36, 45, 54, or 63 erasers
5. 48, 54, 60, or 66 magazines

Page 82
1. C   3. C   5. B   7. A
2. A   4. A   6. D   8. C

9. 2, 3, 5, 7, 11, 13, 17, 19
10. 8, 16, 24, 32, 40

Page 83
Toy boat

Page 84
Doris locked, that's why I knocked.

Page 85
1. $\frac{2}{3}$ 5. $1\frac{1}{4}$
2. $1\frac{3}{4}$ 6. $2\frac{1}{4}$
3. $\frac{1}{4}$ 7. $1\frac{1}{3}$
4. $1\frac{2}{3}$ 8. $1\frac{1}{4}$

Page 86
1. <   5. <   9. <   13. <
2. <   6. <   10. <   14. =
3. <   7. =   11. >
4. <   8. >   12. >

Page 87
1. 2 eggs
2. Jose, because he missed 6 and Molly missed 5.
3. They both got 75 correct and missed 25.
4. Answers will vary. Alec and Sandy, you both have the same amount of money. You each have $0.50.
5. Answers will vary. Yes, if Adam's test had more items, for example if it had 20 items and he missed half, then he missed 10 items and Katie only missed 7.

Page 88
1. A   3. B   5. D   7. A
2. D   4. C   6. B   8. C

9. Answers will vary, but should show models of $\frac{1}{3}$ and $\frac{1}{4}$.
10. Mureta got 18 correct and Juan got only 15 correct.

Page 89
When eating watermelon

Page 90
Friday's five fresh fish specials

Page 91
1. $\frac{6}{7}$ 6. $\frac{11}{12}$ 11. $3\frac{3}{5}$
2. $\frac{6}{7}$ 7. $\frac{6}{7}$ 12. $4\frac{3}{4}$
3. $\frac{5}{6}$ 8. $\frac{7}{8}$ 13. $3\frac{7}{9}$
4. $\frac{3}{3}$ or 1   9. $\frac{3}{5}$ 14. $6\frac{3}{7}$
5. $\frac{7}{9}$ 10. $\frac{3}{4}$ 15. $12\frac{1}{9}$

Page 92
1. $\frac{4}{9}$ 9. $\frac{7}{10}$
2. $\frac{5}{7}$ 10. $\frac{2}{9}$
3. $\frac{1}{4}$ 11. $5\frac{2}{4}$ or $5\frac{1}{2}$
4. $\frac{7}{9}$ 12. $4\frac{2}{9}$
5. $\frac{2}{5}$ 13. $4\frac{5}{7}$
6. $\frac{3}{7}$ 14. $3\frac{3}{5}$
7. $\frac{1}{8}$ 15. $3\frac{1}{8}$
8. $\frac{1}{6}$

Page 93
1. $3\frac{1}{4}$ packages of gum
2. $6\frac{2}{3}$ boxes of candy
3. $2\frac{2}{4}$ or $2\frac{1}{2}$ bags of candy
4. $4\frac{2}{5}$ miles
5. Yes, because it is $5\frac{1}{4}$ pages long.

Page 94
1. B   3. A   5. A   7. C
2. D   4. C   6. D   8. D

9. $2\frac{3}{4}$ pages
10. $4\frac{4}{4}$ or 5 packages

Page 95
He is a great butter-in-law

Page 96
At flea markets

Page 97
1. Answers will vary: $\frac{2}{4}$, $\frac{3}{6}$
2. Answers will vary: $\frac{2}{6}$, $\frac{3}{9}$
3. Answers will vary: $\frac{2}{10}$, $\frac{3}{15}$
4. Answers will vary: $\frac{4}{6}$, $\frac{6}{9}$

EMC 3017 • Basic Math Skills, Grade 4 • ©2003 by Evan-Moor Corp.

Page 97 (continued)

5. Answers will vary: $\frac{8}{10}$, $\frac{12}{15}$

6. Answers will vary: $\frac{6}{14}$, $\frac{9}{21}$

7. Answers will vary: $\frac{2}{8}$, $\frac{3}{12}$

8. Answers will vary: $\frac{2}{14}$, $\frac{3}{21}$

9. Answers will vary: $\frac{6}{8}$, $\frac{8}{12}$

10. Answers will vary: $\frac{4}{10}$, $\frac{6}{15}$

11. $\frac{1}{2}$	14. $\frac{1}{4}$	17. $\frac{2}{3}$	20. $\frac{1}{3}$
12. $\frac{1}{3}$	15. $\frac{3}{4}$	18. $\frac{3}{7}$	
13. $\frac{1}{3}$	16. $\frac{2}{3}$	19. $\frac{3}{4}$	

Page 98

1. D	3. H	5. E	7. F
2. G	4. A	6. C	8. B

Page 99

1. 0.3 is a larger discount
2. $\frac{1}{4}$ cup
3. Answers will vary.
4. Answers will vary.

Page 100

1. D	3. D	5. D	7. B
2. B	4. B	6. C	8. D

9. Answers will vary: $\frac{1}{2}$, $\frac{2}{4}$, $\frac{3}{6}$, $\frac{4}{8}$

10. Answers will vary.

Page 101

A watch dog

Page 102

Seven silly Santas slid on the slick snow

Page 103

1. 3.8	11. 14.79
2. 11.7	12. 14.92
3. 8.9	13. 11.79
4. 8.9	14. 16.31
5. 8.6	15. 16.66
6. 12.2	16. 13.39
7. 15.1	17. 8.84
8. 13.2	18. 12.75
9. 4.27	19. 14.97
10. 11.1	20. 57.84

Page 104

1. 1.1	11. 3.88
2. 3.2	12. 3.51
3. 3.3	13. 3.09
4. 2.3	14. 1.67
5. 1.05	15. 2.32
6. 3.79	16. 43.1
7. 4.07	17. 20.27
8. 4.94	18. 44.64
9. 2.3	19. 0.54
10. 1.41	20. 0.99

Page 105

1. $2.36	4. 6 ft
2. 0.25 m	5. 5.3 ft
3. 18.3 cm	

Page 106

1. A	3. B	5. C	7. A
2. D	4. A	6. D	8. A

9. 7.4 feet
10. 2.7 yards

Page 107

A blazer

Page 108

1. T	3. T	5. T
2. F	4. T	

Page 109

1. <	4. <	7. =	10. <
2. >	5. =	8. =	
3. >	6. =	9. <	

Page 110

1. <	6. >	11. >	16. <
2. >	7. >	12. <	17. <
3. =	8. <	13. <	18. >
4. <	9. <	14. =	19. >
5. =	10. =	15. >	20. <

Page 111

1. Tim
2. 24 centimeters
3. Answers will vary: No, they are equal.
4. both
5. Answers will vary: No, one-tenth is less than two-tenths.

Page 112

1. B	3 A	5. C	7. D
2. A	4. A	6. B	8. B

9. 5.9 feet
10. Answers will vary: No, they are equal.

Page 114
In the river bank

Page 115
Pug puppy

Page 116
1. 11, 13, 15; +2
2. 19, 23, 27; +4
3. 29, 35, 41; +6
4. 16, 32, 64; ×2
5. 16, 13, 10; –3
6. 35, 29, 23; –6
7. 22, 29, 37; +1, +2, +3, +4, etc.
8. 74, 69, 64; –5
9. 84, 92, 100; +8
10. 17, 19, 22; +2, +3, +2, +3, etc.

Page 117
Answers will vary.
1. ⇦   3. ◨   5. ◺   7. ☐
2. ◤   4. ⊘   6. ▲   8. ●

Page 118
1. Answers will vary.
2. lengthwise
3. blue, red
4. chorus
5. Answers will vary.

Page 119
1. B   3. B   5. B   7. C
2. D   4. B   6. A   8. B

9. Two ends of bricks followed by one lengthwise brick. The next one should be an end.
10. Answers will vary.

Page 120
Six sharp smart sharks

Page 121
You hold it's nose

Page 122
1. subtraction
2. division
3. 3 + 6 = 9, 6 + 3 = 9, 9 – 3 = 6, and 9 – 6 = 3
4. 1 × 3 = 3, 3 × 1 = 3, 3 ÷ 3 = 1, 3 ÷ 1 = 3
5. 5 × 5 = 25, 25 ÷ 5 = 5
6. 5 + 6 = 11, 6 + 5 = 11, 11 – 5 = 6, 11 – 6 = 5
7. because of the two 5s

Page 123
1. addition
2. multiplication
3. 4 + 3 = 7, 7 – 4 = 3, 7 – 3 = 4
4. 2 × 5 = 10, 10 ÷ 5 = 2, 10 ÷ 2 = 5
5. 2 × 3 = 6, 3 × 2 = 6, 6 ÷ 2 = 3
6. 8 – 6 = 2, 2 + 6 = 8, 6 + 2 = 8
7. 8 + 7 = 15, 15 – 8 = 7, 15 – 7 = 8
8. 12 ÷ 4 = 3, 3 × 4 = 12, 4 × 3 = 12
9. 6 × 3 = 18, 18 ÷ 3 = 6, 18 ÷ 6 = 3
10. 17 – 8 = 9, 8 + 9 = 7, 9 + 8 = 17

Page 124
1. 4   2. 4   3. 2   4. 2

5. Because when there are duplicate numbers and when you use the commutative property, you don't get a new equation (i.e., 5 + 5 = 10; if you switch the two 5s around, you don't get a new unique sentence).

Page 125
1. B   3. D   5. B   7. D
2. A   4. C   6. C   8. D

9. 3 × 4 = 12, 4 × 3 = 12, 12 ÷ 4 = 3, 12 ÷ 3 = 4
10. 4

Page 126
Because all the fans are gone

Page 127
Lemon liniment

Page 128
1. 5, 6, 7, 8, 9, 10
2. 2, 4, 6, 8, 10, 12
3. 1, 3, 5, 8, 9, 12
4. 6, 5, 4, 3, 2, 1
5. 7, 9, 10, 12, 14, 15
6. 17, 25, 16, 10, 19, 20

Page 129
1. 4, 5, 7, 9, 11, 13
2. 18, 6, 15, 27, 45, 63
3. −2, 15, −4, 1, 5, 12
4. 7, 4, 3, 1, 4, 10
5. 17, 28, 25, 30, 17, 24
6. 5, 1, 4, 6, 10, 7

Page 130
1. 9, 12, 15, 18; 15 cupcakes
2. 75, 100, 125, 150
3. 120, 125, 130, 135; 135 centimeters

Page 131
1. D   3. B   5. A   7. B
2. B   4. A   6. C   8. D

9. Answers will vary.
10. Answers will vary.

EMC 3017 • Basic Math Skills, Grade 4 • ©2003 by Evan-Moor Corp.

Page 132
1. +4
2. +1
3. −1
4. ×2
5. ÷2

Page 133
Umbrella

Page 134
1. +4
2. ×2
3. −2
4. +4
5. −5
6. ×3

Page 135
1. +4
2. ×3
3. −3
4. +3
5. ÷4
6. −5

Page 136
1. Answers will vary: ×2, +2, times itself
2. Answers will vary: the correct function is ×3
3. Number of bananas times 31¢, $2.48, $3.10
4. Answers will vary: Herald is correct, function is ÷2; the output for 14 should be 7

Page 137
1. C
2. C
3. B
4. A
5. A
6. C
7. D
8. A

9. Answers will vary: ×3, +8
10. Answers will vary: ÷3, −4

Page 138

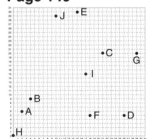

Page 139

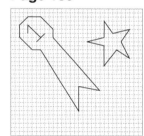

Page 140

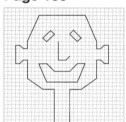

Page 141

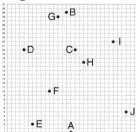

Page 142

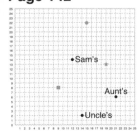

School is (9, 8), Grandparents' house is (19, 13), and grocery store is (15, 22)

Page 143
1. A
2. C
3. D
4. B
5. C
6. D
7. A
8. B

9. (6, 5)
10. Point O

Page 145
Candy

Page 146

Page 147
Point: an exact location in space

Line: an infinite set of points forming a straight line that extends in two directions

Ray: a part of a line that has one endpoint and extends in one direction

Angle: two rays that share an endpoint

Line Segment: a part of a line defined by two endpoints

Page 148
1. right
2. acute
3. acute
4. acute
5. obtuse
6. right
7. obtuse
8. acute

Page 149
1. No, it isn't a line since a line goes on forever in two directions.
2. 4 line segments
3. No, because of the way that they sway down between the poles.
4. Yes, the endpoint is the sun, and the rays extend out in one direction.
5. 12 times

Page 150
1. A
2. C
3. B
4. D
5. B
6. A
7. D
8. C

9. Both extend forever in at least one direction.
10. A line goes forever in two directions, while a segment has 2 endpoints.

Page 151
1. green (yellow and blue)

2. red
3. pink
4. blue
5. brown
6. red
7. no color
8. brown
9. black
10. no color

Page 152
trapezoid 10; square 0; triangle 2; hexagon 6; rhombus 3

Page 153
1–9. Answers will vary.
10. Possible answers include square, quadrilateral, rectangle, rhombus, parallelogram, or plane figure.

Page 154
1. rectangle, parallelogram
2. triangle
3. parallelogram
4. square, rectangle, parallelogram, rhombus
5. trapezoid
6. circle
7. parallelogram, rhombus
8. hexagon

Page 155
Answers will vary: possible answers include right triangle, isosceles triangle, trapezoid, square, rhombus, rectangle.

Page 156
1. B	3. C	5. B	7. A
2. D	4. A	6. D	8. B

9. Answers will vary.
10. Answers will vary.

Page 157
Thunderwear

Page 158
Even Edith eats eggs

Page 159
1–6. Answers will vary.
7. Possible answers include cube, square prism, hexahedron.

Page 160
1. pyramid
2. prism, cube
3. cylinder
4. shpere
5 prism
6. cone
7. pyramid

Page 161
1. Triangular prism, with one triangle facing us and one at the back side

2. Many answers possible, for example:

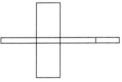

3. Many answers possible, for example:

4. Answers will vary; one example: The container is a tall cylinder and inside are three items that are congruent and each is shaped like a sphere.

Page 162
1. C	3. C	5. C	7. D
2. D	4. A	6. A	8. B

9. Answers will vary: basketball, baseball, marble, orange, grapefruit
10. Answers will vary, for example:

Page 163
Three free throw

Page 164
A horse

Page 165
1. translated (slid)
2. rotated (turned)
3. rotated (turned)
4. rotated (turned) OR reflected (flipped)
5. translated (slid)
6. reflected (flipped) OR rotated (turned)
7. rotated (turned)
8. translated (slid)

Page 166
1. translated (slid)
2. reflected (flipped)
3. rotated (turned)
4. translated (slid)
5. rotated (turned) OR reflected (flipped)
6. rotated (turned)
7. reflected (flipped)
8. rotated (turned)

Page 167
2, 4, 6, and 8 are turns

3, 5, 7, and 9 are slides

Page 168
1. B	3. A	5. A	7. B
2. D	4. C	6. D	8. D

9.
10.

Page 169
A duckseedo

Page 170
Crisco crisps crusts

Page 171
A-1	H-2	O-4	V-1
B-1	I-2	P-0	W-1
C-1	J-0	Q-0	X-2
D-1	K-0	R-0	Y-1
E-1	L-0	S-0	Z-0
F-0	M-1	T-1	
G-0	N-0	U-1	

EMC 3017 • Basic Math Skills, Grade 4 • ©2003 by Evan-Moor Corp.

Page 172
1. 2   3. 1   5. 6   7. 1
2. 4   4. 1   6. 1   8. 5

Page 173
1. Any of the following:

2. Any of the following:

3. Any of the following:

4. There are an infinite number of lines of symmetry on a circle.

Page 174
1. C   3. B   5. A   7. D
2. B   4. D   6. A   8. B

9. Answers will vary.
10. Answers will vary.

Page 176
Black bugs bleed black blood

Page 177
An elephant's shadow

Page 178
1. $2.52   4. $7.07
2. $2.47   5. $10.00
3. $0.11   6. $17.83

7. Answers will vary.
8. Answers will vary.

Page 179
Answers will vary in the last two columns.
1. 75 cents   5. $1.65, 35¢
2. 30¢   6. $5.00, $2.10
3. 80¢   7. $4.82, 18¢
4. $5.15   8. $20.00, $11.01

Page 180
1. 62¢; combinations of coins will vary; fewest coins is 2 quarters, 1 dime, and 2 pennies
2. $1.42; 1 one-dollar bill, 1 quarter, 1 dime, 1 nickel, and 2 pennies
3. $4.25
4. 83¢; Milts and Jinxs or Poxes and Smoths
5. Answers will vary, but they should each total 58¢.

Page 181
1. A   3. D   5. C   7. D
2. B   4. C   6. A   8. A

9. 8 coins; 2 quarters, 2 dimes, and 4 pennies
10. Answers will vary, but should total 27 cents.

Page 182
A meowie

Page 183
A beagle

Page 184
Linear: kilometer, meter, decimeter, centimeter, Millimeter

Capacity: kiloliter, liter, deciliter, centiliter, milliliter

Mass: kilogram, gram, decigram, centigram, milligram

Page 185
Linear: millimeter, centimeter, decimeter, meter, kilometer

Capacity: milliliter, centiliter, deciliter, liter, kiloliter

Mass: milligram, centigram, decigram, gram, kilogram

Page 186
1. meterstick, gram weight, and 2 liters
2. millimeter, centimeter, decimeter, meter, kilometer
3. Answers will vary, but could include something about if the words end in *gram,* then they refer to weight, and if they end in *meter,* then they refer to linear length.

Page 187
1. C   3. C   5. A   7. D
2. A   4. B   6. C   8. A

9. milliliter, centiliter, deciliter, liter, kiloliter
10. meteor

Page 188
end of path is 4

Page 189
You are a star!

Page 190
1. $3\frac{1}{2}$ inches   5. $\frac{3}{4}$ inch
2. $2\frac{1}{2}$ inches   6. $3\frac{1}{4}$ inches
3. 2 inches
4. $4\frac{1}{2}$ inches

Page 191
1. 6 cm   5. $2\frac{1}{2}$ cm
2. 4 cm   6. 8 cm
3. 7 cm
4. 11 cm

Page 192
1. 3 decimeters (30 cm)
2. 3 meters (300 cm)
3. 2 yards (72 inches)
4. $\frac{1}{2}$ kilometer (500 meters)

Page 193

1. C   3. B   5. A   7. D
2. A   4. D   6. A   8. B

9. 16 feet (3 yards is only 9 feet)
10. 2 meters (200 cm is shorter than 250 cm)

Page 194
Thin sticks,
thick bricks

Page 195
The sun shines
on shop signs

Page 196
1. kilometer, hectometer, dekameter, meter,
   decimeter, centimeter, millimeter

2. 100   4. 1,000   6. 100
3. 10   5. 1,000   7. 10

Page 197
1. mile, yard, foot, inch   5. 36   9. 60
2. 3   6. 24   10. 360
3. 12   7. 21
4. 5,280   8. 10,560

Page 198
1. Yes, the board is 36 inches long and they
   only need 28 inches.
2. 5,280 feet
3. Yes, they only need 3 meters of tape
   (6 faces times twice across times 25 cm =
   300 centimeters, which equals 3 meters).
4. Answers will vary.

Page 199
1. A   3. D   5. D   7. D
2. C   4. C   6. C   8. A

9. Answers will vary: 10 decimeters,
   100 centimeters, 1,000 millimeters
10. Answers will vary: 36 inches, 1 yard

Page 200
Truly plural

Page 201
Do drop in at the
Dewdrop Inn

Page 202
1. >   4. =   7. =   10. =
2. <   5. <   8. <
3. >   6. >   9. >

Page 203
1. >   4. >   7. <   10. >
2. >   5. <   8. >
3. >   6. <   9. <

Page 204
1. yes (2 quarts)
2. no (2 quarts + 1 cup)
3. 20 dekaliters
4. 25 milliliters

Page 205

1. D   3. C   5. D   7. B
2. A   4. A   6. A   8. C

9. 16 popsicles
10. No, Nancy will have 0.5 centiliters too much.

Page 206
Glad to meteor

Page 207
Pay and run

Page 208
1. 84°   5. 30°   9. 95°
2. 25°   6. 74°   10. 52°
3. 15°   7. 47°
4. 69°   8. 28°

Page 209

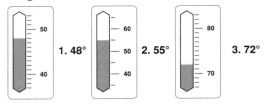

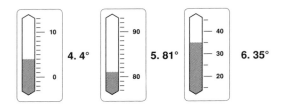

Page 210
1. 48°   3. 79°   5. 31°
2. 87°   4. 39°

Page 211
1. A   3. B   5. A   7. B
2. C   4. D   6. D   8. C

9. thermometer showing 46°
10. thermometer showing 74°

Page 212
A regal rural ruler

Page 213
A tall story

Page 214
1. 68   5. Answers will vary.
2. 39   6. Answers will vary.
3. 48   7. Answers will vary, but should
4. 26.6   include an equilateral triangle
              with three inches on each side.

Page 215
1 184   5. Answers will vary.
2. 6   6. Answers will vary.
3. 58   7. Answers will vary.
4. 16.4

300 Answer Key

Page 216
1. 130 feet, 13 boards
2. 75 feet, 7 rolls

Page 217
1. D   3. A   5. C   7. A
2. C   4. B   6. D   8. D

9. any rectangle with a perimeter of 24
10. any irregular figure with a perimeter of 16

Page 218
Seven silly swans swam

Page 219
She had a pumpkin for a coach

Page 220
1. 10 square feet
2. 4 square centimeters
3. 16 square inches
4. 576 square feet
5. 450 square meters
6. 2,700 square mm

Page 221
1. 64   4. 16
2. 32   5. 1,470
3. 75   6. 1,792

Page 222
239 square feet; you could find the area of the whole 20 by 17 rectangle minus the two smaller rectangles or you could subdivide the original shape into three smaller rectangles and find the area of each.

Page 223
1. C   3. B   5. C   7. A
2. A   4. D   6. A   8. D

9. any rectangle with an area of 24 square units
10. any rectangle with an area of 24 square units and different dimensions than #9

Page 224
A ducktionary

Page 225
Lot lost lots of locks

Page 226
1. 5:00   3. 6:45   5. 11:28
2. 2:30   4. 10:25   6. 7:15

Page 227
1. 8:45   4. 8:40   7. 11:50
2. 2:30   5. 5:20   8. 7:15
3. 8:00   6. 4:45   9. 10:50

Page 228
1. 2 hours
2. 1 hour 20 minutes
3. 8:00
4. 6 hours 50 minutes
5. 25 minutes

Page 229
1. B   3. A   5. B   7. A
2. D   4. C   6. B   8. C

9. one clock showing 4:45 and another clock showing 7:40
10. 14 hours 55 minutes

Page 231
Cell it

Page 232
Dates

Page 233
Answers will vary. One possible answer:

Day of the Week	Morning Temperature
Monday	68°
Tuesday	70°
Wednesday	70°
Thursday	69°
Friday	71°
Saturday	72°
Sunday	64°

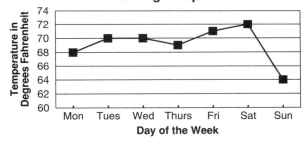

Morning Temperature

Page 234
1.

Stem	Leaves
8	4 6 8
9	2 6 8
10	0 0

2.

Stem	Leaves
6	0 4
7	6 8
8	4 8
9	0 2 8
10	0

Page 235
1. Answers will vary, but should allude to the fact of the y-axis starting with 40 instead of 0.
2. Answers will vary: not starting their labels at zero, having line graphs with uneven spaces across the x-axis, etc.
3. Answers will vary.

Page 236

1. A   3. C   5. B   7. B
2. D   4. C   6. D   8. A

9. any pictograph representing data in table
10. answers will vary.

Page 237

A hood

Page 238

Lisa is 3, Tim is 6, Andra is 9, Marta is 10, Andrew is 12, and Juan is 15

Page 239

1. total absences in Mr. Layden's Class
2. students aren't in school in July
3. December
4. February
5. 13
6. 2 weeks off for winter break

Page 240

1. 5
2. 79
3. number of slices of pizza eaten at the class party
4. one student eating that number of slices of pizza
5. Answers will vary: the pictures are similar if the Xs were bars
6. 6
7. Answers will vary.

Page 241

1. 4   2. 1   3. 3   4. 2

Page 242

1. D   4. D   7. D
2. B   5. B   8. A
3. C   6. D   9. 88

10. Answers will vary. For example: because the scale starts with 60.

Page 243

1, 3, and 4 are good questions and make a rectangle.

Page 244

Answers will vary.

Page 245

Answers will vary, for example:

1. What is your favorite soda?
2. Do you like the Denver Broncos?
3. Do you think that girls are more athletic than boys?
4. Should kids be allowed to ride their bikes on the sidewalks?
5. Do you like the band Hi Rocks?
6. Should your city's water be supplied with fluoride?

Page 246

Answers will vary, for example:

1. What if I liked root beer?
2. Mentioning the black Labrador may sway people to say that type more often.
3. What if you have sisters?
4. "A lot" is a vague term.
5. How much does the "average kid" watch?
6. in what ways (training, feeding, costs, etc.)
7. Are we comparing bedroom size or house size?
8. The negative makes it unclear if you say yes to what you're saying yes to.

Page 247

Answers will vary.

Page 248

1. A   3. D   5. A   7. D
2. B   4. D   6. C   8. C

9. Answers will vary.
10. Answers will vary.

Page 249   **Page 250**

Let lame lambs live   Toadstools

Page 251

1. 42   3. 98   5. 94
2. 107   4. 39   6. 65

Page 252

1. 18   4. 33   7. 60   10. 55
2. 53   5. 33   8. 20
3. 35   6. 40   9. 56

Page 253

1. 73
2. 16 or 19
3. 2 numbers greater than or equal to 19
4. 2 numbers greater than or equal to 19 and less than 29
5. no change

Page 254

1. D   3. B   5. A   7. C
2. A   4. B   6. C   8. D

9. Answers will vary.
10. Answers will vary.

Page 255

Answers will vary.
Challenge: No, there is no advantage.

EMC 3017 • Basic Math Skills, Grade 4 • ©2003 by Evan-Moor Corp.

Page 256

Answers will vary.

Challenge: No, there is no advantage.

Page 257

Answers will vary. (For question 3, the larger the sample size, the closer to ½ of the sample will have heads and ½ of the sample will have tails.)

Page 258

Answers will vary.

Page 259

Answers will vary, one possible answer could be:

1.   2.   3.

Page 260

1. Answers will vary.

2. Answers will vary, one possible answer could be:

Page 261

Knee deep, deep knee

Page 262

Doughnuts

Page 263

1. $\frac{1}{6}$ 5. $\frac{3}{6}$ or $\frac{1}{2}$ 9. $\frac{3}{8}$

2. $\frac{1}{6}$ 6. 0   10. $\frac{2}{8}$ or $\frac{1}{4}$

3. $\frac{2}{6}$ or $\frac{1}{3}$ 7. $\frac{1}{2}$ 11. 0

4. $\frac{3}{6}$ or $\frac{1}{2}$ 8. $\frac{1}{2}$ 12. $\frac{5}{8}$

Page 264

1. $\frac{1}{6}$ 5. $\frac{3}{6}$ or $\frac{1}{2}$ 9. 0

2. $\frac{1}{6}$ 6. 0   10. $\frac{3}{8}$

3. $\frac{2}{6}$ or $\frac{1}{3}$ 7. $\frac{5}{8}$ 11. $\frac{3}{8}$

4. $\frac{3}{6}$ or $\frac{1}{2}$ 8. $\frac{3}{8}$ 12. $\frac{2}{8}$ or $\frac{1}{4}$

Page 265

1. Beth: $\frac{5}{8}$ white (only $\frac{3}{8}$ blue)

2. $\frac{1}{28}$

3. $\frac{1}{25}$

4. fair; even and odd both are $\frac{1}{2}$

5. No, each player will move the same number of turns, but Player B will get to move an average of 7 spaces, while Player A only moves an average of 4 spaces.

Page 266

1. D   4. A   7. C   10. $\frac{1}{22}$

2. C   5. D   8. B

3. C   6. A   9. $\frac{1}{2}$

Page 267

Answers will vary, but should include 12 different outfits.

Page 268

Launch

Page 269

1. 6   2. 9   3. 12

Page 270

1.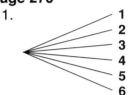

2. A-1   B-1   C-1
    A-2   B-2   C-2
    A-3   B-3   C-3
    A-4   B-4   C-4
    A-5   B-5   C-5
    A-6   B-6   C-6

3. 12 combinations

4. $\frac{6}{36}$ or $\frac{1}{6}$

Page 271

1. Another color (e.g., white)

2. Another vehicle (e.g., car)

3. Another characteristic (e.g., 2-door and 4-door)

Page 272

1. A   3. D   5. B   7. D

2. C   4. B   6. B   8. D

9. 11 sums

10. 16 combinations with sums ranging from 2 to 8

Page 274
Timed Test 1

10	2	2	2
11	3	8	0
5	10	7	8
10	15	6	10
12	9	4	0
11	16	8	7
6	3	6	8
9	8	3	16
3	11	0	7
5	7	18	6
6	9	7	6
5	16	3	4
12	16	5	9
7	5	12	4
8	2	10	10
13	0	14	8
5	7	10	12
5	10	14	10
14	9	4	1
12	4	15	13
1	3	4	3
0	9	8	2
11	6	14	10
8	13	19	5
20	10	3	10

Page 275
Timed Test 2

10	6	4	9
16	7	1	14
5	18	1	11
2	10	5	5
4	9	9	9
1	3	8	8
9	3	8	10
8	1	0	11
1	7	3	10
4	8	1	5
9	12	0	2
1	7	8	6
4	2	10	3
7	0	11	17
5	0	11	6
15	13	17	13
6	9	9	9
13	14	10	5
8	5	9	15
18	1	1	14
7	7	4	8
12	9	13	2
1	6	10	4
6	7	6	5
3	12	4	7

Page 276
Timed Test 3

30	100	16	0
0	24	2	0
27	45	0	36
42	2	42	63
24	0	24	80
6	20	18	25
28	20	20	63
45	6	0	40
24	0	0	54
12	7	49	0
6	40	54	18
20	72	80	18
48	9	8	0
14	60	12	30
5	15	48	3
70	40	14	10
0	4	12	9
32	35	0	60
21	72	0	56
10	6	50	36
0	9	40	64
35	0	30	0
8	21	32	8
12	50	16	81
56	27	4	4

Page 277
Timed Test 4

48	0	8	30
9	2	5	60
40	48	12	56
49	24	7	81
24	8	27	20
18	9	32	20
16	16	42	4
36	35	35	4
0	7	54	1
30	36	40	0
3	80	100	12
0	0	6	30
5	3	6	0
15	0	0	45
16	25	20	72
90	24	10	30
40	14	32	0
8	72	63	4
0	28	18	24
14	18	10	0
40	9	10	50
28	18	8	54
6	10	0	42
0	45	15	20
60	70	12	21

Page 278
Timed Test 5

4	1	2	10
6	0	7	7
7	1	10	6
8	4	9	4
9	6	7	3
2	10	2	1
4	9	1	6
3	6	9	6
5	4	9	8
3	3	8	9
1	0	5	7
2	2	6	9
3	5	7	10
5	7	5	2
7	9	5	1
8	8	7	0
9	4	8	3
10	1	9	4
0	2	0	5
10	0	3	4
6	5	6	7
8	8	3	2
10	6	2	3
7	5	4	10
2	4	8	1

Page 279
Timed Test 6

9	3	6	3
8	4	4	2
1	6	5	1
2	9	8	0
5	9	9	5
8	10	10	8
10	10	8	8
3	0	2	10
0	3	1	5
4	4	4	2
2	6	8	3
3	7	9	5
7	7	10	6
8	1	3	9
10	2	4	10
4	2	3	2
5	5	1	0
6	7	6	3
7	7	7	4
6	10	8	6
9	5	9	7
7	5	10	6
0	2	9	9
1	0	5	1
0	4	4	7

Page 280
Timed Test 7

64	42	7	25
5	10	2	10
4	8	0	6
10	2	1	0
5	40	24	20
8	30	54	35
9	1	35	5
10	16	54	9
2	9	3	9
21	10	7	80
45	14	0	6
24	0	10	3
7	0	2	3
10	3	2	49
90	60	27	18
1	6	8	3
24	3	6	8
4	16	36	40
7	70	12	7
0	0	12	8
6	4	4	40
0	100	9	0
5	6	63	4
8	0	1	6
9	40	5	4

Page 281
Timed Test 8

0	0	30	20
28	0	5	9
30	18	6	2
3	5	8	32
56	48	72	3
1	6	2	0
80	8	15	18
5	3	4	9
7	8	7	8
81	0	10	16
9	0	0	50
6	1	6	9
15	1	48	20
2	4	5	0
1	9	2	60
5	36	32	5
7	10	70	4
30	72	8	42
28	0	6	7
27	4	56	20
12	4	8	2
3	6	9	2
4	0	50	21
4	45	3	10
12	1	2	8

EMC 3017 • Basic Math Skills, Grade 4 • ©2003 by Evan-Moor Corp.